T0164833

—— THE ALTERNATIVE VIEW OF A ——
BOXERS RECORD

A STORY OF PROFESSIONAL BOXING IN THE 1980'S AND 90'S

Jim McMillan

authorHOUSE®

AuthorHouse™ UK Ltd.
500 Avebury Boulevard
Central Milton Keynes, MK9 2BE
www.authorhouse.co.uk
Phone: 08001974150

© 2011 Jim McMillan. All rights reserved.

No part of this book may be reproduced, stored in a retrieval system, or transmitted by any means without the written permission of the author.

First published by AuthorHouse 06/3/2011

ISBN: 978-1-4567-7919-1 (sc)
ISBN: 978-1-4567-7920-7 (e)

Any people depicted in stock imagery provided by Thinkstock are models, and such images are being used for illustrative purposes only.
Certain stock imagery © Thinkstock.

This book is printed on acid-free paper.

Because of the dynamic nature of the Internet, any web addresses or links contained in this book may have changed since publication and may no longer be valid. The views expressed in this work are solely those of the author and do not necessarily reflect the views of the publisher, and the publisher hereby disclaims any responsibility for them.

1 stone = 14lbs.

1kilogram = 2.2lbs

For example:
the welterweight limit of 10st 7lbs = 147lbs
or 67 kilograms

INDEX

INTRODUCTION

In June 2002 Louis Vietch from Blackpool rang to tell me that one of my ex-professional boxers, Simon McDougal, had died in tragic circumstances. Simon was only thirty three years old and I had known him since he was eighteen. He turned professional under my management and had forty four contests before retiring in 1997.

At his funeral I was re-acquainted with his parents whom I had not seen since before Simon's retirement and some other members of his family whom I had never met before. One was an Aunt who lived in the South of England and she told me that although she knew that Simon had been a boxer, she knew very little about his boxing career. She asked me if had any information about his record that she could keep as a reminder of him in the future.

Since I had trained and managed Simon throughout his career and had taken him to fight in venues all over the UK and France, Holland, Italy, Denmark, Switzerland and South America, I promised that I would not just write the cold facts of his record but also tell some of the stories that went on behind the scenes which paint an entirely different picture than a simple win draw or loss recording.

Although I had retired from the boxing business myself around the same time as Simon, after a life times association with the sport, I still had some of my record books and notes plus I had a number of VHS tapes of contests that boxers under my training, promotion and management had taken part in.

Over a period of a week or two I wrote the Simon McDougal chapter. I am fortunate that I have a good memory and many of my boxing experiences are so vividly etched into my brain I find it easy to recall them. I enjoyed reliving them, the high and the low points, the good, the bad and the ugly and by the time I had finished Simon's story, I was pleased by the way it was received by his family and I hope it gave them a little consolation

Some other boxers whom I had managed also read it and asked if I could do the same for them and I promised that some day I would. I was surprised to find some of them had not kept records or memorabilia and I was glad I had not thrown out all the tapes and photographs

With lots of other things going on in my busy retirement, I did nothing more about it until recently when I suddenly thought that if I don't make the effort now, maybe I never will, so over the next few weeks I have written the story of my association with the professional boxing game and the fighters whom I trained and managed.

To make it easier to understand by anyone who may not be familiar the boxing scene other than by what they read in the newspapers or see on the telly, I will start by giving a brief explanation as to what it is about.

For instance I refer to different training programmes whilst preparing individual boxers for contests and also the pre-fight preparations that we went through, so a description of what they entail may make more sense when I refer to them during my descriptions of there contests.

The order that the records are presented in is based on more or less on the date that each individual joined my professional boxing stable.

The make up of a successful professional boxer is complex. There were basic requirements, both Physical and psychological, which a boxer had to display before I would consider whether to train him. The obvious ones were a natural strength, co-ordination, boxing ability, talent and fast reflexes. These things can quickly be ascertained but it takes a little longer to establish some other essential characteristics. Courage, heart and determination, dedication, aggression, self discipline, a high threshold to pain, the emotions of fear and anger

☆ X ☆

and the ability to manage them. If I could add to the above, an instinctive sense of timing and distance, then they had potential.

I was the sole judge of these requirements before signing up a prospective boxer and it would take a few sessions in the gym before I was satisfied that one had enough of them to make the grade. If I rejected them they could either walk away and try elsewhere or train on until I was convinced otherwise. Over the years I experienced both of these options.

I had a specific set of rules and disciplines that I worked too and I always made these clear to everyone. I explained right from the start what I would expect from each individual. I always invited feedback. When I asked them to do things in a certain way I would explain the reason why. There is a fundamental right way and wrong way of doing things in boxing as in anything else, but it is also remarkable how many great boxers throughout history have defied convention. However the unconventional cannot be taught.

Examination of the history of boxing suggests that there are three types of boxing champion. First is the school of pure brilliant boxing. Of perfect footwork, scientific defence, of well-timed punches and perfect craftsmanship. This is boxing practised as a skill and an art. Most of these skills can be taught.

The second is a school of fighters as much as boxers. Men who combine aggression and power with the same skills as the pure boxer, they display stamina and great recuperative power for the long haul. They administer and absorb punishment and they are hard and fit and controlled as they search for an opening for that final blow. They are as cold as ice and deadly as magic. Many of those skills can not be taught only added to

The third are the school of the pure fighter, of relentless energy and whirlwind attack, the tenacity of the bulldog and the enthusiasm of the terrier. There is no brilliant boxing and attack is their defence. Their aim is to subdue with power and to win by all means. Again those skills are instinctive and cannot be taught but they can be enhanced and developed

Boxing is a contentious subject. People watching the same contest may come to different conclusions as to the winner. With the experience of watching thousands of rounds at close quarters, professional trainers have a qualified opinion. Personal bias, pre-fight expectations, ignorance and hype can influence an opinion

Under BBB of C rules the referee is the sole judge. It is a ten points must system where the winner of a round is awarded ten points, based first on the number blows landed on the target area cleanly and with force with the knuckle part of the glove. If the referee deems both fighters to have landed an equal number of blows, the boxer who does most of the leading off gets the ten points. If that is deemed to be equal the referee can take defence and style into account. The loser of a round receives nine and a half points. If a boxer has been outclassed or has been knocked down for a count in a round, he receives nine points. If a boxer is knocked down and cannot get up unaided and in a position to defend him self within ten seconds, he is deemed to have been knocked out. If a boxer deliberately strikes his opponent below the belt or on the back of the head or round the side in the kidney area he may be disqualified or at least have points deducted. He can also have points deducted or be disqualified for hitting with the inside of the glove, for persistent holding or holding and hitting or hitting on the break or striking after the referee has called "stop boxing". A boxer can be disqualified for "not trying". If a boxer receives an injury, such as a cut to any part of his face or head which causes bleeding or suffers any other injury the referee may stop the contest immediately or refer to a ringside doctor for an opinion.

By following this system to the letter, it should be possible to find a winner of practically every round, but in practice it doesn't always work that way.

Referees should be impartial. When the referee stands in a neutral corner before the start of a contest, he should begin judging only after the first bell rings. That is not always the case and there are obvious reasons why. In some cases a boxer is "expected" to be superior to his opponent simply because of the way some matches are made or through media hype and publicity, for example a journeyman fighter versus an up and coming prospect. Just like everyone else at ringside, referees can and do pre-judge the outcome and when the contest starts he appears to be blind to the punches landed by the underdog. If the unfancied boxer continues to perform well, the ref may latch on to it and by the end of the contest he will give the right decision. That is one scenario, but there are many others.

Very often an "opponent" is fighting the "House" fighter. This means that the fighter is managed by the promoter of the show, often in his home town. The opponent invariably travels to the show, often with only his second/trainer and has little or no support from the crowd.

In that scenario the referee, appointed by the local Area Council, is under pressure to see that the home fighter gets the benefit of the doubt in any round that is close. Very often he will call a round drawn so "sitting on the fence" until the last round when he can give that last half point to the house fighter. In close fights or when the opponent is clearly winning the points, the referee may look for some other excuse to get him out of there. The slightest cut or an infringement of the rules can in be all that he needs. That may seem cynical and I am not suggesting it happens all the time, but my boxers and many others have been blatantly robbed. An out of area boxer, in the eighties and nineties, fighting in the North east of England or Scotland, will know what I mean. It was often said that in Glasgow "You need to knock your opponent out to get a draw".

Bad decisions happen even at International level and in front of TV audiences. The referee's decision always stands although in some cases referees have been reprimanded and in isolated cases, downgraded. One outstanding example that sticks in my memory goes way back to the fifties. Peter Waterman was British welterweight champion and was being groomed by promoter Jack Solomans for a world title shot. They brought the Cuban ex World Champion, Kid Gavalan, who was thought to be "over the hill", to Earls Court London, to give Peter a step up in class. The step proved to be too high. The referee was the "A" star class, Ben Green. After a ten round beating, with The Kid a mile ahead on points on everyone's card, we were shocked when Peter's hand was raised. It caused uproar and afterwards Ben Greens was downgraded but the decision stood.

Incidentally, Peter Waterman and Kid Gavalan fought a return two months later and Gavalan again won on points only this time got the decision. Peter Waterman was a great fighter although he never did get that World title fight. He died when he was a young man after contracting poliomyelitis. He was the older brother of TV star Dennis Waterman.

Between 1983 and 1996 I managed and trained seventeen professional boxers. Of those, four joined the professional ranks from the Preston and Fulwood ABC where I had coached and developed them through their amateur careers. Ten turned professional with me after boxing amateur with other clubs and three of them came under my management after boxing professionally with other managers. In addition I had many fighters who didn't make the grade to a professional licence or whom I didn't want to be involved with for various reasons.

Of the seventeen boxers in my stable, seven fought for Central Area titles and four became champions. Two went on to win British, Commonwealth and International titles.

★

I have a lifetime association with boxing starting from just before I was born. On the 9th of September 1935, Glasgow's Benny Lynch became a Scottish hero and a legend when he won the Word Flyweight title by stopping the Champion, Jackie Brown, in the second round at Belle View, Manchester.

Benny was from the Gorbals district of Glasgow and lived only a couple of streets away from my Mum and Dad.

On the 10th of September, some 30.000 delirious Glaswegians, my heavily pregnant Mum and Dad amongst them, were at Glasgow's central railway Station to welcome their hero home. Whether the excitement of it all started her off or not, on the morning of the 11th my mother gave birth to me, so I can legitimately claim to have been there. To be born in a "single end" on the second floor of soot blackened tenement in depression hit Glasgow in the mid thirties is as low a point in society as you can get but the advantage of that is the only way is up!

The streets were a tough playground. My first experience of being stitched was at the age of four when, during one of the frequent street battles, I suffered a direct hit on the head whilst picking up ammunition for the big boys to throw back at the raiders form another street gang. I wasn't wearing a tin hat. Where were the health and safety brigade?

My Dad didn't box, he was an artist and musician, but my uncles from both sides did and Mum's brother Jackie Swan was a professional who had sparred with Benny. As a child of the Gorbals I was surrounded by boxing. The outbreak of WWII brought the migration of my immediate family to Cambridgeshire in the South East of England where my dad was stationed with the RAF. It was like moving back a hundred years in time from the slums of Glasgow to a tiny rural village in the fen lands. The village was called Reach and our cottage was in the outskirts with no running water or sanitation, no electricity or gas and down an unmade track. Strangely the locals didn't understand plain Glaswegian and we didn't understand the Cambridgeshire drawl but that is another story and it is sufficient to say that my boxing education continued in the Cambridgeshire Fen Country.

I fought constant battles with my eighteen month older brother but we fought together against the local boys

In 1948 when I was twelve years old, a professional boxer called George Lovell gave me a hard cover book simply called "Boxing" by Viscount Knebworth in association with W. Childs, coach to the Cambridge University Boxing Club. From that day on it became my "bible". It covers the history of boxing from the prize ring to The Queensbury rules, with many illustrations and it fired my imagination reading about the exploits of the great fighters of that era. It was published in 1931 and although the presentation is "old fashioned" the content is as valid today as it was then and it opened my mind to all aspects of training. When I first began coaching at an amateur boxing club, I read many coaching manuals and attended ABA coaching courses but I learned very little, if anything, that was not covered by Knebworth and Childs all those years before. Some sixty three years later, I still have the "bible". It is the keystone to my philosophy of boxing

As well as boxing my self, I was an avid fan. By the time I was in my early teens I could reel off every champion at every weight throughout the history of the game. I read every book on boxing that I could find and I followed the current scene by reading the weekly editions of Boxing News. In fact I probably learned more from reading those books than I ever did at school.

In the forties went to professional boxing promotions in Cambridge and other Fen towns with my Dad and my older brother Danny. Places such as Bury-St-Edmunds, Wisbeach and Chatteris. We were well known by the professional boxers on the circuit. I still remember many of them, Wally Beckett, Stan Purcell, Gus Harris, Tommy Bailey, Mark Hart, the Giles brothers and little Charlie Waters as well as our own locals, Fred Clements, Johnny Burling, Johnny Newman, "Bumbler" Barton and George Lovell. Charlie Waters was a flyweight and under five feet tall. His seconds had to lift him up onto the stool between rounds which left his feet dangling. Heavyweight "Bumbler" Barton was the opposite. He was massive with huge bulging biceps. He drove trucks for a living and even on the days he was fighting he could be found loading tons of sugarbeet by fork. As a consequence, by the second round of his fights he would already be exhausted and he would spend the rest of the fight waltzing with an equally torpid opponent. We went into the dressing rooms to watch the boxer's gloving up and we talked to them and their trainers before and after their contests.

Those are indelible memories, along with times spent huddled round our old 'Marconi' battery radio listening to Raymond Glendenning's commentaries with Barrington-Dalby's inter round summaries of fights featuring our hero's Bruce Woodcock, Freddie Mills, Nell Tarleton and many others. I remember Dad tuning into an American station to listen to one of the great Joe Louis's World heavyweight title defences. We worshiped the "Brown Bomber" and "sugar" Ray Robinson, Archie Moore and Henry Armstrong. It was a great grounding for what was to come in the future.

In the years after WWII we had our own boxing "camp" complete with open air ring and my Dad trained a couple of local professionals whom Danny and I sparred with. By the time I was thirteen or fourteen, I could spar fifteen three minute rounds, but that's enough about me. This book is about the boxers I managed

The years that followed are part of another story which I don't want to get into at this point, except to say that after serving time with the Parachute Regiment, in 1955 I moved from the Fens of Cambridgeshire to Preston in Lancashire and married Jean Parkinson.

In 1971 a new amateur boxing club was formed in Preston and was named Preston & Fulwood ABC and affiliated to the East Lancs. ABA. Its first tournaments were held at the London Road Labour Club but the first show that I attended was at the new Guild Hall in Preston. I had not been involved in the sport for some time, having been to busy with our young family and in starting a business although I had attended Professional boxing promotions in Preston, Manchester, Blackpool and Liverpool.

To be frank, the level of boxing I saw that night in the Guild Hall, left much to be desired, but to be fair it was a new club and many of the boxers were very young, but the lack of basic skills was apparent. The upshot of it was that Jean said to me "instead of criticising why don't you go and help with the training". A couple of days later, I went to the club and met the chief coach Harold Blackburn who had been a good pro himself boxing under the pseudonym of Johnny Black. I was good friends with his younger brother Terry so when I offered my services they were gratefully accepted and I was back in a boxing gym.

Harold's son, Peter Blackburn was the first P&F amateur champion when he won a National Schoolboy title at aged fifteen

Over the next ten years, many of them as chief coach after Harold retired for health reasons I devoted three evenings and Sunday mornings to coaching many young boxers with Terry Blackburn as my assistant. I had the pleasure of seeing them develop their skills as they matured from schoolboy and junior boxers to the seniors, winning and losing along the way but mostly winning. During that period some my boxers won national schoolboy and ABA titles.

My days with the Amateurs came to an end in January 1982 when I could no longer tolerate the political infighting and the trivial upmanship of some of the ABA officials who were more interested in their own importance than in the welfare of the boxers whom they were supposed to be supporting. As a result of their childish shenanigans and incompetence, my entire team of senior boxers, most of whom I had coached since boyhood, were disqualified from the preliminary round of the ABA championships of that year simply because our club secretary had missed a date for submitting their entry forms.

When the mistake was realised there were still ten days to go before the first night of the prelims. I tried to move heaven and earth to have the entries accepted but to no avail. Individuals of the so called East Lancs Executive Council of the ABA had political points to score over one another so insisted on enforcing a new rule. Up until that year amateur boxers could turn up on the day and be accepted.

I had high hopes for some of my senior team progressing to titles. Gary Bully, Alan Dickenson, Steve Hardman, Dean Charles, Sammy Sampson, and Tony Chadwick, all now eighteen or nineteen years old, had boxed well all year and were looking forward to their chance at an ABA title. I walked away from amateur boxing.

Amateur boxing survives because of the dedication and selfless contribution of the many people who devote their time to helping the clubs. From the coaches who work with the boys week in week out, to the unpaid officials such as MC's, judges, timekeepers and referees to the mums and dads who help run the local shows and especially the young boxers themselves who make their parents and friends proud with their efforts in the ring. Some go on to win ABA titles and even represent their country. I have nothing but respect and admiration for them, some of whom have spent a lifetime in the sport. It's just a pity that there are also a few who can make decisions that can detrimentally affect the careers of these youngsters.

Chapter one
SAMMY SAMPSON

It was January 1981 when Sammy Sampson came to see me at P&F club. He was twenty two years of age and a bit older than the usual recruit to amateur boxing. He had been born in Jamaica and came to live in Preston with his parents when he was four. At first he asked me if he could do some boxing training but added that he was not interested in actual competition. He explained that he had spent all his teenage years in body building gyms but he had become bored with the routine and wanted to try something different. He had won the Junior Mr Great Britain body building title the year before and also various power lifting titles so he was a seasoned weight trainer

I told him that I ran a competitive club and I had a team of senior boxers who needed my coaching in preparation for contests and so I did not have time to spend on non competitors, especially at the elementary stage, but I told him he was welcome to become a club member and use the boxing facilities providing it did not interfere with their use of the equipment. He gladly accepted those conditions.

Over the next few sessions I noticed this muscular West Indian kid punch the heavy bags without seeming to have a clue as which way round to stand, He obviously had never had a boxing glove on in his life. He joined in with the group warm-up routines that preceded training and had an easy going personality and obviously got on well with rest of the boys. He never missed a session and so, after a couple of weeks I had a talk with him and decided to teach him the basics. First I put him on the scales and, at 5'9" tall, he weighed 12st 7lbs. He was a good pupil and his bag work and footwork quickly improved.

By the end of each training session, after two or three rounds of pad work with each of my senior squad, I was tired and my heart would sink when I saw this twelve stone odd hunk of muscle gloved up and patiently awaiting his turn in the ring. Any trainer will tell you that the hardest, but the most valuable, part of coaching is the time spent in the ring with the technical pads and tech-spar gloves, but it is hard on the elbow joints especially when coaching novices.

Sammy became a solid member of the club and attended all the shows that our boxers fought on. With the change in training routine his physique began to alter and he lost half a stone in weight. He worked hard and gradually improved so much that by the time the 1981/2 season started after the summer lay off, he was joining in the sparring sessions. Of course he was still a long way from the standard of my best young senior ABA boxers, but he was getting better all the time and could give them a useful workout when sparring. He had improved so much that I asked him if he would changed his mind about boxing competitively. His reply was that if I thought he had reached the novice standard he was willing to give it a go.

I arranged for him to have his first contest at a show in Morecambe. The Lancaster lads ABC coach Alan McCabe; also had a late starter aged twenty five, making him even older than Sammy, so a match was made at 11st 5lbs. On the night as we prepared, Sammy was nervous but controlled. His mother, who was a seamstress, had made him a beautiful pair of shorts in club colours plus a white towelling dressing gown with his name and the P&F club emblem embroidered in a circle on the back. With his West Indian colouring and his body building experience of flexing and posing, plus an application of oil, he looked more like a world champion than a raw novice. Added to that he oozed self confidence and when the referee called the boxers to the centre of the ring, his opponent was obviously overawed.

At the sound of the bell, Sammy was across the ring quickly and he slammed out a solid left jab. From the start Sammy was one of those fighters who tended to hurt with any punch he landed. He was not yet a KO puncher, but against another novice who wasn't used to taking punches, they were effective. Anyway, after about a minute of one way traffic, during which the Lancaster Lad had been down twice, the referee called it off and Sammy had, in the space of nine months starting from scratch, won his first amateur contest.

During the rest of that season, Sammy had several more contests and won them all. As mentioned, in January 1982, I walked away from the Amateur Boxing scene. Some of my boxers left P&F club and joined other out of town clubs, including Sammy. He joined St Helens ABC which was in the West Lancs ABA area, along with Steve Hardman.

For the twelve months following my fall out with the ABA officials, my only contact with Boxing was reading the weekly Boxing News magazine.

In early January 1983 Sammy came to see me. He said that he had been entered into the ABA championships by his St Helens club but was dissatisfied with the level of coaching he was receiving. He had been offered the use of a makeshift gym in Preston and he asked me to coach him on a one- to- one basis. I couldn't resist the temptation because it wasn't boxing per se that I had fallen out with but the politics surrounding it.

It also gave me the luxury of having time to develop Sammy's boxing and my coaching techniques and explain the intricacies of the game without the limit of time. He was still attending his amateur club and fitness classes so my sessions were devoted to pure technique. The limitations of this arrangement were the fact that I would have no access to sparring or the immediate pre-contest input. Anyway, the result was that he won the West Lancs ABA title. He lost in the next round of the championship tournament when he met the eventual ABA champion and future British professional champion, Ensley Bingham. That ended our amateur boxing association and my brief return to coaching.

In August 1983, some six months after my last sessions with Sammy, he was back to see me. This time he came to ask for my advice on the prospect of him turning professional.

This was serious and required a lot of thought and discussion.

I asked him if he had any contact with the pro game, suspecting he may have been approached by someone at his amateur club, but he assured me that he had not. This was his own idea and he hadn't a clue about how or where to start, accept to ask me because he knew I would be able to advise him of his next move.

Although my boyhood was spent more involved with the pro boxers than the amateurs, there was a lot of stuff to sort out. I knew it would be easy enough to send him to one of the Manchester or Liverpool professional stables, there were no pro trainers active in Preston or the immediate area at the time, but that would have been like sending a lamb to slaughter. Sure they would have loved the look of this big strong young guy with an ABA district title no matter how elementary, but I knew that Sammy was still a raw novice in boxing terms. With his late entry to the sport he had not had anywhere near enough time in the ring to survive in the rough tough dog eat dog world of a professional gymnasium let alone the contest ring.

I couldn't do that to Sammy Sampson. He was married with two children and by now I knew and liked his family and he mine. It became obvious that the only way into the pros for him was with my knowledge and guidance.

The thought of entering the professional game as a trainer was exciting but there were many obstacles to be negotiated. I had no doubts about my ability to train boxers at a higher level but I was running a business with two retail shops and an aquarium manufacturing workshop. I could only proceed with the help and support of my wife Jean, who was working full time in one shop and we had a manager in the other. Jean agreed that I would have to spend less time in the business so we re-scheduled our operation so that I could give enough time to the boxing.

The next thing I had to do was find premises for a gym and I eventually found an old cotton mill, of which there were many in Preston, close to the town centre. I negotiated a three year lease at a reasonable rent. I only had Sammy as a potential pro fighter, but I was sure that once he was licensed and in trained, it would attract more local boxers looking for the chance to turn professional. I could also open the gym to other members of the public for general fitness training.

I couldn't afford to employ decorators and joiners to fit the mill out but Sammy and a friend of his, John Middleham, were willing to work at it with me and by the end of September 1983, after a lot of hard graft and my bank account £5,000 lighter, we had it ready to open complete with a full size ring, six punch bags, two speed balls, mats, benches, weights, sparring and bag gloves, a shower and dressing rooms and even a sauna and sun bed. It was a heroic effort because even as we were putting it all together, I was still breaking off each evening to put Sammy through a training routine and in between, building fish tanks and cabinets for Jean to sell in the shops.......How did we do It?

I even sectioned off one end of the mill and used it as a workshop so that I could open the gym all day whilst I worked at my aquarium manufacturing and still be there to help and give advice in the gym. My eldest daughter, Deborah was studying for a PhD so was able to combine her studies whilst acting as the gym receptionist!

We called the place "The Ringside Gym" and had T shirts and seconds jackets printed with a logo.

I contacted Ted Tulley the secretary of the Central Area of the BBB of C. By phone and asked for licence application forms for myself as a trainer/second and for Sammy Sampson as boxer. Ted was a decent guy and he was very helpful. As well as the forms I got a date for me to attend the next Area council meeting, the 1st of October, at the Piccadilly Hotel, Manchester. Licence approval was subject to appearing before the council. Nat Basso was the Chairman and the council was made up from representatives of all categories of licence holders including steward's referees managers matchmakers promoters and boxers. I answered all their questions and my licence was approved. One year later I was a member of that same Central Area Council

I learned that no one could hold a managers licence until they had held a licence in another category for one year but I was given the telephone number of a Blackpool boxing manager who might be interested in signing Sammy with me as his trainer. His name was Manny Goodall and I knew of him. He managed boxers from all over the area and had been managing and promoting since the fifties. He owned the Yorkshire Executive Sporting Club based at the Norfolk Gardens Hotel in Bradford and he ran dinner shows once a month throughout the boxing season.

I had not jumped into the professional boxing business with my eyes shut. I was well aware of some of the shady goings on in the sport and the characters associated with professional boxing, but I reckoned that I was experienced enough to look after myself and my protégés.

I rang Manny and arranged a meeting for Sammy and me. A few days later we met at the Castle Casino on North Shore Blackpool where Manny was a member. At that meeting we agreed terms for Sammy to sign a one year contract. Manny was not too happy because he said he normally insisted on a three year deal. I also insisted that I would have to approve Sammy's opponents and again he wasn't to pleased but when I told him about the Ringside Gym and how much I had already invested he must have thought that he would be able to sign up more fighters who came to my gym so we agreed terms.

I knew more about Manny than he knew about me. I had already asked questions about him and Ted Tulley had given me a run down on his existing stable. I also remembered how Manny had been in the headlines a few years earlier over a run in with John Conteh.

So we were making good progress. Sammy's boxers licence was approved without him attending a meeting on the strength of my interview and Manny's association. The gym was doing OK with a lot of Sammy's workmates at BAE becoming members. Sammy was a sheet metal worker having served an apprenticeship there and he still worked full time.

John Middleham was a Policeman based at Lancashire Constabulary HQ at Hutton and was a member of the team training police cadets. He began to bring the whole cadet squad to the gym two or three times a week and I coached them on basic boxing techniques. We paired them off and put them in the ring for bouts of "Milling". Good for self discipline and character building. I primed John for an application for a second's licence which was granted so he was able to work the corner with me

The gym also attracted a few of the kick boxing clubs from as far away as Manchester. One of their World Champions, Ronnie Green, signed up to use the gym for a few classes a week. Other Muay Thai schools were regular members and some of them asked to spar with Sammy as a way of improving the Western style boxing element of their sport.

I began to take Sammy to other gyms in Manchester and Liverpool to spar with professionals and he was able to handle himself well in their company. He was never short of confidence or bottle

By the beginning of December 1983, Manny began ringing to ask when Sammy would be ready to fight. I told him that I felt he needed another two months before I was confident that he could handle it. Sammy said he was ready now but I knew differently. After all, he had not boxed since his last amateur fight in March and his serious preparation for the transition from three rounds to six had only started when we opened Ringside gym in October. I agreed with

Manny that he would be ready for his Yorkshire Executive Club show on the second of February.

We now had a date, a weight (Sammy would operate as a light-middle) and a distance, six two minute rounds. I was told that the purse would be the standard going rate for a six two minute round contest less 25% managers commission and I would receive 10% as his trainer. These were the BBBofC regulations. Since I wasn't charging Sammy gym fees, the 10% didn't go very far towards my overheads.

I was soon learning a bit about the inside manipulations of the game. Manny wouldn't, or couldn't, give me an opponents name at that stage. Manny's matchmaker for his shows was Tommy Miller. Tommy was from the old school. He was in his mid sixties at that time and was a manager/matchmaker. He had been in the business so long that he knew everybody, which is the key to matchmaking, one of the most stressful jobs in boxing. Tommy was as crafty as a bag of monkeys and an expert at manipulation. Often he would give you the name of an opponent only to change it at the very last moment leaving you in a "take the opponent or no contest" position. I was subjected to this move several times in the next few years as I will relate.

I quickly learned that ninety nine per cent of boxing "contracts" are verbal. Terms are agreed over the phone and are binding only by trust. The BBB f C does have a comprehensive contract form which is legally binding but it is unusual to be offered a written contract unless it is for the more important fights such as championship eliminators, title fights or International bouts.

Ringside gym had now settled into a routine and I was able to concentrate on getting Sammy ready for his debut. He was already "fit to train" and I had the benefit of eight weeks to prepare him. I had the advantage of only having one boxer to concentrate on and he had learned the basics from me so I didn't have the problem of correcting faults that had become bad habits, as I was to come across in later years. If anything, the most difficult thing was the conversion of the heavily muscled physique of a body builder into one that was suited to the demands of the boxer, plus the fact that as a late starter, Sammy needed the rounds in the ring to smooth out his style. But he was a model pupil. I got feedback from him and a total trust in what I was doing with him, in other words he was turning into a good solid professional boxer.

In between all the furore of putting the gym together and running my business, which was paying for all this, I was also studying physiology and psychology. I have always been a great believer in that anyone can be an expert on anything if they work at it. All the information is out there. It is a question of absorbing it, interpreting it and practice, practice, practice. Look, listen, learn.

One advantage of having John Middleham in the team and coaching the Police Cadets, I was able to get access to courses on things such as sports injuries, first aid and sports psychology. I also got the use of the running track at Police HQ at Hutton where I took Sammy on Sunday mornings.

Sammy's improvement was apparent in the sparring sessions we were getting in Liverpool and Manchester and at the same time I was able to learn a lot by talking to the trainers in those gyms. I quizzed them about Manny Goodall and other managers whose fighters they were training and this information stood me in good stead in my dealings with them over the years.

A week before the fight, Manny informed me that Sammy's opponent was Dave Dunn, managed by Tommy Miller. The match was made at 11st. 4lbs. When I checked Dunn out, I found that he had already had twenty two contests but had only won three and drawn two of them, so he was experienced. He was from Manchester, was four years older than Sammy and had been a pro for eleven years. His last win had been in 1981 but he only fought once in 82 and had lost on points. He had in fact lost most of his fights on points and he was one of those boxers who are the life blood of the professional game who put the up and coming fighters through their paces and don't fall over the first time they get hit. It was going to be a good test for the former junior "Mr Great Britain"

The day of the fight arrived. The venue was the home of the Yorkshire Executive Sporting club, the Norfolk Gardens Hotel in Bradford, an hour and a half drive on the motorway from Preston. The guests were invariably professional people, businessmen, their employees and clients. The format of those dinner shows was a three course meal with lots of booze, followed by a half hour comedy turn, usually a "Blue" comedian and then a guest speaker, often a leading sports personality, followed by four boxing bouts. As a result, the boxing didn't start until well after 9.30pm.

The weigh- in was at 8pm which allowed plenty of time for the pr-contest preparation. That evening I picked Sammy up from his home at 6pm. He was on good form and relaxed. I checked out what he had eaten that day but needn't have worried as he followed my instructions to the letter. I had weighed him in the gym the night before and he was 11st. 3lbs.

We made an easy run along the motorway and even stopped for me to have a coffee at the last service area just before we exited for Bradford so that we were not there too early. We were to follow that format many times in the next few years.

On arrival at the Hotel we made our way to the dressing rooms where we were amongst the first boxers to arrive. I found a corner where we could settle and prepare. Before long we were called to the scales. I waited to see Dunn on the scales first and he weighed in at 11st. 7lbs, three pounds over the agreed limit. Sammy weighed 11st 3lbs, a pound under.

Now I was learning about how Tommy operated. He came to see us in the dressing room and when I questioned him about the weight he said "what are you worried about, Dave is one of my fighters and he's not worth two bob". He then said to Sammy "Now don't show off in there to-night, we don't want any knock outs" Sammy was pretty peed off with Tommy and I had to calm him down which I soon did. We went out to the hall to get the feel of the atmosphere. The guest speaker that night was Ian Botham and we stayed out to listen for a few minutes.

When we got back to the dressing room I began the process of preparing Sammy for the contest by getting him into the "Zone". I will be referring to this in future with other boxers so I will give a quick description of what this entails.

It starts with the boxer getting changed into his boxing gear. Socks and boots, groin protector, shorts and dressing gown. His hands are then bandaged with the specified eighteen feet of two inch bandage for each hand plus nine feet of one inch zinc oxide plaster tape. I always prepared the tape by cutting it into a pattern of lengths to support the metacarpals, the base of the thumb and the knuckles with narrow strips between the fingers to hold it all in place.

During this time the boxer should start to shut down from surrounding distractions and begins to focus on the fight. I would talk about the tactics we have practiced and the action I wanted them to take after the first bell. The boxer then stretches as a preliminary to warming up with some shadow boxing to get the heart rate up a little. The glove "whip" at the show usually brings the contest gloves, 6ozs for weights up to light middle and 8ozs from middleweight up, when the previous contest starts. That night we were second on.

The gloves are laced on and the laces bound with tape to make sure they don't come loose during the fight. Fighters go through a moment or two of nervous apprehension around this time as their adrenaline starts to flow. It varies tremendously from fighter to fighter. It's not a bad thing and most fighters are able to keep a little fear under control and it usually heightens their reactions. I apply a smear of oil to the face and body. This helps prevent abrasions especially before a fighter starts to sweat. Vaseline is rubbed into the eyebrows and around the nose and ears for the same reason but has to be kept to a minimum.

The ref will ask for the surplus to be wiped off before the fight starts if too much is used

By the time we were called to the ring the boxer should be warmed up, focused and in the mood for the job. He would be 'switched on' or as I put it, in the Zone.

Before leaving the dressing room I would check that I had everything with me that I would need during the contest and as allowed by the regulations. First the boxer's gumshield, then a full water bottle, a sponge and a clean white towel, Vaseline, ice bag and cold iron (to apply to local swellings) and a pair of scissors. The all important kit in case of a cut was a bottle of 1000to1 adrenaline solution and swab sticks to apply it and packs of sterile gauze. I always had a screw top jar with a few carefully prepared swab sticks pre-soaked in adrenaline which fitted into my second's jacket pocket.

At this point I will explain the job of a chief second before and during a contest. The coaching of the boxer should be left in the gym. By fight time he has to go with what he has learned and the tactics, if any, that have been rehearsed. A second should know the capabilities of his charge and his job is to bring the fighter into the ring motivated and ready for the fray. If the second is himself nervous at this stage he must disguise it and he must be both encouraging and reassuring.

From the first bell I always concentrated on watching the opponent rather than my own fighter. I would be looking for any faults he may be showing that could leave openings for my fighter to exploit, or dangerous punches he was throwing that my fighter had to defend against. I know it is the fighter himself who has to do this during the round, but there are times when the right word of advice between rounds can improve a fighter's performance.

The main job is to refresh a boxer at the end of a round and provide a haven for one minute. The second should stay calm. If there is blood from mouth nose or eye, the chief second's job is to instantly access the injury and stem the flow. In the case of cuts to the eye, he must first dry the wound with sterile gauze then apply a solution of 1001 adrenaline into the injury. The adrenaline acts by shrinking the capillary veins, so must be applied right into the wound and then covered with Vaseline. Some seconds build a reputation on their skill at doing this and are known in the trade as cuts men. Broken noses are not uncommon and from my personal experience a badly bent septum can be straightened if it is done immediately after the blow. Mine was and I have straightened a few. Not all.

Swelling around the eye can be reduced by the application of an ice pack or a cold "iron" pressed against it. All the time, whether injured or not, the chief second should be motivating the fighter or calming him down. Fighters, according to their temperament, can be discouraged or become angry during the fight. Losing your temper during the contest can be disastrous. At the same time, losing concentration can be just as lethal and it is a second's job to see that it doesn't happen. Finally the chief second must have compassion. If a fighter is being well beaten and perhaps being too brave for his own good a second can pre-empt a referees decision by "throwing in the towel" or retiring a boxer on his stool before a round starts.

The one thing I always told my boxers was that I needed to get "feedback" from them during the interval. It didn't have to be words just a nod of the head and eye contact was enough. From that it was possible to know what state they were in at any stage. I always knew if their head was down, if they were stunned or if they were getting angry and from that I could take the appropriate action. This brief explanation means I won't have to refer to it again when describing individual fights.

Sammy was in the zone and when the first fight was over we were called to the ring. Sammy looked the business with Black and silver grey shorts and embroidered black satin dressing gown. As he went through a light shadow boxing routine in the ring and the MC introduced the fighters, I took a good look at Dave Dunn. By contrast he was subdued with no sign of having warmed up or of any pr-contest activity. He was obviously unconcerned having seen it all before. He had the thick waisted look of a man half a stone heavier than his best weight.

Referee Harry Warner called the fighters to the centre of the ring and Sammy gave Dunn a stare but I don't think he was intimidated. I popped Sam's gum shield in and gave him a pat on the back and the bell rang for start of the contest and the start of Sammy's and my professional boxing careers.

Sammy was quickly across the ring to lead off with a long left and a hopeful but ineffective right. Dunn was compact and methodical but not offering much by way of leading punches. At the half way point in the first Sammy bundled Dunn to the ropes and slammed in a good body shot but Dunn was unperturbed. The round ended and Sammy had won it clearly.

The pattern of the second and third rounds was pretty much the same. Sammy was making the fight but had not shaken Dunn at any stage. At the same time, he had not taken a shot of any meaning him self and he was clearly three rounds up. Round four, in contest terms was new ground for Sammy Sampson having previously only gone the three rounds of amateur boxing. I had urged him to step up the pace and try to draw a lead punch from Dunn to open him up for a counter. Again Dunn was just content to cover then throw a few out of range shots, then get close and spoil. His experience at that stage began to show as he tied Sammy up and held him.

In the fifth round signs of Sammy's physical type began to show. The problem with big muscles is that although they store lots of Glycogen, fuel for instant energy, the bi- product of burning that fuel is lactic acid which the blood supply can't get rid of quickly enough. This result's in a slow down of reaction time. The effect is obvious, it was as if Sammy was wading through water and Dave Dunn knew that Sammy was tiring and for the first time he became aggressive. I was glad to hear the bell for the end of the round, which Sammy had lost.

I knew that I needed to get him to relax in the one minute interval and was glad that we had covered this scenario in training and that his powers of recovery were good. All he needed to do was control his output for the last round and use his boxing ability.

Dunn, for the first time started the last round aggressively which opened him up to counter punches and at the final bell Harry Warner had no hesitation in raising Sammy's hand as the winner. His scoring was the same as mine. Sammy had won the first four rounds, lost the fifth and drawn the last.

I was satisfied with Sammy Sampson's performance. Dunn had been a tough opponent, mature and experienced and WE had learned a lot from the six rounds compared to what could have happened if he had fought a lesser fighter who may have been stopped early.

Who would have thought that the twelve and a half stone body builder of just three years before would be winning a six round professional boxing contest weighing just over eleven stones?......Not many I can assure you.

I was amazed when, the following day I got a phone call from Manny Goodall. He told me that he was disappointed with Sammy's performance and that Tommy Miller had told him he was wasting his time with him. My reply was something like "How is it wasting *your* time. I am the one working with him, your not paying for his training or gym fees, your just taking 25% of his purse" There were probably one or two expletives referring to Tommy as well.

After a couple of days off it was back to the gym. Now with that first experience behind us I was able to adapt the training regime to work on Sammy's weaknesses.

There are many examples in the history of boxing where men with muscular physiques have to learn how to cope with the lactic problem. The great middleweight champion, "Marvellous" Marvin Hagler suffered two defeats early on in his career when he "blew up" during hard fights. It is a question of training the body to build the energy systems and then the intelligence of the fighter to control his output during a contest. Big Frank Bruno is the classic example of having a massive lactic problem. If he could not overpower an opponent early in a fight he would go into the lactic state as he did against Bonecrusher Smith and then in fights with Tim Witherspoon and Lennox Lewis, all of which he was winning for the first few rounds and then he was "Walking in Water". Just watch the decathlon athletes who can sprint and jump and throw in all the explosive events but are labouring in the 1,500m, the one long run they have to do. They have the same problem.

Anyway, back to Sammy's record. We continued with the routine of going to other gyms for sparring and by this time getting other trainers to bring boxers to our gym. A couple of ex-amateurs from P&F, as expected, came to see me but after a few sessions they faded away. I think that the training regime was too hard for them.

Manny's March Dinner show came and went with no word from him then I got a call to see if Sammy was fit to box on the April 16th show. Manny didn't even know that Sam hadn't been out of training since his first contest. He was so used to his other fighters disappearing off the scene after a fight and not showing up in the gym until they were given their next date. As usual Tommy couldn't give us a name so there was no way of checking an opponent out or preparing for a specific style.

A few days before the fight I was told that Sammy's opponent was Mick Dono of Liverpool. Mick had had fourteen fights winning seven and losing seven. We had not come across him during our sparring sessions but I knew him from his amateur days when he boxed under his real name, Michael Donahue. He had always boxed at welterweight but the match was at 11st 2lb which suited us and gave us a natural weight advantage but again we were giving away experience.

I was cautious in view of Tommy Millers comments after Sammy's first fight so I rang one of the Liverpool trainers whom I was now getting to know quite well after our sparring sessions. He said he knew Mick and his trainer/manager, Chris Moorcroft. He thought that Sammy should be able to handle him on the strength of his sparring but warned that Mick was known as a "Rough handful". That was good enough inside information for me. I could just imagine Tommy reassuring Dono that Sampson was "now't special"

Everything had gone well with the preparation and we set off and followed the same routine as the last time. This time we were on the scales first and were spot on the eleven two. Dono, with a surly scowl, weighed in at 10st 11lb so sure enough we had a five pound advantage.

This time we were first on the bill after the guest speaker. Sammy as usual was perfectly turned out and warmed up and in the zone. The referee was Alan Richardson, and soon the first round was underway. In contrast to his first opponent, Dono was soon across the ring and punching but the physical difference was obvious. Sammy was out reaching him and knocking his head back but it didn't deter him.

The first round was pretty even due to Dono's aggression, but Sam was calm between rounds. In the second Sammy was first to land and slowly began to give Mick a beating. In the third and fourth, Dono began to fall back on the rough stuff. He was holding and hitting and banging in with his head. The ref seemed out of his depth and didn't know how to control him, but it was good for Sam's learning curve and providing he didn't get cut, he was never in danger. Three quarters through the fifth, after a particularly rough close quarter's exchange, Sammy broke away and began to gesture to the ref and was complaining about something. I was up on ringside in a flash but just then the bell sounded for the end of the round. As soon as I got Sammy's gum shield out he said to me "The bastard just bit me" sure enough there was a bite mark bruise on his chest. I immediately called the ref over and lodged a complaint. He said to me "Don't worry I'll have a word with him" Don't worry he said, Cheeky swine.

Sammy was pretty mad and I had to calm him down. I said "make him pay for it" At the bell he was on him in a flash slamming home big left and rights and he dropped Dono with a left hook. He got up at eight but was cowering against the ropes as Sammy rained shots on him. There was no sign of the lactic problem. The ref called it off and Sammy had scored his second win and his first by stoppage.

Manny called the next day and this time he was "quite pleased" with the result and said that Sammy would definitely be on his next show on the 21st April

The training went well but again no name was given of the opponent but I was getting the picture. Two days to go and I was given a name. Lee Roy. This time my research showed that Lee Roy had fought eleven times, lost eight, won one and drawn two. It looked like an easier fight

The venue was the same and by now we knew the routine pretty well but I was about to learn more about Tommy Miller's devious ways. As soon as we arrived at the Hotel he came to me and said "we have got a bit of a problem, Roy is out, he got injured in the gym (the usual lame excuse) but don't worry, Dave Dunn is standing in" I was mad because it was so obvious that he was giving Dunn, his fighter, a chance for revenge. Dunn had had one win since our first fight with him and he fancied the job. It was fait'accompli and we had to accept. Sammy showed how good a professional he was becoming by accepting it without a murmur and we knew that he would do a better job the second time around. Dunn was even closer to the weight and was just a pound heavier than Sam.

Again Harry Warner was the ref but this time, because Dunn was more confident, he began to lead off. It left him open and Sammy was soon punishing him. Round after round went by and Sammy was well in control but still could not find a stoppage punch against the tough pro. He won a comfortable point's win with only one round drawn according to Warner's score card and that must have been in sympathy. So Tommy's plan had backfired again. Sammy had shown no sign of the lactic acid problem he had in their first fight.

It was the last show of the Yorkshire Executive SC season and there wouldn't be another until September. I had a meeting with Manny and asked him to find some fights for Sammy until about mid July when it would be time to lay him off from training for couple of weeks before picking up again for the new season. Manny said he would see what he could do but that didn't leave me feeling to confident in him as a manager.

We now went into the mode that most professional boxers are in if they are not with one of the big promoter/managers stables. They cannot be kept in a state of peak fitness indefinitely, but must be fit enough to take a contest at short notice, even sometimes very short notice. The chance of getting enough time to be able to reach a "peak" is remote.

With someone like Sammy it wasn't really a problem but many fighters do not have the discipline to train relentlessly.

A month after the second Dunn fight I got a call from Manny. He said he had a good fight for Sammy in about ten days time. He had a call from Frank Warren seeking an opponent for Mick Courtney over eight three minute rounds. I couldn't believe it! Courtney had been an ABA champion and an international amateur. He had fought fourteen times as a pro and had won eleven and he was rated number ten lightmiddle in the Boxing News ratings. It was as I pointed out earlier, a typical "lamb to the slaughter" match.

He defended the match by saying he could get good money for the fight and that as Sammy's manager he wanted him to make some money and in any case, he and Tommy didn't think he would get very far in the business so he may as well cash in. The fact that Manny was on 25% of the purse didn't influence him then??

I turned the match down flat although he said he wanted to speak to Sammy about it and since I was only the trainer I didn't have the authority to turn it down. I told him that if he insisted I would ask the BBB of C to arbitrate on the fairness of the match. That shut him up. As a result of that head to head, no other matches were offered, but at least Sammy still had all his marbles!

The summer came and went. We had a holiday break and the gym was ticking over with my aquarium workshop keeping me busy and keeping the wolf from the door. Jean was doing a sterling job in managing the shop. We had sold the lease on our town centre shop so we just had the one shop in Ribbleton.

By the middle of August we were back into routine and Manny, for the first time, came over to our gym to see Sammy and me. He was full of apologies about the Courtney affair and said that it was actually Tommy Miller who had got the call from Warren and that he didn't know anything about Courtney's record. He said his first show at the Sporting club was on the seventeenth of September and that we would be on it. I asked him why he had not found work for us since May and he just said it was difficult to match Sam. After just three contests, I didn't think so. Of course no opponents name was given but we were used to that.

Three days before the fight I got a call from Tommy Miller direct for the first time. He asked me if I would accept Frankie Moro as an opponent. Now this was a big change in attitude which meant that he and Manny were getting the picture. Frankie was a Ghanaian fighter with experience in Africa and had come over to the UK to box and had been signed up by Tommy. We knew Frankie pretty well having sparred with him over in Liverpool and I had seen a couple of his fights in Bradford. He was 6' tall and muscular, a slippery box-fighter and a class up from Sammy's previous opponents but Sam had held his own in sparring. I told Tommy we would take the fight but only over six *three* minute rounds knowing that Sammy would need the extra time to wear Frankie down. Tommy complained that they couldn't afford to pay the extra money, it was worth a bit more than the six two's. After a bit of whinging he agreed, providing Sammy could be inside 11st 2lb since Frankie was really a blown up welter. That was not a problem.

Why was I having to haggling over purse money with Manny's matchmaker?

We were back to the old routine with the drive over to Bradford. We were looking forward to, some day, boxing at other venues, but what the hell. On the scales Sammy weighed 11st 1 and 1/2lb Frankie weighed in at 10st 12lb so, for the second time, we had a slight weight advantage.

The ref was Brian Hogg. His name will come up again in the story of another of my boxers but I will just say that he wasn't one of the best. From the first bell Sammy took charge. He was so much stronger than Frankie and was able to force him onto the back foot but Frankie was very good at slipping around on the ropes and Sammy wasn't able to land any big shots. Frankie was counter punching neatly in rounds two three and four but was not hurting Sammy. By the start of the fifth I thought that things were fairly even points wise but Sammy needed to close Frankie down and by the last minute of the round he caught him with some good body shots and trapped him in a corner with some combination punching. The most satisfying thing from my point of view was that, even over the three minute distance, there was no sign of the lactic effect. The last round was the same as the fifth and Sammy had again won on points

I could tell by the look on Tommy's face when I went t to collect Sammy's purse. He thought he was onto a good thing with Frankie. He was beginning hate us.

A month later, 22nd October, and it was back to Bradford. This time the late notification was a surprise. We were told it was Lee Roy again; the fighter who was supposed to have pulled out on the day Sammy fought Dunn for the second time. Roy had only won one of eleven with a couple of draws. Would he turn up on the night? He did and weighed in half a pound lighter than Sam's eleven stone two.

Ron Hackett refereed but didn't have much to do. The first round was very one sided with Lee showing the attitude of someone thinking "what am I doing in here?" He saw it through to the bell. A minute into the second round Sammy feinted with his left then feinted with his right and Lee Roy fainted. It was goodnight Mr Roy. Win number five

Three weeks later and glory be. I got a call from Tommy on the 7th of November to see if Sammy was fit to fight on the 12th at the Civic Hall in Nantwich. This time against a middleweight called Dave Scott. I told him I would call him back in an hour after talking to Sammy. I didn't need to speak to Sammy; I just needed to check out my records to access the strength of Scott. He had won nine, lost four and had two draws, so he was reasonably tough opponent on paper. Knowing how Sammy was coming on and realising he needed to keep progressing I accepted the bout. The match was made at eleven stones seven. Sammy was delighted to be boxing at a different venue and was unconcerned about the weight. As he always said "if you say it is right it's right with me" It is good to have that sort of trust but it is a responsibility not to be abused.

It was a shorter trip to Nantwich. It was an open show so not an audience of boozed up diners, but people who have paid to see some decent boxing.

On the scales Sammy was the heaviest he been since turning professional. It was deliberate since I didn't want to give to much weight away. Sammy was eleven four Scott eleven seven. Scott was tall at 6'1". The dressing room area was a bit bizarre, an open room with screens separating the boxers. As we were getting changed I spotted Dave Scott trying to get a look at Sammy so knowing all about his posing abilities from his body building days, I told him to step out a little and do some big lat spreads making him look half as big again. It worked like a charm.

From the first bell Scott was in counterpunching mode allowing Sammy to back him up and Scott smothered at every opportunity. By virtue of doing all the leading off, Sammy won the round clearly. The second was pretty much the same and in the third Sammy began to land some good right crossers after drawing the counter punch. Scott went back to his corner with his left eye swollen. Half way into round four, Sammy landed the best right hand of his career up to that point. Scott was hurt and badly cut and the ref jumped in and stopped it. It had been a solid, one sided performance from Sammy Sampson.

One week later Tommy was back on the phone. He was offering us fight at Leeds Town Hall on the 28th of November this time over eight two minute rounds against a Manchester's Wayne Crolla. This was better, a bit more regular action. I knew Wayne way back to his amateur days and thought of him as a welterweight but the match was at eleven two, Sam's best weight. The purse was the best yet. Crolla had fought professionally twenty times winning fourteen of them, so he was no mug. Apart from that we had sparred with him at Nat Basso's gym in Manchester. Nat was his manager.

Wayne was a pound lighter than Sammy on the night.

I didn't know the ref Ricky Nicholson, but we didn't need him anyway. Wayne was competitive in the first round and until halfway through the second, than suddenly he was in trouble from a big left hook. This time it was a cut under his right eye, but not a stoppage type injury. In the third Wayne spent most of the time avoiding more damage to his eye, with his gloves held high. I told Sammy to switch to the body at the start of the fourth and he did to good effect. Wayne was being hurt and he brought his hands down and got clipped by Sampson's big right cross. Wayne was down for a count of eight. He got up but the fight had been knocked out of him and the ref jumped in to save him. That was stoppage win number four out of seven. Not too bad for someone who was going nowhere.... eh Manny!

This was Sammy's last fight under Manny Goodall's management. On the first of October 1984, a year after taking out my trainers licence I applied for a manager's licence and it was granted.

I rang Manny and told him that when Sammy's contract with him ended in January, He would be signing up with me. He was pretty peed off and said "after all I have done for him, getting him seven wins" Yes, Manny, and in the process you tried to get him turned over on at least three occasions not counting the attempt with Courtney. I had spent hundreds of hours in the ring with him, taken him all over the place at my own expense for sparring and haggled to get him more money and the right distance contests. You had just taken 25% of his purses.....We were learning fast and playing them at their own game.

We took a break over Christmas and the New Year. I knew there would be nothing I could do until the end of January as far as getting fights for Sammy anyway. Besides that, I was very busy with the aquarium business on the run up to Christmas, with lots of tanks and cabinets to make.

It also gave me a chance to step back from boxing and access the year. A lot had happened. I had learned a lot more about the game. I watched a lot of fights apart from Sammy's and also observed the goings on in the dressing rooms and corners. The good, the bad and the just plain stupid!

I was under no illusions about Sammy Sampson. He certainly had come a long way in a short time and I had nothing but admiration for his attitude....but to observers it was obvious that he was a "Manufactured" fighter. Because of his limited experience in boxing....at that time he had been in the game for less than four years starting from scratch...he didn't" flow" the way a fighter does when he is either naturally gifted or very experienced. He didn't have the lightening fast reflexes that the very best fighters are born with, or the god given talent of perfect timing which the hardest punchers posses even without coaching. No, he didn't have those things but what he did have was a great body, intelligence, an athletic aptitude, a big heart, self confidence, a willingness to learn and a wonderful work ethic. No coach could ask for more and in spite of the sceptics I was sure that Sammy had enough of what it takes to go a lot further in the business. Because I knew him so well I was confident that when the time came…as it always does…I would know when it was time to get him out of the game before he got too badly hurt.

I attended the Central Area Council's AGM in early January. I was nominated for a seat on the council and seconded by Tommy Miller (he was now my friend) and voted in by a comfortable margin. It was important to be on the inside where the main players collude!

Serious training was commenced on the 5th of January 1985. Sammy was still only eleven stones four after his break once again illustrating his professionalism and we were soon picking up from where we left off after his last fight.

I got an offer for a fight again at Leeds Town hall on the 5th of February. They had liked Sammy's last fight there. The opponent was a Birmingham based Ugandan called John Langol. It was over six threes at eleven stone two and the money was right. I did my usual check on Langol's record and found that he had won six and lost five. Of his wins, four had come by way of stoppage. But he had been stopped himself in four of his losses. So he could bang a bit but he didn't take a shot either. I accepted the fight.

The preparation went as normal by now. Sammy was spot on the weight and Langol a pound heavier. From the first bell Sammy was right on him. It was important to impose his authority and not allow the puncher to get too confident. Rounds two and three were pretty one sided during which Langol had taken a count. In the fourth Langol had already lost the will to fight and was "Looking" for the canvas which Sammy found for him with the help of a left hook.

Chapter two
KARL INCE. JOE THRELFALL. SAMMY.

Things at the ringside gymnasium were beginning to get interesting when two of my ex Preston & Fulwood ABC boxers came to see me. They were Karl Ince and Joe Threlfall.

Karl first came to my notice when he was fourteen or fifteen years old. He was one of those all action boys who was madly enthusiastic about boxing, just Like I had been at his age. His hero was The British Welterweight Champion Dave "Boy" Green and his one ambition in life was to be like him. He actually came to work as a Saturday boy at my shop and soon he was like another son with Jean and my children. Over the next two years Karl became a solid member of my competition squad with P&F and we had many good nights at shows with Karl usually dominating with his sheer aggression. When the bell rang it was like letting a little bull terrier off the lead.

Karl left school and started work and was of the age of making the difficult transition from Junior to Senior ABA contests. I remember taking him to fight in a tournament at Lancaster Town Hall. I think his opponents name was Hargreaves. Any way the kid had a bit of a reputation but I was confident that Karl would see to him with his growing strength and aggression. But, as sometimes happens, Karl didn't perform up to his usual standard that night and lost on points. He was bitterly disappointed but it was only a club show and no big deal.

It obviously was to Karl for he completely disappeared from the club. He didn't come to see us at the shop or telephone me and I eventually put it down to the sort of thing that young men do as they mature and find that there other things to life apart from gymnasiums and getting your nose punched. I was very disappointed all the same.

So when he turned up nearly five years later I was, at first, surprised but pleased to see him. I didn't question him about what had happened in the past, just what his intentions were. He was now a mature twenty two year old about 5' 7" tall and weighing around eleven stones of solid muscle. He said that the work he had been doing had taken him off around the Country and at one time when he was in the South of England he had gone to see Denny Mancini in London to ask him about turning pro. Denny was big time in the pro game as a manager, agent and cuts man. He had a gym in Carnaby Street just around the corner from the Lonsdale shop in Beak Street of which he was a director and manager. Denny, like most of the London "Big Shots", was used to handling ex-ABA champions so he wasn't interested in Karl and suggested he try one of the provincial mugs…oops I mean managers. So here he was.

He had not been trained or coached since his amateur days so I was anxious to get him back in the ring to see how far back he had gone. He was impressively powerful but at least half a stone above his fighting weight which would make him a welterweight. He was one step closer to his dream. I agreed to manage and train him providing he met my conditions.

Joe Threlfall was a different story. He first appeared in the P&F gym when he was eighteen. His family were farmers were into Cumberland wrestling and at that age he was well up the rankings in that field (literally). He had come along to the amateur boxing gym to try out the sport. I gave him the same basic training I would give to any boy new to the sport and he, as a proven athlete, was quick to learn. Even then he was big and powerful weighing around thirteen stone so it would have been difficult to find suitable sparring for him at our amateur gym. Anyway it didn't matter because he didn't stay long enough to get to that stage. I don't think the Boxing training was fitting in with his wrestling.

But here he was now, also twenty two years old and asking about a professional boxing career with no amateur experience at all. He was now the British Cumberland wrestling champion which proved he was a competitor and a winner although in a vastly different sport. I thought I had taken on a handful with Sammy Sampson, but this was something else.

It was no co-incidence that he had come along with Karl because they both lived in the same neck of the woods and had both been members of a local rugby club. Anyway, as you may have gathered by now, I am not someone who backs down on a challenge. I agreed to have a look at him in the ring. Joe had a great physique. At just over 6' tall, he weighed fourteen and a half stone and carried very little spare weight. In 1985 the cruiserweight division didn't exist so Joe would box at heavyweight.

When I thought they were nearing the fitness level for a six two minute round contest I took them for the regulation medical and skull X-ray which they passed easily and I applied for their professional licences. Now the gym was beginning to buzz.

Two weeks after Sammy fought John Langol, I got a call from Nat Basso. Nat was Mr Boxing in the North West. He was well known as an MC and he knew everybody in the business and I mean *everybody*. As well as being an MC. He managed quite a big stable of boxers from Manchester and farther a field. He also ran the Anglo- American Sporting Club which was based at the Piccadilly Hotel in central Manchester where the Central Area Council, of which he was the chairman, was based. The Anglo-American Club ran a series of shows throughout the season, just like Manny's YESC.

Nat wanted Sammy for one of his shows on the eleventh of March. It was an eight rounder at eleven two but once again it was against an experienced Welsh pro called Steve Davies who had a twelve win twelve loss fight record. He had been a Welsh International amateur. He had boxed in good company. When I hesitated, Nat said "well Jim, your fighter is getting a bit of a reputation and he is undefeated. It will be good experience for him and a loss wouldn't do him any harm" That was typical of that school of thought but it was not mine. Anyway, I accepted the match. Sammy took it in his usual way.

At least we were getting more sparring in our own gym which was helping us all.

At the weigh in for that fight I queried the scales. Sammy only weighed 10st 12lbs and Davies was three ponds heavier. Nat just brushed it off with the "same scales for everyone" excuse. I knew Sammy was just over eleven stones so Davies was in fact a middle weight

The fight was the hardest of Sammy's career to date. Davies was some tough nut and by the end of the fifth Sammy was having to dig deep, having taken a big right that had him down for the first time in his pro career. We had rehearsed the scenario in the gym time after time and Sammy knew that if he was down but knew where he was, he had to turn to face me in the corner and wait for my signal. This he did and waved him up at eight. The round ended before Davies could follow up and in the one minute interval, Sam's powers of recovery came to the rescue. He held his own in the sixth and seventh and won the points in the eighth by which time Davies was dog tired. It was a sound point's win and another lesson learned. It would be nice to have an easier fight though.

By this time and after having attended a couple of Area Council meetings, I was beginning to get the big picture of this business. The fact was that, as a small time provincial manager, it is extremely difficult to maintain control of an undefeated and unfashionable fighter. To get the sort of opposition a fighter like Sammy Sampson needed and the sort of opponents my new fighters were going to need was a problem. Promoters want a share of a successful fighter otherwise they are not interested, especially if it means their own "house" fighters getting beat. The fashionable fighters ie; ABA champions with big reputations, naturally gravitate to the big promoters with TV connections. Those fighters are then built up at the expense of the journeymen fighters supplied by the small time managers, one of whom I had now become.

I was also getting to know my fellow Council members. They were the sort of men I was going to have to deal with in the boxing business.

They were, by and large, a hard headed lot, some without scruples and little sympathy for the boxers themselves. They saw them as their 25% earners and Nat even said that to me. It was clear that to trust what they said was either stupid or dangerous. With some of them, you had to count your fingers after shaking hands with them. They were motivated more by money than prestige. On the other hand, a few were decent men. Knowing what and who you were dealing with was the name of the game and being on the inside helped

One way to overcome the matchmaking problem was to become a promoter myself which I knew was to take a huge financial risk. It was so risky that I had to discuss it thoroughly with Jean because it had the potential to put our business in danger and it was only the business that was keeping us afloat as it was. The gym had made at a loss in the first year.

I began to look around for a suitable venue to promote a boxing show in the Preston area. I could only make a decision based on establishing the actual cost of a promotion and the potential returns from ticket sales. I had costed projects before in my fifteen years in business so I knew what I was doing.

My reckoning was that Preston had once been a good boxing town. I had attended pro boxing shows way back in the fifties and sixties when Preston had several professional boxers including British middleweight champion, Johnny Sullivan, but it had lapsed for many years. Now that I had established a gymnasium and had fighters from the town, surely, with the right venue and some good ticket sellers it should work. My motive for promoting was not for making profits for myself, although a profit would have helped the gym along, it was to give me some control over the opponents for my boxers.

What surprised me was that, for a town the size of Preston, there were no medium sized venues at all. The new Guild Hall was too big and expensive for a trial show. It held 2,200 in a boxing show format, but the rent for a one off show was way too high and too risky. The nearest place was Park Hall at Charnock Richard, just a few miles up the motorway. The boss there was John Rigby and I had met him before. He was one of the high flying property developer types.

We had a good meeting and he showed me round the events hall. With a boxing ring in place he worked out that there would be seating for about four hundred plus maybe another hundred standing. That would be within his fire regulation limit. I got some dates from him so I had enough information to cost a show. He said he would keep the hire cost down as a first timer in the hope that if it was successful I would be repeating the booking plus they would make money on the bar.

My next move was to contact Ted Tulley who had all the costs of the officials, ring hire and boxer's purses. He was very helpful and posted to me all the relevant information. He also told me how to go about getting a promoters licence which is not as straight forward as it seemed. I would need a bankers guarantee to start with plus the backing of the Area Council, which he didn't think was a problem.

All of this was on top of my now very busy schedule in the gym. Working with the dual power houses that were Karl and Joe put a huge strain on my elbow joints. Unless you have actually held punch pads for professional boxers, you have no idea of the power they generate. Going through a range of punches from both hands covering straight shots, hooks and uppercuts, movement around the ring and a whole range of defences with one boxer in a session is hard. Doing it with two or three, one after another is exhausting. The pain in the elbow joints is doubled by mis-hits. This is when a boxer mis-times a punch or lands a punch late when you are not braced to take it. The harder a fighter hits the more it hurts. Big Joe especially, with his lack of experience but his huge punching power, caused many an aching joint.

By contrast, although Sammy was hitting very hard and getting harder, because we had been going through the routine for so long, mis-hits no longer happened with him.

The boxers were pleased with the prospect of me promoting shows for them and were confident that they could sell tickets. I would be relying on them!

I got the figures from Ted and I wrote down a detailed plan. It was just feasible but it would have to be a sell out at Park Hall. I bit the bullet and decided to go for it. The date was set for the 30th of April 1985 and the whole thing set in motion.

Now we had a date, I had six weeks to get Karl, Joe and Sammy ready for our first show. Sammy was not a problem and Karl was responding well to his new training programme. Joe Threlfall was a bit more of a problem in so much as I was starting from scratch with him as far as boxing technique is concerned. I had no doubts about his cardio/vascular fitness but instilling even the rudiments of ring craft takes time. He was a willing pupil and was encouraged and helped by his ring mates.

Karl was now beginning to look like a welterweight and his previous ring experience was standing him in good stead but naturally his long absence from the ring was obvious. He had a lot of power but his hand speed and timing had suffered by what ever he had been doing since I last had him in the ring. His sparring was improving and I was confident that I could get him the right sort of opponent for his debut.

Tommy Miller had offered his services as matchmaker, for a fee of course, and I accepted. I realised that I had a huge amount of organising to do as well as my training schedule and the Aquarium business in the background. Nat was to be the MC and Ted Tulley's job as Area secretary was to provide all the Board of Control officials ie: Two referees, a timekeeper, two Doctors, the officer in charge and whips. I had to get a ring ordered, Tickets and posters made up and printed, programmes set out and printed and a five bout bill with two other contests apart from my own three fighters, who were what this was all about in the first place. Sammy was top of the bill over eight rounds and the other four bouts were over six rounds.

Getting my priorities right was the main problem and maybe it had an affect on the mistake I was about to make.

On the 25th of March, some two weeks after Sammy's win over Steve Davies, I got a desperate telephone call from Charley Shorey, one of the London matchmakers. It was the sort of call I was to receive and make myself over the next ten years or so. He said that he needed a short notice replacement to box Lightmiddleweight Graeme Ahmed whose opponent had pulled out at the last minute. He had spoken to Tommy Miller who had given him my number so he was calling me to see if Sammy was available.

With still five weeks to go before the Park Hall show and with Sammy in full training, I promised I would call him back after checking out Ahmed's record. The show was in Gateshead, Ahmed's home town. I knew we would get no favours over there. Ahmed had had a good start to his career, winning his first twelve contests which was similar to Sammy's, but he had lost four of his last five fights. I gave Sammy a quick ring to see how he felt about the short notice but his response was as expected, bring it on. I rang a relieved Charley Shorey back and asked for some extra cash for the short notice. He complained but agreed to pay another £100. The fight was on the 27th, two days later

Our drive across to Gateshead in the morning went well and Sammy was in good spirits. The show was at the Gateshead Leisure Centre and the top of the bill fight featured Glen McCrory, who was still boxing at heavyweight, was undefeated and his manager, Doug Bidwell, also managed Ahmed.

The weigh in was at 1pm at a Hotel and there were quite a few journalists and photographers present creating a fresh experience for us. Ahmed weighed in first and I was shocked when they called his weight as 11st 11lbs and was ready to protest but first I let Sammy on the scales and when he weighed 11st 11 1/4lbs, I realised that the scales were way out and probably set to weigh heavy so as to make Glen seem bigger than he actually was. It was all bull shit. When Doug Bidwell saw Sammy on the scales he nearly had a fit. He got hold of Charley Shorey and asked him what the hell he was doing getting this big undefeated fighter for Graeme and he was even going to call the fight off. He didn't, but he wasn't a happy man.

We spent the afternoon after the weigh in at the new Metro shopping precinct. We had some lunch then went to a cinema to pass an hour or three.

The pre fight preparation went well and we were called to the ring. It was a full house and the atmosphere was the best we had experienced so far. The referee was Fred Potter. When he called the boxers to the centre of the ring it was apparent that Sammy had all the physical advantages. He was taller and altogether more powerful looking. At the first bell Sammy was quickly across the ring and shooting out a jab. Graeme was on the defence and was obviously a slick mover but Sammy stayed on top and at the end of the round, even the home town biased ref would have to give him although, now knowing how these referees operate, Fred would probably have called it a draw.

The second round started the same as the first until about two minutes through when, for the first time, Ahmed came inside Sammy's lead and bundled him to the ropes. The next few seconds were farcical. Sammy moved to his left along the ropes but his foot slipped on a wet patch on the canvas and for a moment he was off balance and against the ropes. Ahmed pressed forward in an attack and as Sammy went to counter with a left hook, he was leaning back on the ropes and his arm became tangled in the strand that holds the top and middle ropes together. The next moment he was unbalanced on one knee but not from a punch. Fred Potter jumped in and waved Ahmed to a neutral corner and started to count. Sammy looked across at me and I signalled to say to him to keep calm and get up at about seven. He hadn't taken a punch and Ahmed knew it so he didn't immediately follow up.

Now the farce got worse. During the hundreds of hours I had talked to Sammy about ring craft, I had warned him that a fighter can be at his most dangerous when getting up from a knock down if he hasn't actually been stunned. The fighter who has just scored the knockdown has an adrenaline rush and can become careless, defence wise and wide open to a counter. In fact when Sammy won his ABA title it was exactly one of those occasions. That time his opponent knocked Sammy down and then, certain he could finish the job, he walked in with his hands down and Sammy promptly knocked him out with a right hook.

This time though, Ahmed was too canny to fall for that so he didn't press forward, Sammy did a little shimmy as if to say "come in and get me" but he was ready to throw his right. We were amazed when Fred Potter jumped in and called the fight off. Sammy said "come on ref, I was fooling him" Fred said "well son, you fooled me". It was the classic opportunity he needed to end a fight that looked like it was gong to be a hard one for the home town fighter.

It was a hard lesson to learn and an indicator of what a boxer is up against when he is fighting in his opponent's home town. Referees are supposed to be unbiased.

The conversation on the return drive to Preston was full of if only's and regrets. I told Sammy that he had overdone the acting, which he now realised, but he said he was feeling confident of winning after the first round and confirmed that he had not taken a punch prior to the tangle with the ropes.

It was the end of his undefeated record so it was straight back to business in the gym.

The next four weeks flew. I was beginning to realise the enormity of the task I had taken on. My priority was definitely in the gym and I was satisfied that everyone was achieving the targets I had set for them. Karl was well up for his debut but Joe was concerned that his lack of boxing experience might be against him. I was confident, on the strength of the lack of fitness and competence I had observed in the lower levels of the heavyweight division, that providing I could get one of those fighters, he would be OK, but the final decision was with him. He said he would trust me.

Close to the date I was in constant touch with Tommy Miller. Several names were put forward and rejected until finally I had the right opponent. Blackpool manager George Hill had two heavyweights.

The first of these was Mike Creasy who was a 6' 1" twenty eight year old with a nine fight, three wins six losses record whom I had seen box twice. He was a bouncer on night club doors. I had also seen him in the training ring when I had taken Sammy over to George Hill's gym in Blackpool to spar with another of his fighters called Dougie Isles. Mike would fit the bill and also maybe sell some tickets.

George's other heavy was a Scot called Brian McCue. Brian was a bit of a character. He was only five foot five inches tall and almost round. He weighed around fourteen stone and had been around the gyms for years. He was physically strong and he had a reputation for courage and gameness. As far as I was concerned he was an unknown quantity so I reckoned Mick Creasy was a better bet. The match was made. Tommy also matched Brian McCue with another of the circuit's heavies called Mick Cordon who had beaten Mike Creasy twice.

For Karl, Tommy came up a welter from Doncaster called Mick Joyce with a two fight two loss record. The match was made at 10st 10lbs

Nat was the MC for the show and as his manager he persuaded Wayne Crolla to fight Sammy Sampson in a return with Sammy's loss to Ahmed as an incentive.

Another local pairing made up the bill and tickets were selling quite well.

I had the centre pages of the programme printed at the last minute hoping there would be no late pull outs as often happens. The last few days before the show were very stressful.

On the morning of the show I went to the bank and drew out in cash enough money to pay the boxers and officials. Every one had a pay packet and Jean was appointed as paymaster with the cash in a brief case and a minder by her side.

The show went OK but I was under pressure in the dressing room for the first time with three fighters to prepare. As the promoter I was having a constant stream of people enquiring about this that and the other, including Tommy Miller. In the end I blew my top and banned everyone from our dressing room until after I had bandaged Sammy, Karl and Joe's hands.

I had set the order of the programme with an opening six rounder between Blackpool's Brian McCue and Doncaster's Mick Cordon. I wanted to have a look at them as potential opponents for Joe. The pairing looked ridiculous, almost laughable. Brian was looking up at the 6' 1" Mick, but at the bell it was a different story. Brian was a buzz saw compared to the plodding Mick and surprisingly out jabbed him. Little Brian had a deceptively long reach and already I was glad I had gone for Creasy who was at least conventional. The crowd were delighted when McCue won a points decision.

Joe was nervous, much more so than Karl, so I decided to put him on second with an interval before Sammy's eight round top of the bill fight, then Karl's bout and finally another six rounder to close the show. I started to get Joe warmed up and in the zone. Once he began to put some punches together on the pads and I told him how good he looked, he began to relax a little, and the adrenaline was flowing.

On entering the ring to plenty of cheers he began to look the part. Creasy on the other hand just stood in his corner with that 'seen it all before' look. Creasy was half a stone heavier but didn't look it when they shook hands in the centre of the ring. Joe looked impressive but he would have turn looks into action.

From the first bell it was, more or less, one- way traffic. Joe opened up with some heavy left jabs and clumsy but thought provoking right handers. Creasy was content to cover and grab as an experienced fighter does.

In the interval I just had to keep Joe calm and make sure he kept Mike on the defence but not to punch himself out. With a physique like his, I didn't want a repeat of what had happened to Sammy in his debut with Dunn.

Rounds two and three were pretty much the same and by the half way mark Joe was three rounds up. Mike was obviously thinking that the inexperienced Joe would blow up and in the fourth began to throw some shots back, catching Joe now and again and he may have won the round. Joe was coping well in the interval so I told him he needed to pick some targets especially to the body when Mike clamped his hands to his face. He did so in the fifth and knowing how hard Joe was hitting, they even made me cringe. Mike must have thought that discretion was the better part of valour in the sixth and was content to see it through without taking one of Joe's bone crushing rights clean on the chin. Joe was a wide point's winner and he was delighted. So was I

Taking into consideration that it was Joe's first ever boxing contest and Creasy's experience, it was a good performance.

Sammy's fight was routine. Wayne, remembering how he was hurt in their first fight, didn't put up a great deal of resistance. He was no push-over but didn't fight as though he could win. He did go further than their first fight and lasted into the seventh before Sammy began to bust him up again and he was down just like the first time and looking at the ref who had the compassion to end it.

Now it was Karl's turn but unlike Joe he was raring to go. Joyce had weighed in a couple of pounds heavier than Karl but from the bell you wouldn't have thought so. Karl was tending to wing punches from too far out of distance giving Joyce the chance to cover and Karl wasn't stunning him. Most rounds were the same although Joyce threw more shots back at Karl than Creasy had at Joe.

I had no concern about Karl running out of steam. Although muscular and extremely powerful, he was a different physical type. The decision was a formality. We didn't need any home town help from the ref.

So, on our first promotion we got the three wins that I was hoping for.

We had more or less sold out. Jean had done a good job as paymaster and sorted out the few chisellers who had tried to claim money when they were not on the list.

As well as everyone else getting their cut out of the show, after all the accounts for the promotion were completed and I did them myself, a profit and loss account had to be forwarded to HQ, the BBBofC wanted a cut of the profits. After all the hard work and stress I just about broke even. Park Hall would not be worth doing again but at least it had confirmed my assessment and we had learned a lot. The search was on for somewhere better.

I remembered that in the fifties and sixties I had attended boxing shows, both amateur and professional at the King Georges Hall in Blackburn. I knew there were professional boxers active in the East Lancs area and I knew their trainers. Being only seven miles from Preston I reasoned that a show there might be profitable. A visit to the Town hall and a talk with the entertainment manager confirmed that the capacity of around eight hundred and the cost of hiring the venue were feasible so I stuck my neck out and booked it for the 30th of May.

Again I got Tommy Miller to help with the matchmaking making sure he used some local boxers. Since he was managing some of them anyway, it wasn't a problem.

I contacted George Hill myself and offered him a fight for Brian McCue against Joe Threlfall. The way Joe had handled Mike Creasy and having seen Brian in action I was confident that Joe could handle it. I also told George that I would get an opponent for Mike. Jimmy Ashworth from Burnley was a match and Tommy arranged it.

Manny Goodall had a Liverpool fighter called Tony Smith who was really a blown up welter and they jumped at the chance of an eight rounder with Sammy as a bill topper. Tommy came up with a fighter called Dave Heaver as an opponent for Karl. Dave had lost twenty four of thirty and was from the same camp as Mick Joyce. He was obviously a 'fight anyone for money' type but quite experienced. Would Karl's aggression and power be enough? I asked Tommy to find someone else. Another two matches were made involving local fighters including a couple of heavyweights whom I could put an eye over as potential opponents for Joe.

I once again dived into all the preparations involved in the promotion just as I had with the Park Hall show except that this time I had a little more idea of what was involved and the fact that I had a lot more contacts. I got some airtime on local radio and BBC radio Lancashire but even so ticket sales were slow.

The day before the show Tommy rang to say that he had matched Karl in a return with Mick Joyce. It wasn't ideal but it was too late to do anything about it. When I put the phone down I made the decision that I would not use Tommy as a matchmaker again. He was too manipulative for my liking.

On the day of the show everything went well until the weigh in. Sammy was a pound under the eleven stone limit that I had agreed because Smith was really a welter. Smith weighed in three pounds lighter. Joe had a slight weight advantage over the roly-poly Brian McCue, but Brian was totally unfazed by it. Karl weighed in at 10st 10lbs but Joyce was just over 11st. I was furious and took his manager, Ken Richardson from Doncaster, to task. He showed the disrespect that some managers have for their fighters when he replied "what are you worried about? Shit weighs heavy" What chance does a fighter have with manager who talks like that about him?

Ticket sales had been a disaster. The Blackburn and Burnley fighters had sold very few of their allocation and this meant that the bulk of the supporters there were those who travelled from Preston and the last minute "walk up" was poor. I knew that it was going to be a financial disaster

Sammy's weight and power were too much for Tony Smith's extra experience and although it went to points the decision was clear and Sammy had another win. Karl was like a raging bull. He rampaged all over poor Mick Joyce for a minute and a half before connecting with a huge right hook that had him spark out. Joe and Brian had a much more even contest for three rounds. Joe was methodical but had difficulty landing his big shots on the mobile little guy who had some cute moves learned from years around the gyms and his deceptively long reach. After a gee up between rounds three and four and my orders to get to grips with his frustration, Joe went out with a much more positive attitude. He closed Brian down in a corner and rained a barrage of power punches on him until the referee jumped in and stopped the one way traffic. Brian McCue protested to the referee and to give him his due, he was not really being hurt but it was one way traffic.

So another step along the boxing road had been taken. My boxers had handed out three good hidings to their opponents. Blackburn Town Hall had handed me a good financial hiding. When all the accounts were finalised I had lost two grand!

It was back to the gym and to forget the local shows. By now I was getting known by more of the boxing fraternity especially since the first of the edition of the British Boxing Yearbook by Barry Hugman had been published. In this comprehensive record book, every British boxer, manager, promoter and official was listed complete with contact numbers. I was listed in my BBBofC licensed capacities of Manager/ trainer, Promoter and matchmaker.

As a result I was receiving phone calls on a regular basis from other matchmakers and promoters to see if I had a boxer available for this or that fight. Some calls were from matchmakers desperately trying to find last minute substitutes to replace boxers who had pulled out at short notice and it wasn't unusual to get a call well after midnight. Most calls though, were from matchmakers working for big promoters looking for "opponents" for their fancied fighters. Over the next few years I turned down many more fights than I ever took for my stable, but more of that later.

Chapter three
PETER CROOK. JOE. KARL. SAMMY.

During the period after the disastrous Blackburn show, with my boxers working in the gym and improving all the time, PETER CROOK came to see me. I knew Peter from his amateur career going right back to his school boy days. He was one of a family of three boxing brothers from Chorley and was twenty two going on twenty three years old. I hadn't seen Peter for years and he told me he had just come out of the army after serving five years with 1 Para, the Parachute Regiment. As an Ex-Para my self (3 Para) he immediately got my attention.

Peter had been to my show at Park Hall and after watching the standard of the boxers he had decided he could do as well if not better in the pros. I agreed to take a look at him in the gym and see if we could get on together. I told him what I would expect and that my training "style" was probably different from what he was used to, especially if his army boxing was anything like mine had been. I knew his old amateur coach, Reece Bretherton, at Chorley ABC who taught sound boxing technique to juniors and who had remained with the amateur code throughout his career. Peter seemed happy with my conditions.

He weighed around ten stone and at 5' 9" he was whipcord. I decided that he would make lightweight but would start as a Lightwelter.

After my experience of working with Sammy Sampson and Joe Threlfall, both big and strong but starting from scratch in every aspect of the game from punching and defensive techniques through footwork and ring craft, and then sharing the ring with the powerful in- your- face Karl Ince, working with Peter was pure pleasure.

His style was established and he was fast and clever. His punch range was excellent and his build was obviously suited to the longer distance of the pro game. His footwork was sound and, at his age and with the hard core Para training behind him, I knew it was only a case of raising his fitness level and modifying his technique to suit my criteria. Going way back to his early amateur days with Reece Bretherton, he wasn't a heavy puncher. He tended to punch too the target, not through it. His hand speed recovering after the punch to the defensive position was impressive. All in all he was a welcome addition to the gym. He added another dimension to the sparring and he had some blistering sessions with Karl.

From the outset of my venture into the World of professional boxing with Sammy Sampson and each boxer after, I told them that my objective was to help them to achieve their maximum potential. When they got to the point where they were no longer likely to improve or progress or were at a stage when they were going to take serious punishment I would ask them to retire. I also told them that if they were not happy with my methods or attitude, then they were free to leave. The history of boxing is full of examples of boxers who carry on to long and taking beatings that result in long term health problems and I didn't want to be part of that. The longer I was in the game the more I saw of the immoral side of the profession and some of the unscrupulous people in it.

I knew that if and when I could no longer justify my own presence in it, I would walk away.

I trained and managed seventeen boxers in the professional ranks. Every one of them won their first contests.

I was now in the position of having four pro boxers in my stable but relying on the phone ringing with offers. Apart from Sammy's farcical loss to Graeme Ahmed, they had won all of their fights so other managers were not queuing up for their services. I couldn't take the risk of another financial loss with a small hall promotion. So far, with the gym set up costs and eighteen months running at less than the overheads plus the Blackburn show losses, my venture into the pro game had left me about eight grand down.

My next step in promoting had to be up market. The Guild Hall in Preston was a superb venue and a meeting with the events manager to explore the possibilities of a show there indicated that, with capacity of 2,200 seats, it was a safer bet than the small capacity halls, even though the overheads were greater. Obviously I would have to put on a significant event to attract public interest.

I had a talk with Sammy Sampson and suggested that he was ready for a step up to Area title level. He was full of enthusiasm at the prospect. If I could secure a challenge for a title and feature the other three boxers I would only need two other fights to fill the bill.

The Central Area light middleweight title was held by Paul Mitchell from Leeds who was managed by one of my fellow Area Council members, Trevor Callighan. Trevor was experienced and he seemed like a decent, straight talking guy. I rang him and we discussed terms and, after a bit of wrangling, came to a purse agreement for Sammy to challenge Paul for the title. We then put it before the Board and, with us both seated on the council plus Sammy Sampson's record, it was unanimously approved.

I went back to the Guild Hall management and secured a date, 2nd July 1985. Now the ball was rolling and I had committed myself to either another big financial loss or, hopefully, a profit. By doing my own matchmaking I had control over the opponents for my boxers and I was saving £200 in matchmaker's fees.

I had six weeks to prepare Sammy for a ten round title fight and to get Karl, Joe and Peter, ready for six-round contests. The intensity and duration of Sammy's training sessions were steadily increased as we worked towards peak fitness

I matched Karl with a Birmingham fighter called Mark Hynes who had a one win two loss record. I matched Joe with a one of the heavyweights I had used on the Blackburn show. His name was Steve Garber. He had lost and drawn with Mick Cordon in his two fights and of course Joe had beaten McCue who had in turn beaten Cordon so taking a form line it was a good match. Garber was 6' 6" tall and a stone heavier than Joe but I was confident that Joe's big punch would equalise that. Peter's debut opponent was Clinton Campbell, again from the midlands. Clinton had won six and lost eighteen but his recent form suggested that he was a good opponent for Peter's debut.

Everything went well in the gym. The guys were getting good sparring and were injury free and I was spending most of my time on their training.

I also had to do all the things a promoter has to do in the run up to a show. I had agreed a deal with Brendan Ingle for two of his fighters, World Class middleweight Herol "bomber" Graham and British Champion Brian Anderson, to box a four round exhibition as an added attraction.

The week before the event I arranged a press conference to which I invited Trevor Callighan and Paul Mitchell. It gave me a chance to take a look at Paul. He was the same height as Sammy and of a similar build. I had done my homework on him and I knew he was a decent fighter. He had boxed twenty two and won more than he had lost against some good fighters. Trevor asked me casually if Sammy was an orthodox or southpaw fighter. I confirmed he was orthodox but it gave me an idea.

Over the last few training sessions Sammy practiced boxing from the southpaw stance and the plan was to box southpaw for the opening round. I reckoned that that might throw Mitchell at the start of the first and his seconds would be advising him on his tactics against a southpaw. Sammy would then come out for the second round in his natural orthodox style leaving them wondering what to expect for the third. For the last few days of training, as we were winding down, Sammy shadow boxed from the southpaw stance,

On the day of the show things were looking good. Tickets had sold quite well and my boxers had done their share. I was confident I would at least break even. My younger brother John was now a licensed whip and I put him in charge of managing the show on the night so I knew it would run smoothly.

At the weigh-in Sammy and Paul both weighed a half pound under the Championship weight of eleven stones. Joe weighed 14st 6lbs against Garber's 15st 2lbs. Karl weighed 10st 9lbs and Hynes was 10st 10lbs. Peter and Clinton were both 10st 2lbs.

Joe again was nervous and I had arranged for him to be second on the bill. He warmed up well and by the time he got in the ring he was fine as he got a big cheer from his fans in the crowd. When the ref called him and Garber to the centre of the ring, the difference in size seemed even greater but Joe looked the part with his powerful physique.

At the first bell Joe carried the fight to Garber who was content to cover up and then use his reach advantage with a few long left jabs, which were not landing. Joe was trying to reach him with big right crosses over the jabs but he was out of distance and the hooks were turning into swings. I saw enough to be able to give Joe some instruction at the end of the round. Coming up to the bell to end the first, Joe had Garber trapped in his own corner and was raining punches on him similar to the situation with McCue in his last fight.

As the bell rang to end the round, Joe turned away just as Garber released a right of his own which hit Joe behind his left ear. Technically it was a rabbit punch, although it was not a deliberate foul, the effect was dramatic. As Joe walked to our corner, his legs seemed to turn to jelly. He looked as if he was drunk and if hadn't been so serious it would have been funny.

When he sat down his eyes were clear and focused but we couldn't understand what had happened to his balance. I hoped that in the one minute interval the effect of the blow to the back of his head would pass but at the start of the second it was obvious that it hadn't. Joe's mobility had gone and although he tried to fight back, Garber was on the offensive and the ref, realising Joe had a mobility problem, jumped in to stop the fight. Even at that point Joe wasn't dazed or hurt, more angry and frustrated.

It had not been a good start to my Championship show but it soon got better. Peter was next on and his pre-fight warm up had gone well. He was confidant getting into the ring and at the first bell he immediately had the look of a very good fighter. Clintons own professional experience meant that he was not overawed which made for a good contest. I was pleased with Peters hand speed and ringcraft. He was composed and alert between rounds and all I had to do was refresh him, he needed no instructions. He clearly won an entertaining contest.

I had arranged the bill so that Sammy's title fight would be after an interval and the "Bomber" Graham/Brian Anderson exhibition. My brother John, who was now a licensed whip, was in charge of organising the programme had arranged for the ring lights to be dipped and Sammy's entrance music played as we came to the ring. The excitement and tension built as we got into the ring and it was the highest point so far in our professional careers.

At the first bell Sammy went out leading with a right jab and for the rest of the round he dominated the action so it was clear our ruse was working. We were one round up

The second round saw Sammy back in his natural orthodox style and again he was dominant, two rounds up. In the third Paul began to get into his stride and was letting shots go but Sammy was dealing with them and still edged it, on my card anyway. Between rounds Sammy was alert and I was getting good feedback from him. I was making suggestions as to what shots to use and he was responding.

The fourth and fifth were fairly even although Sammy was ahead on points. In the sixth Sammy began to land some significant punches that I could see were beginning to hurt Paul. The shots that Sammy had taken were causing no damage. As Sammy sat down I was pleased that there were no swellings or bleeds that needed attention. We were more than halfway through the contest already and Sammy was showing no signs of the lactic condition he had suffered earlier in his career.

At the bell for the seventh I asked him to start to wind up the pressure on Mitchell and that is what he did. With a minute of the round to go he landed a great right hand to the head and Paul was down and hurt. He took an eight count and Sammy looked across at me from a neutral corner and I warned him to be careful. I knew that Paul was hurt but not stunned and there is a big difference. Sure enough when he got up and the ref ordered them to "box" he came back with a few big shots but they were mistimed and Sammy easily defended against them.

Again in the interval Sammy stayed calm but he was eager to get back into action. I felt that Mitchell was now weakened enough for Sammy to set up a sustained attack and he was hitting Paul hard with nothing much coming back and then half way through the round Sammy landed a great left hook. Paul was stunned this time but instinct and a fighter's heart got him up at eight, but this time Sammy was right on him and another shot had him down again. This time the ref had seen enough and the fight was over and the muscle bound ex Junior Mr Great Britain of five years previously was now the Central Area Light middleweight professional boxing Champion. Who would have believed it?

After the excitement of it all, I still had Karl Ince to take into the ring for his third pro fight against Mark Hynes. Karl was raring to go and his fans were there in the crowd cheering. The referee was Brian Hogg and he obviously had taken a dislike to Karl from the moment we got in the ring. When he called the fighters into centre for instructions, Karl gave Hynes the old intimidating stare treatment. Hogg didn't like it and warned him even before the first bell rang.

Karl was instantly into action at the bell. Hynes was a few inches taller than Karl but he was swept around the ring by Karl's power shots. Whenever they got close enough for Hynes to try and tie things up, the ref was warning Karl about his head and rough tactics. Half way through the round, Karl landed one of his crunching left hooks and Hynes was down and hurt. He got up at eight and Karl was straight onto him and it was so one sided that the referee should have stopped it.

At the end of the round Karl sat down and I began to calm him down. It was obvious that all he had to do was set Hynes up for one good clean shot and the fight would be over. At this point Hogg came over to us in the corner and again warned Karl to cut out the aggressive stuff. I was amazed and thought he was totally out of order. It was my job to do that not his.

At the start of the second it was back to work for Karl. Mark Hynes was at his mercy and just trying to survive. He was being driven round the ring by the force of Karl's attack. A minute into the round and Karl had Hynes backed against the ropes when Hogg called "break". Since the boxers were not tangled or in close and holding, Karl let go with a big right that knocked Mark Hynes clean off his feet. Brian Hogg immediately disqualified Karl.

So my first Guildhall show was over and I went home with mixed feelings. There was the overall elation at Sammy Sampson's championship win and Peter Crooks excellent display, tinged with the disappointment of the freak punch that wiped out Joe Threlfall and then the disqualification of Karl when it really should have been a KO win. I was learning more about this business.

I looked up some information on the Threlfall incident and found that the area of the brain that controls locomotion is indeed in the rear lobe exactly where Garber's blow landed. A study of the video replayed in slow motion proves it beyond doubt.

A few days after the show, I was able to draw up the final accounts and I had indeed made enough profit to more or less cancel the losses from the Blackburn show.

Jean and I took a couple of weeks off for a well earned holiday. What with my multitasking and the inevitable extra work load on Jean, we were physically and mentally exhausted and in any case the boxers themselves needed a break.

By the middle of August we were all back in harness and I was planning my next move promotionally. It was all soon to be interrupted in a violent manner. I was woken early one morning by a call from the Police. Overnight the gymnasium and entire mill building had burned to the ground. The fire brigade had been called out in the early hours but by the time they arrived there was nothing that they could save. The roof had gone in and only the walls were left. I had lost everything we had worked so hard to put together plus all my tools and personal effects such as books, accounts, contacts and all of Deborah's PHD paperwork and notes.

I just cannot describe how I felt when I arrived on the site where the firemen were still hosing down the smouldering wreckage. There were a couple of newspaper reporters asking for my comments but I could hardly find words to describe my despair.

I was insured but as anyone knows, getting a claim sorted and paid out is a lengthy business. The source of the fire was never fully decided. The Fire Brigade officer could only offer the suggestion that the TV which was in the reception area was still plugged in and could have been the source of the fire but it wasn't certain. The insurance accessor asked a lot of questions and tried all ways to get the claim reduced and delayed but they paid out in the end.

My priority was to find new premises. I found another town centre site, this time it was a hall attached to another mill that had closed a few months previously. The process of fitting it out started all over again. We had rescued only a few things such as the weights and bars and the steel bench frames from the fire but I had to re-purchase everything else including a boxing ring. It was better than the first gym when it was finished but I felt like I needed another holiday.

Whilst all this was going on I was still taking the boxers to another local gym so that there continuity was not interrupted and they were soon settling into the new surroundings.

I planned another Guild Hall show for the eighth of October 1985 we had four weeks to prepare. This time I had the benefit of the experience of my July show behind me so it was only a matter of repeating the process.

As a bill topper the thought that a return with Sammy's only conqueror Graham Ahmed was a good match that would pull in the punters. I rang Doug Bidwell, Ahmed's manager and negotiated terms. Doug was a slippery customer as I was to find even more in the future. Anyway I tied him down and it was on.

Joe had got over his experience with Garber and was improving all the time. I matched him with Burnley's Jimmy Ashworth who had boxed on my Blackburn show and who had now a one win and one loss record. I thought he might sell some tickets in the East Lancs Area and I also booked one of his stable mates, Danny Glover, in a supporting bout.

I matched Peter Crook with Dave Heaver of Doncaster who had been offered to me for Karl Ince at Blackburn. He was a full division heavier than Peter but I was confident that Peter's slick style and speed would negate the weight difference.

Karl was harder to match after the way he blasted out Mick Joyce and Mark Hynes, word was getting round about how dangerous he was becoming. I had him matched twice before the last few days but both opponents pulled out. I rang Tommy Gilmour Jnr. In Glasgow to see if his fighter Mike McKenzie was available but he offered me instead a boxer called Manny Romain. Manny had won five and lost four of his previous fights but more significantly he had been stopped quickly in his last two. It seemed a fair match with his extra experience against Karl's power.

I went through the matchmaker's nightmare in the run up to this show, with pull outs and rematches for the supporting contests right up until the last minute. Finally I got the programmes printed on the morning of the show.

The weigh in went well. Sammy was three pounds lighter than Ahmed who came in right on the eleven two that the match had been made at. Again Sammy looked the much bigger man. Joe for the first time was a good ten pounds heavier than Ashcroft although an inch shorter. Joe's attitude was much more confident than he had previously been and I thought he was now getting over his complex of not having had amateur experience. Peter was at ten three was giving ten pounds in weight to heaver, but looked a lot fitter and he was his usual professional self. Karl, at a fraction over the ten stone seven welterweight limit was three pounds lighter than Romain but he seemed unperturbed.

For this bill I put Karl on second, since he had to suffer the nerves of being last on in the July show. Because I had not seen Manny fight I asked Karl to go out and box for the first round then, from what we saw, we could plan the tactics.

It wasn't to be though, instead, at the first bell Karl charged out just as he had against Mick Joyce fight and Mark Hynes. He seemed hell bent on destroying Romain in the first round and for one minute it looked like he would do just that. Suddenly Manny Romain fired a left hook as Karl was charging in, wide open, with another bombardment. The punch caught Karl on the right eye and dropped him for a count of eight. When he got up, blood was running down his face and the ref called it off. It was a hard lesson for Karl and he found out that he just couldn't rush in and overwhelm every opponent.

Peter was next on and by contrast he gave another boxing lesson to the bigger Dave Heaver and won a wide points decision. Peter boxing was neat and precise and with a bit more power he could have stopped Heaver but it was a good win and a pleasure to watch

Now it was Sammy's turn to avenge his only loss. The run up to the fight was on a lower key than the Title fight but Sammy was his usual confident self. For weeks we had worked out the tactics. From what I had seen of Ahmed in the two rounds of their first fight, I knew that Sammy's reach advantage gave him an edge but we also worked on a right uppercut counter to Ahmed's left lead. Graeme had been well schooled and he boxed with his chin tucked behind his shoulder. The usual counter punch, right hand over the top of the left lead, wasn't likely to work but an uppercut under the left would, so we practiced it in sparring.

The first two rounds went exactly to plan. The referee, Mickey Vann from Leeds, was one of the better refs, or so I thought. Vann had nothing much to do. The action was clean and fast with Sammy making the fight and landing with solid jabs and mixing his shots well. Ahmed was also boxing well although more defensively. Sammy was calm between rounds and in control.

Half way through the third round, Sammy slammed home the right uppercut we had worked on and Ahmed was down and badly hurt. For some crazy reason, Sammy stood over him with his hands in the air instead of going straight to a neutral corner. The timekeeper was calling out the seconds but Mickey Vann put his hands on Sammy's shoulders and pushed him into a neutral corner. When Vann turned back to take up the count, which was at eight, Ahmed was pulling him self upright but he was groggy. The next few seconds were another farce. Vann, as refs do, indicated for Ahmed to wipe his gloves but instead he went back down and, incredibly, Vann took up the count again from "ONE! So Ahmed got another eight seconds to recover.

This time when he got up Vann waived Sammy back into action. By now Sammy, who had for a moment thought the fight was over, was hyper. He attacked Ahmed with a crazy barrage of punches with Ahmed covering up against the ropes. Suddenly, to my horror, I saw the old problem of the lactic acid effect taking hold and in a moment Sammy was punching in slow motion. The bell sounded and Ahmed had survived the round. Sammy slumped down on the stool and I went to work trying to get him to relax and draw in the oxygen he desperately needed. The fight had all but been over but he had to get out there and do it all over again.

As the fourth round started, Sammy again carried on where he had left off, but Ahmed had recovered well in the interval and was on defence with his hands clamped over his face and rolling on the ropes. For a minute and a half Sammy was desperately trying to open him up to land a clean shot but couldn't get through then suddenly everything left him. He had "hit the wall", the term used to describe the condition when an athlete has used up every bit of muscle energy. He was totally wasted. Ahmed, sensed it and for the first time in the fight came on the attack and, with Sammy offering nothing back, Vann waved the fight over.

I was in shock. I was angry with Sammy in the first place for not immediately going to a neutral corner when he dropped Ahmed. If he had done so Ahmed definitely would not have survived when he got up after the eight count, but I was also angry with Referee Vann for allowing Ahmed to go down a second time without taking a punch, which is strictly against the rules, and it allowed him a total of eighteen seconds to recover from the punch. Then I was mad at myself for thinking that we had overcome the old lactic acid problems of the ex-body builder.

I had to get a grip of myself because I still had to get Joe Threlfall ready for his fight with Ashworth. There was another bout in between which gave us time to get in the zone. Joe was more confident than he had been for any of his other fights.

Jimmy Ashworth was two or three inches taller but Joe was more powerful and from the first bell that is the way he boxed. In his first three fights Joe had to cope with the mauling tactics of Mike Creasy, the unorthodoxy of the short Brian McCue and the very tall Steve Garber. By contrast Jimmy was "normal" and what is more he was a boxer and not a fighter. In the first, Joe was able to match everything that Ashworth threw and his superiority in power was obvious. He hurt Jimmy with left hooks and overhand rights in the second and by halfway through the third he was right on top after dropping Jimmy for an eight count and the ref had seen enough. It was a welcome return to winning ways for Joe and a relief for me after first Karl's and then Sammy's losses.

When the dust had settled a few days after the show and I had finalised the account's I was back into debit. The boxers had sold there share of tickets but the walk up had been poor and as a result I was another thousand pounds poorer.

The fighters were back in the gym and concentrating on learning from their experiences. From this point I will concentrate on their individual records, continuing with Sammy Sampson's.

Chapter four
SAMMY SAMPSON

Next up was Sammy's first foreign opponent. I had been looking at the figures from the last Guildhall show and after the loss to Ahmed; I thought that maybe if I could get a bigger named fighter to top the bill plus the come backs of Sammy and Karl backed up with six round supporting contests for Joe and Peter, it should be possible to get back into the black.

I spoke to Brendan Ingle at a Council meeting and He offered his Middleweight Brian Anderson, who had of course boxed an exhibition with Herol Graham on the Guildhall show when Sammy had won the Area title, providing I could come up with a suitable opponent.

Brian had, just a few weeks before, lost a disputed decision in France to Andre Mongelema and they wanted a return with him. John Gaynor, who was an international agent, said he would broker the fight and at the same time find an opponent from the same stable for Sammy thus keeping expenses down. I agreed terms with Brendan, always a hard haggle.

John Gaynor rang the following week to say he had made contact with the French manager who had provisionally accepted the match for Anderson and he offered a fighter called Abdelkader Souihi, a Moroccan based in France, as an opponent for Sampson He had a five wins three losses and one draw record. I had no way of checking the strength of his opposition but I accepted.

I booked the Guildhall again for the 12th of December 1985. It would either be a good Christmas or a bad one!

Training went well for everybody. I worked hard on Sammy's routines and again impressed on him the need to control his output after the way he had lost his head against Ahmed by getting over excited at knocking him down then tearing in without guile or control. He had learned the lesson.

I had booked Hotel rooms for the French party, who were booked to arrive the day before the show. I had paid for their tickets weeks before. I met John Gaynor at the arrivals area at Manchester and we waited for them to come through. John was holding up a name card and two guys came up to him. It was Souihi and his trainer but there was no sign of Mongelema. My guts turned over and I asked Gaynor what the hell was going on. He said he had spoken the French manager only the day before and everything was OK and he could only assume they had missed the flight and would probably get the next one, which wasn't due for another four hours. I had the other two Frenchmen to get back to Preston and couldn't expect them to hang around the airport. They said that there was no sign of Mongelema in Marseille where they had flown from.

I got back to Preston and booked Souihi and his trainer into their Hotel. Neither of them spoke English and my French was no better but Deborah and a friend were able to translate for me to explain that I would pick them up for the weigh in etc the next day.

I rang Brendan Ingle to put him in the picture but there was no chance of finding a late replacement for Mongelema if he didn't show. Gaynor rang me to say he had been in contact with the French manager who claimed that the fighter should have met up with the other two at Marseille airport and that he wasn't answering his phone so he had presumed he was on his way.

I now realised that promoting shows at the same time as being a manager and a trainer was a mistake. There was too much to do when I should have been concentrating on the final preparations of my fighters. When everything was going straight forward it was difficult enough, but with set backs like this it was nerve wracking.

Gaynor rang again to say he had met the last flight from Marseille for that day and there still was no sign of Mongelema. There was one more flight at ten am the day after but with the weigh in at 1pm there wasn't much hope of him turning up. I was p****d off. Anderson weighed in at the match weight and passed the doctor so I was obliged to pay his purse. I had lost the cost of the airline ticket and John Gaynor still stuck his hand out for his agent's fee even though he had done a bad job. More importantly I had lost the main event of the promotion. At ten pm the night before I had rung around and managed to put on another eight rounder at short notice with inflated purses to give some value to the punters.

Sammy had a seven pound weight advantage over Souihi who looked like a welterweight, tall and slim. He turned out to be a slick boxer and Sammy learned a few tricks and moves from him. Sammy was much stronger than him and ran out a clear point's winner but he couldn't land a stopping shot. At least there was no further sign of a stamina problem.

Again the show closed out at a loss but not as bad as the one before.

I had to keep the boys busy so I booked the Guildhall again for the 16th January 1986. I had at last secured a TV date in the Fight Night series after a meeting with Frank Warren in London. To secure the deal I had to bill it as a joint promotion with Manchester promoter Jack Tricket who had some sort of deal with the Warren outfit over the TV dates in the Central Area. I got a sponsor for the show in the form of the local Mercedes car dealership, Ciceley Motors, and Frank Warren put on a match for the British Super featherweight title between John Doherty from Bradford and Pat Doherty from Croydon as top of the bill. I provided the supporting contests.

I had, through Tommy Miller, booked Phil O'Hare from Manchester for Sammy Sampson as the chief support over eight three minute rounds. O'Hare was very experienced but had only won twelve out of thirty seven fights with three draws. He had been in with everybody including a few of Sammy's old opponents so it should have been a good learning contest.

I should have known better than to trust Tommy though. Three days before the show he rang with one of his tricks. O'Hare had pulled out with some excuse or other but not to worry because he had another fighter to take his place. It was Judas Clottey from Ghana. Judas was really a welterweight who was the current African champion at that weight. He had lost four out of his twelve contests in the UK.

I spoke to Sammy about the situation and we decided that once again Tommy was trying to stitch Sammy up like he had with Frankie Moro. It had back fired on him that time a so we could do it again. At least we would have a weight advantage again as we had with Souihi.

At the weigh in there was only a one pound advantage. Clottey had three inches in height over Sammy. We had a good preparation and went into the ring confident and in the zone but from the first bell it was obvious that Judas was in a class above Sammy. There wasn't much in it for the first three rounds simply because Sammy tried to make the running but Clottey was just to clever and was moving and counter punching well. For the first time I saw Sammy being unable to use his power to get into a fight. In the fifth he was still trying his best but suddenly Clottey caught him with a solid combination and Sammy was genuinely knocked down for the first time in his career. He turned to look at me and nodded his head indicating that he knew where he was so I signalled for him to get up at eight. He tried to get Judas as he came in for the kill but his timing had gone and he was down again. This time he got up on his own but the ref had seen enough and Sammy had been well beaten. It was another hard lesson.

I promoted the first of my series of shows at the Winter Gardens in Blackpool on the 20th of March. Dave Garside topped the bill against Belgian Heavyweight Champion Al Syben. I matched Sammy with Manchester's Billy Ahearne who was managed by Nat Basso who was also the MC for the show. Like O'Hare who never made it for Sammy's last fight, Billy had been in with everyone and had a twenty two wins sixteen losses and five draws record.

This time the fight went ahead except that Ahearne was seven pounds over the match weight. He looked fleshy and under trained so we didn't make a fuss. Just like Dave Dunn in Sammy's first fight, Billy was just fighting for money. He was tricky and set a few problems but it was mostly one way traffic and in contrast to Judas Clottey, he was there to be hit although he took some good shots he never looked like going down. Sammy won a shut out decision.

Two weeks later the devious Tommy Miller was back on the phone. This time he was asking if Sammy could top a bill at the Hospitality Inn in Glasgow on the 28th of April against Home town favourite John McAllister over eight threes at eleven stone.

McAllister had won eleven lost one and drawn one and he had won a hatful of ABA titles. At that time Sammy had won fourteen and lost three and was the Central Area Champion. In spite of knowing all about the refereeing in Scotland, I accepted. Tommy must have been rubbing his hands even though I had screwed him to the wall over the purse.

Sammy looked impressive against John McAllister on the scales. They both weighed eleven stone exactly but John had that pale Scottish bluey-white complexion and although an inch taller he looked a division smaller.

The atmosphere in the hall at the start of the fight was hostile but Sammy seemed to thrive on it. From the first bell it was a cracking good contest. Sammy was making the fight and at times McAllister looked as though he was losing heart, but he fought well. By the halfway mark the audience warmed to Sammy and I could even hear a few shouting or him.

Sammy fought the best fight of his career so far and I was even enjoying it myself which was unusual because I am normally so involved that I don't get to actually watch the way I would if I was just sitting at ringside. I had Sammy three rounds up at the start of the eighth and he won that round as well so I was not surprised when the referee called it a draw. It would have been a win anywhere else. The crowd cheered them both out of the ring.

Tommy's face was a picture at ringside!

The summer of 1986 was a difficult one for our family when my Dad died in July. He had been ill since the April, adding to the pressure I was under.

I promoted three more shows at the Winter Gardens that summer in which Sammy didn't fight. His next fight was again in the Guildhall Preston in what was to be my last promotion there on the 25th of September 1986.

This time I matched him with the big southpaw, Ian Chantler, from St Helens. Like Ahearne, Ian had a thirty one fight record with fifteen wins against sixteen losses but he was an "awkward" type with an unconventional style.

At over six feet tall he presented Sammy with problems he couldn't solve and after an inelegant eight rounds, Chantler won a deserved decision.

It was the nineteenth of February 1987 before Sammy fought again. Gary Stretch of St Helens had been a high flying amateur before turning pro with Mike Barrett, one of the London manager/promoters. He had suffered only one loss against thirteen wins and was the mandatory challenger for Sammy's Area title. Mike had a TV show in Stretch's home town and we had to accept the challenge or forfeit the title. Sammy had sparred with Gary in the amateur gym back in 82 before he turned pro and was happy with the match. At least I was able to get him a decent purse.

We prepared well with plenty of sparring although we didn't have a six foot southpaw to spar with. On the scales Sammy was exactly on the weight and Stretch half a pound lighter.

It was a Saturday BBC Grandstand show with Harry Carpenter commentating. At the first bell Sammy attacked Stretch and backed him into the ropes where he was able to land a few shots. Two minutes into the round, Sammy landed a solid left hook and momentarily, Stretch was shaken but he tied Sammy up and survived to the bell.

In the second, Stretch used his long reach to keep Sammy off then landed a big shot of his own. Sammy was down and hurt and he didn't turn towards me but got up at eight. Stretch was too good to let the chance go and he was in again with another big right and this time Sammy was down for the full count.

His title had gone and maybe we had come the point where he had reached his potential and was on the way down but it was too soon to make that decision, after all Stretch was a very, very good fighter.

Sammy took a few weeks off for a well deserved rest from boxing. He popped in for a few sessions and he was still only a couple of pounds over his fighting weight. We had a good talk about the future and Sammy decided he was not yet ready to call time on his boxing.

By this time I had other fighters in the gym but I had promoted my last show, at least for the foreseeable future. After promoting a total of thirteen shows between April 1985 and September 86, I had lost a lot of money in the process. I had taken my eye off the aquarium business during this time and the guy who was helping Jean to manage the shop had helped himself to some of the takings. We parted company with him.

Sammy Sampson left his job at BAE and went into partnership with a friend he had worked alongside for a few years. They opened a sports wear retail shop. This project kept him busy for a couple of months but he carried on with a fitness training programme and was in the gym regularly until Mid April 87 when he decided he was ready to get up to contest fitness again. He put total commitment into his training as he always had and by the end of the month I was looking for a fight for him.

I got a telephone call from Frank Maloney who was looking for an opponent for Johnny Williamson for one of Frank's own promotions in Lewisham on the 27th of May. It was for an eight by three minute rounds contest at eleven stone two. Williamson had won six fights by KO and lost just two so we knew it was not an easy fight but the money was right and Sammy keen for the job. Johnny had been bragging in the Boxing News magazine that he was the strongest light Middle in the Country.

When we met up with Frank Maloney before the weigh in, he had that smug, cocky sort of attitude that told me he thought he pulled off the perfect match for his protégé. At the weigh in Johnny Williamson was arrogant but they both must have had some doubt because Sammy looked good and at eleven one he was in top condition. Williamson was a pound lighter and when he tried to stare Sammy down Sammy just grinned at him.

The boxers entered the ring to a trumpet fanfare and most of the crowd were behind Williamson although there was the odd shout for Sammy. The referee was Dave Parris of London, an A class ref.

Sammy started the fight from a southpaw stance just as he had done against Paul Mitchell. The action was fast and furious with Williamson hurling power shots from both hands and Sammy Jabbing away with his right and counterpunching with a left hook. At the end of the round I thought it was about even which meant that on Parris's card it would have gone to Williamson.

Williamson again was very aggressive from the bell for round two and he caught Sammy with some good shots, particularly with some right hooks but Sammy fought back every time he took a punch and he showed his growing experience by tying Johnny up then scoring in close. The ref seemed to be going out of his way to warn Sammy about his head when in fact they were both just as rough as one another. With about thirty seconds to go in the second, Sammy landed a terrific right cross and Johnny was down but jumped up before a count started but he was definitely hurt and Sammy finished the round strongly. Apart from the knockdown, which would have given Sammy the round if a count had started, I think that Williamson would have edged the second.

From the start of the third, Sammy was busting Johnny up mainly with his left jab. His left eye was swelling although he was still fighting back strongly but there was that slight look of desperation in his work and I knew he was being hurt by everything Sammy was hitting him with. At the end of the third I was sure that even Dave Parris would have had to give it to Sammy.

When Johnny came out for the fourth round I could see that both his eyes were swollen although his left one was worse from taking Sammy's big right hands. Sammy was again dominating but Williamson was a long way from giving up and was throwing some dangerous punches of his own and landing some, then suddenly Sammy landed a peach of a right hook. The next few seconds highlighted the actions of the home town referee symptom. This wasn't supposed to be happening. Williamson was supposed to be knocking out his opponent; Sammy's right hook dropped him to his knee. Amazingly, Parris grabbed him by the arm and hauled him upright before the timekeeper could take up a count. If he had left him on one knee and taken up a count, at least Williamson may have survived the round although Parris would have had to score the round to Sammy by a full point. Instead he allowed him to walk toward Sammy, who had already gone to a neutral corner as he now immediately did when dropped his opponent. Sammy stepped forward and crashed home probably the hardest right hand he ever threw. It landed flush on Johnny's jaw and spun him round so that he slammed down on his back out for the count.

I still watch the video of this fight and cringe as Dave Parris leads Johnny over to meet Sammy's right hand.

It was a great win for Sammy Sampson and I was proud and impressed by the professional way he had handled himself from the start to finish of this whole experience. It also popped him into the Boxing News top ten ratings.

Williamson recovered from the fight but it more or less ended his career. He only had one more fight after this crushing KO

Sammy's next contest was on the 15th of September1987. Gary Stretch had moved on from the Central Area Title and Derek Wormald of Rochdale and Sammy Sampson was nominated to fight for the vacant title. I knew Wormald way back to his amateur days and now with a professional record of ten wins and a draw he was a tough opponent.

The fight was promoted by Wormald's management at the Frontier Club, Batley in Yorkshire, and a venue I would come to remember in the future.

We had plenty of time to prepare thoroughly and to peak for the fight. It was just as well because it was a hard ten rounder. Once again Sammy nearly upset the applecart early when in the second round he caught Wormald with that big right hand and dropped him on his backside, but it was early enough in the fight for Derek to shrug off the effect and the fight went on to a points decision. It was close all the way with both fighters in great physical condition and it was a good fight to watch. I thought Sammy was probably two rounds ahead at the end but once again with Ron Hackett refereeing, the home town fighter won by half a point but Sammy once again could hold his head up high after a good performance.

Two weeks later I had a call from Dennie Mancini offering Sammy a fight in Saint Nazaire, France against French favourite Pascal Lorcy.

Lorcy had a sixteen wins two losses and one draw record and was a leading contender for the French welterweight title. It was in his home town so I knew we couldn't expect any favours. The one advantage we would have was in size although they wanted the fight at under eleven stones. The money was decent and it was Sammy's first overseas opportunity and he jumped at the chance.

Although Sammy had had a hard fight with Wormald only two weeks before, he had not suffered any physical damage and he was already at a high fitness level.

We flew into La Rochelle the day before the contest and were met and well looked after. The fight was on French TV and we were interviewed by the reporters and local press during which, once again, Sammy handled himself with credit.

The venue in St Nazaire was a circular sports hall and it was packed to the rafters. At the weigh in again Sammy was much bigger than Lorcy although only a 1Kilo heavier at 69.5 Klg (in France the weigh in was in Kilos). I had a good look at Pascal up close and, as he was shaking hands with Sammy for the benefit of the TV and press, he had a look of apprehension in his eyes.

From the first bell that is how he boxed. He was a neat boxer but Sammy made all the running without being able to quite catch the elusive Pascal. That was the pattern throughout the contest. It was a good fight though Lorcy didn't have the fire power to hurt Sammy at any stage but he was clever enough not to get hurt. At the final bell I half expected that, against the odds, we would get the decision based on the fact that Sammy had made all the running, but of course Lorcy's hand was raised. I bet there were ructions over the matchmaking in Lorcy's dressing room.

I got the French newspaper the following morning and one of my house seconds at our gym, Andy Sumner, who was a language teacher in his day job, interpreted it for us. They were full of praise for Sammy's performance and not so happy about Lorcy's

After Christmas and New Year 1987/88 Sammy was back in the gym. Near the end of January I had a call from Dennie again offering a match for him this time in Paris on the 13th of February against Jean-Claude Fontana.

This was another toughie. Fontana had a sixteen win one loss record with eleven wins inside the distance. His only loss came in his pro debut way back in 1981, just when Sammy was thinking about taking up boxing. Fontana was in training for a title fight in 1983 when he was involved in a serious motor accident which put him out of the game until 87 since when on his comeback he had scored three KO wins.

The money was good and by now Sammy really had become a good professional fighter in every way. He trained hard and his head was right. He had learned plenty of tricks and was up to fighting at any domestic level. He knew as well as I did that the top flight was out of reach but he had not suffered any real damage in his career so far, not even a cut, and so he accepted the fight without hesitation.

We travelled out with Noel Magee and his trainer since Noel was fighting another French light heavy on the bill.

We were met at the airport and taken to a nice Hotel in Paris city centre. It was a televised show from a night club called the Wiz Discotheque. We weighed in at the Hotel and Sammy weighed 70k (11st) the same as Fontana. Fontana had the look of a typical French gypsy with a face that left no doubt as to his profession.

With the boxing only starting at midnight, it was 1am before we got in the ring. The referee was from Belgium and we were not expecting any favours. From the first bell Fontana came out fast looking for a quick finish but he was met by a barrage of lefts and rights from Sammy which gained him respect. Fontana then became more methodical and I knew we were in for a hard night.

For three rounds the pattern was the same with Fontana forcing the pace but Sammy boxing well and counterpunching but he was three rounds down. The fourth saw Fontana up the tempo even more, but he was still not having things all his own way until, with about a minute to go in the round, he hit Sammy with a terrific body shot. Sammy had his back to me when it landed and he sank to his knees and took a count without turning to face our corner so I knew he was hurt. He got up at eight and Fontana went in for the kill.

We had rehearsed this scenario in the gym. Sammy knew that if he was put down but his head was clear and he knew what he was doing, he had to be prepared to fire back when his opponent came in to finish him, and that is exactly what he did. As Jean-Claude walked in, Sammy hit him with a solid right smack in the centre of his face and it knocked him back into the ropes. If Fontana's nose hadn't already been broken it would have been now. It certainly stopped him from following up.

When Sammy came back to the corner I asked him how bad he had been hurt and he confirmed that his ribs were sore. I told him that at the start of the next round Fontana would be coming out strong to end the fight. He had to dig deep and meet him with an attack of his own so as to give him something to think about just as he had when he got hit by Sammy's big right hand.

At the bell to start the fifth Sammy was across the ring fast and firing in two handed combinations, he was getting through and Fontana was in trouble and desperately rolling on the ropes. Sammy won that round clearly but more importantly, Fontana was so busy defending himself, he couldn't hurt Sammy again.

The sixth followed the same pattern and at one point Fontana was looking like a beaten man but he was a tough guy and he wasn't going down unless he was stunned. It was another round to Sammy which left him just two rounds down on my score.

They rallied Fontana between rounds because he came out hard at the start of the seventh but it didn't last long and Sammy weathered the storm and was coming on again, but by now he was tiring after his big effort following that hurtful body punch in the fourth. I would have to call it an even round.

They both started fast in the eighth but again by halfway through they were both just surviving. Sammy tried his best to land his big right cross but Fontana was blocking well and the fight ended with them locked together having given everything. Fontana got the points decision which he deserved but Sammy came out of a hard fight with great credit and the admiration of the spectators. I myself didn't expect him to survive the fourth after that body shot but Sammy proved he was no quitter.

There was a champagne dinner laid on after the boxing ended and Sammy and Jean-Claude got on well and spent an hour or two exchanging experiences.

Sammy took the rest of the year off with only occasional spells in the gym and only returned to serious training after Christmas when he asked me to find another fight for him. I put the word out that he was back on the market and early in January 1989 I got a call from Terry Toole who was matchmaking for Mickey Duff. They were looking for an opponent for Winston May, an ex ABA champion who had now turned professional. He had won his first two fights. It was a big change for Sammy to be the more experienced fighter and it was only a six rounder but the purse they were offering was good so we accepted. The date was the 31st January at the York Hall, Bethnal Green

Sammy was fit enough and seemed sharp in sparring and on the pads but it was almost a year since his last fight and there is a vast difference between gym fitness and the competition ring.

He was his usual confidant self during the run up to the fight and at eleven stone two pounds; he had a one pound weight advantage.

At the start of the first round, Sammy was on the front foot and Winston was giving him plenty of respect. He was fast both with his hands and feet and Sammy wasn't able to pin him down to land anything solid.

In the second, with Sammy still in pursuit, Winston was having success with fast counter punches and Sammy was just that bit slower with his own punches but it was early yet and I thought maybe by round five or six Winston would slow down and Sammy's firepower would come into play.

By the middle of the third round, May, who was five years younger than Sammy, was looking like it. A minute to go in the round and, for the first time in his career, Sammy was cut over the left eye. He sat down at the end of the round and I got to work with the adrenaline. It wasn't a bad cut, in the hairline, and I was able to stop the bleeding. I told Sammy that he needed to step up the pressure on May in the fourth.

At the bell he was quickly across the ring but Winston was quicker with some neat footwork and was able to keep the distance he needed for his fast counter punching. Suddenly I realised that Sammy was bleeding again but this time from a cut over his right eye. The first cut was also opened again and after another half minute referee, Ritchie Davis, called it off.

In the space of four rounds, Sammy went from never having been cut to having cuts over both eyes.

Back in the dressing room the doctor stitched both cuts and shortly after, looking at himself in the mirror, Sammy put words to my thoughts. "I think it is time to call it a day"

On the way back to Preston we discussed the situation. We agreed that at the outset of his professional career, I would help him to achieve his potential and once he had peaked and before he suffered damage to his health I would ask him to get out of the game. He had done that and now he would just be a stepping stone for young fighters on their way up.

From the start there had been many doubters who thought Sammy Sampson would achieve nothing as a professional boxer but he had proved them wrong. He became an area champion and fought with distinction both at home and abroad. The highlights of his career were his area title fight with Paul Mitchell and the KO of Johnny Williamson. Up there also was the 'draw' with John McAlister and the half point 'loss' to Derek Wormald. I was proud of his performances in France where they rated him highly for his professionalism and sportsmanship. The guts and determination he displayed against Fontana was exceptional. I would miss working with him in the gym. I invited him to carry on as a trainer but he declined.

I was proud of what I had achieved with him over the last eight or nine years and he had been a pleasure to work with.

He always tried to win and never gave in easily even when out of his depth. A trainer can ask nothing more of a fighter.

A year later he came to ask me if I would train him for one more fight. He had been speaking to Barry Hearns who offered him a comeback fight at the Guild Hall in Preston on one of his Matchroom promotions. I tried to persuade Sammy against it and explained that he was displaying the symptom of every retired boxer in history who thinks there is one more fight left in him. He had made his mind up though and since he had never trained under any other coach; I reluctantly agreed to help him.

He was matched against another young ex ABA champion, Carlo Colarusso, on the 21st of March 1990.

Sammy was just a shadow of the boxer he was at his best. Just like the Winston May fight, he looked like the old pro in with the young lion only this time the young lion could really punch and by the middle of the third round the ref had seen enough and this time Sammy's career really was over.

Chapter five
KARL INCE

So now back to 1985. KARL INCE was back in the gym after his reckless assault on Manny Romain which had resulted on him getting cut in the first. I had talked it through with Karl and tried to impress on him that he had to concentrate more on his boxing ability to develop openings for his attacks. His heavy build and comparatively short reach, coupled with his aggressive nature meant that he was never going to be a fancy counter puncher, his head didn't work that way, but he needed to practice more ring craft. My next show in the Guildhall was on the 12th December and his opponent was Cliff Domville, a stable mate of Liverpool biter Mick Dono. It was six threes at 10st 9lbs.

Karl weighed in at 10st 6lbs two pounds lighter than Domville, who was a few inches taller. Karl was his usual pent up self in the warm up but he was keeping calm and listening to my pre-fight instructions. The referee was Keith Garner.

From the bell Karl was on his front foot but not rushing in. Domville was happy to just keep away from Karl's inevitable big overhand rights. Karl won the round as he did the second and third. The fourth saw Domville getting more involved then suddenly it was developing into another tear up as Karl began to get some power shots in. Domville was trying some dirty tricks but Karl was having none of it and he had a few of his own.

At the start of the fifth Karl was back on full throttle and Cliff Domville must have realised he was out of his depth as he was driven round the ring and could do nothing about it. Keith Garner had seen enough and called it off. It was a good win for Karl.

The next show at the Guildhall was the TV show and finding the right opponent for Karl was again proving difficult. London manager Darkie Smith had another fighter on the bill and he had a kid called Dean Barclay at Karl's weight. Dean had only had one pro fight which he had won by TKO and although he had been a good amateur, it looked like a good match for Karl.

Karl's preparation went well and his confidence seemed to be back after his win. At the weigh in Karl, at ten eight, was a half pound lighter than Barclay and again was the shorter by a couple of inches. Again the ref was Garner.

From the first bell the action was fast and furious but Karl wasn't rushing in as recklessly as before. It was an even round with Karl making the fight but Barclay was a neat boxer with a good straight jab which was just beating Karl to the punch although not stopping him from marching forward.

It developed into a good close contest with Karl pressing forward all the time but not quite landing that telling big punch that could turn it around. During the middle rounds I was getting a few negative vibes from Karl although he was boxing well. I reckoned that the winner of the last round would get the decision and Karl pressed forward harder than ever but at the bell referee Garner raised Dean Barclay's hand. He gave it to him by half a point but Karl had boxed well and I would have given it the other way.

Karl was not happy with his performance and I couldn't understand why.

Less than four weeks later, Nat Basso rang and offered me a fight at the Anglo American club for Karl with just a few days notice. The opponent was Frank Graham who had lost his only two previous contests. Frank was a light middleweight but I doubted whether he would be as strong as Karl.

As it turned out, he was only six pounds heavier than Karl but from the bell he was overpowered. Karl drove him round the ring for three rounds then in the fourth began to get through with his big shots dropping Frank a couple of times before referee Harry Cowsell had seen enough. It was another good win.

On the 20th of March 1986, the action for Karl continued at my Blackpool show in the Winter garden. I got Neil Patterson from Hartlepool who was managed by Trevor Callighan. Neil had a four win six loss record and was a tall slim kid who had started out as a flyweight but had grown into a welterweight. Karl was altogether bigger and stronger.

It turned into a good though one sided battle with the lighter fast punching Patterson trying to keep away from Karl's power punching. There were times when I thought that Karl was on the brink of stopping him but Neil was a tough kid and survived to lose on points. It was another good win for Karl and he had learned a bit more.

A month later and it was the Winter Gardens again on the 17th of June. This time I got Manny Goodall's fighter Tony Smith whom Sammy Sampson had out pointed at Blackburn. It was a support bout on the Joe Threlfall Area Title fight show. Since losing to Sammy, Smith had won four and lost one and his record now stood at ten wins, eight losses and a draw.

Like Mick Dono and Cliff Domville, Tony Smith came to have a bust up with Karl. Smith was a welterweight and had given away natural size to Sammy so it was a more even match except that with Karl he was up against someone who would be hard to intimidate. From the first bell it was all action. This time I wasn't too bothered about Karl boxing Smith, it was more important to keep pressure on him and that is what Karl did. It was not a pretty sight but Karl was landing the quality shots and dictating the action.

By the third, I could see that Smith was bruising up and he was holding and hitting and generally trying to spoil. Referee Ron Hackett had to warn Smith about various infringements including using the head. Halfway through the fourth, Smith was only just surviving and finally after a blatant deliberate head butt he disqualified him and Karl had won his third consecutive fight.

On the 17th of July I promoted my last show at the Winter Gardens. I had problems all the way with this show. Fight after fight fell through. When I first booked the venue I had planned for Joe Threlfall, the new Area cruiserweight champion to top the bill, but when you read Joe's record next you will see why I couldn't.

Next Peter Crook got injured so he was out. Sammy was having the summer off so I was relying on Karl. Getting a suitable opponent was proving difficult since, in those days, most managers and their boxers were taking a summer break. I was taking a risk by putting on a show in Blackpool during the holiday season and it was backfiring on me because, contrary to the venue managements promises, Blackpool just wasn't that busy in July.

In desperation I finally got through to Tommy Gilmour Jnr in Glasgow and did a deal with him to use three of his fighters on the bill plus a four round exhibition match between his lightweight Billy Buchanan and Karl Crook of Chorley who was Peters younger brother and an undefeated contender for the British title.

Tommy agreed to let Mike McKenzie fight Karl over eight rounds as the top of the bill but he screwed me for money because he knew I was getting desperate for fighters. He said that Mike really didn't fancy the job with Karl but with a seventeen pro fight record against Karl's nine, was he a professional or not?

From a financial point of view the show was shaping up as a disaster. With only Karl on the bill from my stable, pre ticket sales were poor and with the town deserted the walk up was non existent.

At the weigh in McKenzie was the same weight as Karl but there the resemblance ended. Karl definitely intimidated him. When we were warming up I told Karl that this was the perfect opportunity to use some boxing skills and practice his ring craft in setting McKenzie up for a finish after a few rounds.

It was not to be though. From the first bell Karl was a raging bull slamming in big hooks from both hands and heavy straight lefts. By the end of the first minute he had Mike pinned against the ropes and bent forward trying to cover until Karl stepped to his left and slammed in a left hook to the side of the body. Mike went down and stayed there. It was Karl's fourth straight win.

I know Karl was doing his job and if that meant destroying his opponent in one minute, so be it. My immediate feelings were, what did he learn? It would have been more beneficial for him to practice his boxing skills for a few rounds and then open up with the bombs. Now how hard was it going to be to get him a follow up without taking on much better fighters than McKenzie?

All these emotions were mixed up with the knowledge that I was looking at anther four grand down the toilet. I was not blaming the fighters for that. I had taken a series of gambles and lost most of them.

A few days later I had a talk to Karl. He was not happy and I felt that something had changed between us. Was he listening to the same whispers that his friend Joe had been influenced by?

Karl had now won seven of his ten contests, five inside the distance. He had lost one by disqualification which really should have been a KO win and he had lost a very close points decision which again could have gone either way. By rights he had only really "lost" one fight legitimately when he was reckless against Romain.

He continued to train OK and a few weeks later I got a call from Ernie Fossey offering Karl a fight on a Frank Warren promotion in London. It was against an eighteen year old ex ABA champion called Tommy Shiels who was making his pro debut. Fossey said he didn't really want anyone as tough as Karl for the kid but he was up against it, matchmakers always are. I reckoned that since Karl was one of the strongest welters out there he should be able to overpower an eighteen year old novice, even if he had an amateur background. It would also raise his profile in the business. When I told Karl about the offer he was reluctant to take the fight and I got the feeling that I was losing touch with him.

The trust and confidence that I asked for from my fighters was in doubt.

Just as had happened in his amateur career, Karl disappeared from the scene. We didn't fall out or have an argument or anything. I was looking forward to him joining Sammy Sampson and Joe Threlfall as a Central Area Champion in the future. I was sure he could attain that at least. It was September 1986

In 1989 I got a phone call from George Bowes. He was training boxers for managers in the North east and he asked if Karl was free to fight for them. I had no objection. Karl had three fights with them winning one and losing the other two.

My thoughts all these years later are tinged with regret that the young fire brand that Karl had been as a boy had somehow been lost for a few vital years in the transition from boy to man. When he re-appeared he never quite hit the heights. He did become a fearsome competitor and he should be proud of what he achieved.

I have questioned myself as to whether I had mis-managed Karl? I know that he did not fulfil his potential. It is something we can never know but I think I did my best for him. Like all of the fighters I managed, he was never beaten up or financially robbed.

Incidentally, Tommy Shiels won his pro debut on points against a fighter who had won one and lost two of his previous fights. He only had eight fights in his career. I still think that Karl Ince, at his belligerent best, would have blown him away.

After he retired Karl went on to become a very successful businessman and then I was pleased to hear he was running his own gymnasium in Bolton and training professional boxers himself. He had added to his own personal experience by spending time as a cornerman and trainer with some top trainers such as Brian Hughes in Manchester and Enzo Calzagie and Joe Calzagie in Wales. Karl is now one of the country's top trainers. I am proud of him.

Chapter six
JOE THRELFALL

Let me continue with JOE THRELFALL'S record. On the 30th of October 85, three weeks after his win over Jimmy Ashworth, I got a call from Harry "Arry the orse" Griver from London. He was desperate for a heavyweight after a late pull out for a show in Wandsworth London the following night and he had heard about Joe. His fighter was Mick Fawcett. I told him to call back in a couple of hours so that I could check Fawcett out.

He had a three win, two loss record, just one more fight than Joe, but I needed more information so I rang Ernie Fossey, who was the front man and matchmaker for Frank Warren promotions and had been on the London pro scene for ever. Ernie knew of Fawcett and told me he had been around the London gyms for years before turning pro. He said "if your Kid can bang a bit, take it". Well Joe could bang more than a bit. I rang Joe and told him about the offer and he said "if you think it is right I'll take it". When "Arry", who got his nickname from having a deep gravely voice, rang back I negotiated a short notice purse and expenses.

The following morning I drove us to London. It was the first of many trips I would make in the future. We got to the Battersea Leisure Centre and when Joe weighed in he was eight pounds lighter than Fawcett at 14st 6lbs.

I figured that by not having too much time to brood over the fight, Joe might be more confident during the preparations and as I bandaged his hands and we warmed up and got in the zone that seemed to be the case. Joe's fight was a supporting contest to a British title eliminator and we were second on the bill. There were a lot of boxing journalist's at ringside and of course a biased London crowd.

Fawcett got a big cheer when the MC introduced the boxers and the atmosphere was slightly intimidating for Joe. At the bell Joe went out and, as instructed, was the first to lead off with a jab but, as I suspected after Ernie Fossey's tip off, Fawcett knew his way around a ring and had no difficulty in avoiding Joe's punches. For the next two minutes Mick Fawcett enjoyed making a fool of Joe who, by contrast looked like the absolute novice that he was. Joe was getting frustrated at not being able to connect with anything and I knew that I had work to do between rounds. When the bell rang, Fawcett got a big cheer and I heard a few smart ass remarks from the cockney fans.

As Joe came to the corner he banged his fists down on the top ropes and I could see he was mad. He had really lost it and it was difficult to get a response out of him. He was actually looking around me to see Mick in his corner and as the bell sounded he tore out and across the ring. This time the sheer force of his aggression took all the fancy moves away from Fawcett who was now desperately covering against the ropes and then grabbing hold of Joe. Referee Tony Walker forced them apart and at that moment, Joe stepped in with the hardest left hook he had ever thrown. It hit Fawcett flush on the jaw and lifted him off his feet and sent him crashing on his back, out for the count. Joe jumped up on the middle rope facing the crowd who were nearly as stunned as Mick. It was a great moment for the British Cumberland Wrestling Champion…and me!

On the 12th of December Guildhall show, finding an opponent for Joe was even harder after having won his last two by KO. I tried to get a return with Steve Garber who had won their first fight by a fluke. There was no chance and the same went for the other "local" heavies that I had used on my first promotions. I found a match whom I thought was ideal in Alfonso Forbes from Birmingham. He hadn't won anything in the amateurs and his pro record was one win and two KO losses. He was Jamaican and the same height and only a few pounds heavier so it looked an ideal match.

On the night, Joe warmed up well and he seemed confident going into the ring, but he just didn't perform that night. He was hesitant and he was punching short and out of distance Referee Keith Garner gave it to Forbes on points after a fairly dull fight. It was a huge contrast to Joe's performance against Fawcett

Next up for Joe was one of the most memorable and controversial fights of Joe's and anyone else's, career. After coming out of the December show slightly ahead financially, I booked the hall again for the 16th of January. This time I spoke to Trevor Callighan who had a heavyweight called Carl Gaffney, from Leeds. I agreed terms for a six by two minute rounds against Joe. Carl had a five win and one loss record, but significantly, his loss was by stoppage against Alfonso Forbes who had just out pointed Joe.

The antics started on the scales when Gaffney towered over Joe and out weighed him by a stone and a half. Joe was definitely intimidated and I had to work hard at convincing him that in the heavyweight division, height and weight did not always count. It was power that mattered and he had loads of that.

The warm up before the fight went OK although Joe was still apprehensive, but when the adrenaline kicked in, he began to loosen up. When the ref, again Keith Garner, called them together in the centre of the ring, Gaffney looked gigantic.

At the first bell Gaffney came out leading with a long left and caught Joe with ease, whilst Joe tried to counter punch over the top. When Joe did manage to close the distance Gaffney was able to tie him up before he could land effectively. The first round ended and it was Carl's. Just as in the Forbes fight, the aggression that Joe had shown in previous fights was missing.

The second started the same. Joe was out of distance and the big man was winning the points and then a right hook from Gaffney had Joe down. He wasn't stunned and he looked at me for the signal to get up at eight. He was able to use some of his wrestling moves to tie Gaffney up and the round was over.

In the one minute before round three I had to somehow get some of the fire Joe had shown against Fawcett re-kindled. I told him that he was giving Gaffney too much respect and he was standing off exactly in Carls range but out of his own.

It must have worked because Joe started the round much more aggressively and immediately it became a different fight. Gaffney didn't like the action coming at him and Joe at last was connecting. Suddenly Joe landed one of his sledgehammer right hands and the giant, in a slightly delayed action effect, as if half a second after the punch landed, the signal got through to Carl's head that he was hurt, he sank to one knee. Joe was standing over him with a big left hook cocked but not sure whether to throw it. The referee was slow to react as well and with Gaffney clearly down on one knee, Joe let go with the hook anyway. It landed on the side of Gaffney's head and knocked him from his one knee position to a sprawl on his back. I was appalled and fully expected the referee to disqualify Joe, as did Gaffney himself, but instead he started a count. At around seven or eight Gaffney got up protesting to the ref. He had been hurt by the right but not stunned and the referee ordered them to box on.

By now Joe had the bit between his teeth and he sailed straight into the now bewildered Giant and landed the hardest left hook you have ever seen, just as he had against Fawcett. The moment it landed Gaffney went stiff and landed flat on his back with his head resting on the bottom rope. He was out cold and Keith Garner didn't even start a count because Carl needed the doctor's attention.

I jumped into the ring with mixed emotions. I was happy that Joe had pulled off a great win but at the same time mad that he had so nearly got himself disqualified. He said Gaffney was so tall, even on one knee he didn't know he was down and the ref hadn't sent him to a neutral corner so he was just making sure! Of that he was right, but it was a close call.

I love watching my recording of it

Trevor Callighan lodged a formal complaint about the referees handling of the contest and I was present at the Council meeting and questioned about Joe's action. Keith Garner was reprimanded.

In 1986 the BBB of C re-introduced a cruiserweight division in line with the rest of the World governing bodies. The weight limit was set at 13st 8lbs. Joe was definitely on the small side for the heavyweight division in spite of the fact that he had the power to equalise, but the height and weight disadvantages against fighters like Garber and Gaffney were a lot to give away. Although Joe had a great physique, we thought that with a bit of revision to his diet, the drop of around half a stone was possible with no loss of power, so that was the plan.

I had still been taking a financial hiding on my promotions at the Guild Hall so I had decided to try my luck at promoting in Blackpool. I did a deal with First Leisure, who owned the Tower and Winter Garden complexes, to run a series of shows at the Winter Gardens.

The first of them was on the 20th of March 1986 at the Winter Gardens. Dave Garside, the top ten rated heavyweight from Gateshead, had come to live in Blackpool. Dave was managed by London's Dennie Mancini and Dennie had asked me if Dave could train over in my gym and under my supervision. I agreed and also offered to promote him in the hope that a higher profile fighter might sell tickets in the resort. I matched him in an International contest against the Belgian champion Al Syben as the top of the bill. Garside beat Syben in three rounds

Joe Threlfall was now working well in the gym and benefiting from sparring with Garside and another young heavyweight called Sean Daly from Leigh, near Wigan. His weight was well below fourteen stone and he was still hitting harder than ever.

Coming up to the show I was experiencing difficulty finding a suitable cruiserweight for Joe, particularly after the way he had destroyed Carl Gaffney.

After dropping weight off Joe, I couldn't risk looking for another heavyweight because of the psychological effect it might have on him and at that time there weren't too many cruisers around. I was using one of Wally Swift's fighters on the bill and I asked him if he had or new anyone in the midlands area. He was managing Roy Smith who had been a good amateur and had won nine out of ten fights as a pro and I thought he would be to cute for Joe. Then again, Smith was not known as a puncher and with Joe down in weight it was logical to expect him to be faster than he had been at heavy….and he still had that equaliser. Four days before the show I had to decide and I made the choice to accept Roy Smith.

It turned out to be a mistake. Joe again showed a lack of confidence. I could tell from the moment I told him about his opponent. I tried to get him fired up about the fact that for the first time since he fought Brian McCue, he was up against a naturally smaller man and that if he was aggressive and took the fight away from Smith, he could negate the difference in experience, after all Smith had only had three more professional fights.

It was no good. On the night we went through the motions but there was no fire. I am the first to admit that it was a mistake to take the fight knowing that Joe had never really got over the fact that he had no amateur experience. He had inhibitions that, even after having KO'd four heavyweights, he couldn't overcome.

From the first bell Roy Smith out boxed Joe. He never hurt him and at no stage did it look like he could stop him, but Joe fought without conviction and by the middle of the seventh round, with Joe never looking like he was going to stop Smith, the ref called it off with Roy Smith having won every round. Joe thought I had "overmatched" him. I thought that Joe never even tried to win. He had accepted second best before the first bell rang.

A couple of weeks later I had a good talk with Joe. He came back to the gym after a break to get over the fight and we were able to talk without the emotions we were feeling right after the loss. I then realised what I was up against. Other people were talking to him away from the gym, people who had nothing to do with boxing were "advising" him. It is a well known fact that out there, in every pub and club there are "experts" who can manage and train every sportsman better than the actual professional trainer whether it be a footballer, boxer, cricketer or any other athlete and these were Joe's advisors.

I explained the position and the fact that I had more confidence in his abilities than he seemed to have in himself. For instance, I pointed out, during his wrestling career he must have grappled with much bigger guys who had been wrestling since before he was born and yet he had beaten them. Boxing was different but the analogy was the same and he seemed to accept it.

I had another date booked at the Winter Gardens on the 17th of June. After Sammy Sampson's Area Championship win, I was keen to get all of my fighters a shot at an Area title if I could. That way they would at least be in the record books for all time long after they had retired. The newly adopted Cruiserweight division championship had not so far been fought for so I looked at the possibilities for Joe. My old adversary, Manny Goodall, had a fighter called Bernie Kavanagh who had a five win eight loss and one draw record in the lightheavy division but had been struggling at the weight. Bernie was from Liverpool and had been a decent amateur. I had seen him in the gym several times when we were over in Liverpool with Sammy Sampson for sparring. I had also seen him when he lost a Central Area Title fight in Bradford on one of Manny's shows where Sammy was boxing.

I reckoned that he was a good opponent for Joe at this stage of his career. After my talk with Joe I was hoping he would now get a grip on his lack of confidence. He was working well in the gym and with plenty of time to "peak" for a title fight; I decided to go for it.

I spoke to Manny who jumped at the chance of a decent pay day for him and Bernie. In light of Joe's showing against Smith, Bernie was also keen to get another crack at a title and the Area Council approved it unanimously.

I matched Dave Garside against fellow north East heavyweight Glen McCrory in a British title eliminator as top of the bill. Karl Ince was fighting another of Manny's Liverpool fighters, Tony Smith, whom Sammy had beaten at Blackburn, and Sean Daly was matched against Tony Hallett, one of McCrory's stable mates.

Again as fight time approached, Joe was nervous. I had tried to hammer home the fact that it was Kavanagh who was over matched this time. On the scales at 1pm they both weighed in half a pound inside the cruiser limit but Joe was by far the bigger man and with the loss of half a stone since his heavyweight fights, he was in magnificent shape.

The warm up went well and Joe was in the zone going to the ring. I was feeling confident this time as apposed to the concern before the Smith fight.

From the first bell, it was as if we were carrying on with another round against Smith. Joe was totally negative and allowing the experienced Kavanagh to dictate.

This time when Joe came back to the corner I jumped right on him just as I had done between rounds in the Gaffney fight, I impressed on him that he had to get out there and close Bernie down.

At the bell for round two he did just that. He powered forward and took the play away from Bernie. He backed him against the ropes and released that blaster of a left hook. The effect was the same as it had been against Gaffney and Fawcett. Bernie was out cold before he fell on his face. The referee could have counted to fifty and he still wouldn't have moved.

Once again Joe had shown what he could do when he lost those inhibitions.

Now Joe, just like Sammy Sampson, had a professional boxing title to go alongside his wrestling Championship. I was hoping that it would at last help to instil some self belief in him, but to no avail.

We had a talk a few days later and I was astonished to hear Joe say that he thought he had been overmatched against Kavanagh. He said "If I hadn't knocked him out he would have out pointed me". With logic like that there was no where forward to go. The words were spoken by Joe but were coming from somewhere else and I knew it was time to call it a day.

It was a huge disappointment for me after two years of hard work in transforming this big powerful wrestler into a champion boxer. On analysing his record I can see only one contest where Joe was out of his depth and that was against Roy Smith and even then, if Joe had fought with aggression and confidence, he may have pulled it off. He performed way below his best in the Forbes fight which, on form, he should have won. The loss to Garber was a fluke. Under my tuition he had developed a terrific left hook and the smoothing out of his style would still take time, after all it was only two years since he started boxing from scratch.

We parted without acrimony, we had always got on and I respected his decision if not agreeing with it. He had not suffered an injury of any sort other than to his pride after the Smith fight.

Joe enrolled at Newcastle University to study for a Sports Science degree

Six months later I got a call from George Bowes, who was training fighters over in North East, to say Joe was working out in his gym and would I release him to fight over there. It seemed that whilst studying he fancied another try at the pro game. I gave him my blessing and released him from his contract. He had three fights in Gateshead and lost them all.

Many years later, after reviewing video footage I have of some of Joes early fights, I came to the conclusion that if Joe, say at the age of fourteen or fifteen, had dedicated himself to boxing instead of wrestling, he could have become a very good boxer. He was brave, he had the physique and he had that hell of a KO punch. He was ruthless when he lost his inhibitions. But, at twenty two, he lacked that little bit of arrogance and self belief that all successful fighters must have.

There is no doubt that he was blessed with that ability to render an opponent unconscious with one blinding punch. If only he had believed it.

Chapter seven
PETER CROOK

And so to continue with PETER CROOK'S career. After the comprehensive win over Dave Heaver; I had a call from Graham Lockwood who was now doing the matchmaking for the Yorkshire Executive Sporting Club which had been taken over by John Celebanski from Manny Goodall. He asked if Peter would be available to box on their show on the 21st of October 1985. The opponent was Gary Lucas from Liverpool. Gary really had been around the circuit for a few years. He had been boxing pro since 1978 and I had seen him box Barry McGuigun way back in 1981 where he went four rounds before being stopped. He now had a fifteen win, twenty eight loss and four draw record. He was a lightweight and three inches shorter than Peter. I accepted the match.

Peter trained in usual diligent way and on the night he weighed exactly ten stones, three pounds heavier than Gary. The referee was Mickey Vann and on the night he didn't have a lot to do in Peter's fight. It was a good clean exhibition of smart boxing with no holding or mauling but with Peter in control all the way but with the experience of Gary it was a good learning contest for him. Peter won a wide point's decision.

On my next Guild Hall show I matched peter with a Southport boxer called Brian Wareing from Southport. Brian was managed by Mike Smith, a Liverpool manager who was on the Area council at the same time as me which is how I made the match. For a change, Peter was boxing an opponent who had boxed only three times, winning two and losing one. Brian was the same weight and height as Peter.

Even though Wareing had only the three fights, he boxed really well that night and although Peter deserved the points win, it was a good fight to watch for those who appreciated the boxing skills of two fit and evenly matched men.

It had been such a good fight that a return was easy to make for my next Guild Hall show on the 10th of January 1986. Again the boxing was fast and furious and again Peter came out on top to record another good win, his fifth on the trot.

Three weeks later we took a job in Doncaster against local Lightwelter Gary Williams. Gary had fought twenty bouts with eight wins and eleven losses and one draw and I thought it was a good match for Peter.

Peter had taken charge from the first bell of all his fights to date and had generally dominated his opponents. This time, although the pre fight preparations seemed to go well, it was Williams who started the better. He was a ruff tough type although not in the same way as the ruffians from Liverpool whom Sammy and Karl had had to deal with.

Peter was far from overwhelmed but he was digging deep for the first time in his professional career and he had to use all of his skills to stay in there. In the third or fourth, I can't remember which, he was down from a good punch for the first time. He was up at eight and fought back well but that knockdown probably sealed the decision for Williams. It was Peter's first loss in the pros.

Next up was another trip to Blackpool to fight on my 20th of March show. Peter had not dwelt on his point's loss and was back in the gym and working hard. His sparring sessions with Karl Ince sometimes were harder than any fight in the ring that they had with nether of them willing to give an inch.

I matched Peter with Les Remikie from Leicester. Les was a Lightwelter with a twenty one fight record, four wins and seventeen losses but again he had been in with some good opposition. Peter had a height advantage and they weighed the same.

It was another classic boxing exhibition and well contested with Peter always that bit better at everything. It was another good win on his record.

At the next Council meeting I talked to Trevor Callighan who managed the Central Area lightweight title holder Michael Marsden. He was looking for a fighter to challenge Michael for the title on a Frank Warren "Fight Night" show at Huddersfield Town Hall on the 20th of May. Was Peter interested? It would mean Peter dropping to the nine stone nine pounds limit but with seven weeks to go so there was time.

I had a talk to Peter and he, as I thought, jumped at the chance. Marsden had a twenty three fight record with fifteen wins and seven losses and a draw so was beatable. I agreed terms with Trevor and we submitted the contest for approval which was granted.

The step up in Peters training routine both in length and intensity for the ten by three minute rounds of a title fight brought his weight down naturally and we had no problems on the scales. At this weight Peter was faster still and I was confidant of a good result.

We were second on the bill so that the TV cameras could get it in the can before the main event. We went through all the pre fight prep and Peter was in the zone.

From the start Peter was well into the fight and by the fourth or fifth I was certain he was ahead on points, although with Yorkshire ref Mickey Van in charge there was always the home town threat, so Peter needed to keep the pressure on and he did. At the start of the tenth and last I was confidant that Peter was home and dried. Marsden came out in a last round desperate attack. Peter was tired and began to wilt. He only needed to survive that assault and he would be champ but it gave the ref a chance to save it for Marsden and Mickey stopped the fight. I was pretty upset.

To be fair, afterwards Peter said that he couldn't remember anything about the fight after the seventh round. He wasn't the first fighter to experience that, for many a time a boxer will fight in auto mode, often winning without remembering a thing. Although Peter had made the lightweight limit without a struggle I was left wondering about my wisdom in taking the fight at lightweight.

In March 86, a month after his loss to Peter Crook, Brian Wareing came to see me in the gym. His manager Mike Smith had decided to get out of the boxing business and Brian asked if I would take him on. After his two great little battles with Peter I said "yes" without hesitation. He was the head chef at a posh Hotel on Lord Street, Southport. He had two wins with me and I was going to feature him on my next (and last) promotion at the Guild Hall on the 25th of September 86.

When looking for an opponent for him I was offered a match against Peter's old adversary, Gary Williams. Since his win over Peter, Gary had been nominated for a shot at the Central Area Light welterweight Title and his management were seeking an opponent acceptable to the Council. Brian fitted the bill and as a title fight, I could use it to top the bill. Brian was delighted that coming from nowhere he was actually going to get a title fight.

Brian trained well. He was enjoying his workouts now in contrast to the "drive to exhaustion" style of the Liverpool gym he been in during his time with Mike Smith.

He was working hard until, with less than three weeks to go, I put Karl Ince in the ring to spar with him. We knew how tough and strong Williams was after his fight with Peter and working with Karl seemed a good way to get him used to it. After a couple of rounds, with Karl as aggressive as usual he had Brian backed up to the ropes covering up from one of his onslaughts when Karl stepped to one side and slammed in a big right to the body. Even with sixteen oz sparring gloves, it crashed against Brian's side around his elbow and dropped him. I stopped the session immediately but Brian was badly hurt and couldn't continue. He showered and changed and I suggested we should go to casualty to get him checked out since he was still in pain. He said he would rather go home and see how he felt in the morning.

I rang him at 10am by which time he had been to see his GP. The report was not good. He had suffered bruising to his ribs and a kidney and was passing blood. He would need to rest for as long as it took to heal which, with that kind of injury, which is not uncommon and usually happens during a contest, it takes about four or five weeks to clear up.

That was Brian out and I had to find a replacement at a couple of weeks notice. Peter was in training for the September show, not having fought since his loss to Marsden four months ago. He was back up to Lightwelter and he was keen to step in for Brian. I rang William's manager, John Rushton, to explain what had happened to Brian and said that Peter was willing to stand in. He was happy with that since Gary had already got that points win over Peter. Nat Basso as chairman of the Council OK'd it, so now Peter was lined up to top the bill and for the second time in succession fight for an area title but this time at his more natural light welterweight.

I had to step up Peter's training again for the additional four rounds. Two weeks is not enough to plan a peak of fitness, but he was already in good shape and I didn't think it would be too much of a problem.

On the day Peter and Gary both weighed in half a pound under the ten stone limit. Peter was on good form and was up for the fight.

He opened much faster for this fight against Williams than he did in their first meeting and won the first couple of rounds by virtue of his fast left jab, neat footwork and general ring craft. By the end of the third, Williams was getting more into his stride and was rough on the inside especially with his head.

The fourth saw Williams attacking and Peter, lacking of a really hard punch, was unable to hold him off, but I was still confidant that as the fight wore on, his speed and accuracy would see him get the points.

In the fifth though, the sheer strength and heavy hitting of Williams suddenly began to tell and when he landed a sharp left hook, Peter was down. He was up at eight but Williams had the bit between his teeth and with Peter in trouble, the referee quite rightly ended the contest. Williams was the Champion and had become Peter's bogey man.

Peter rested up for a few weeks and just before Christmas 1986 he came to see me. He told me that he wanted to join his younger brother, Carl, at John Celebanski's gym. Celebanski was working with Graham Lockwood who was making a name for himself as a matchmaker and they had promised to get plenty of work for Peter who was popular on the circuit because of his slick boxing style. He could always be relied on to put on a good show and since he was not a dangerous puncher, it was easier to match him

I was sorry to see him go but as I told all my boxers from the start, if and when they wanted to move on, I would not stop them. I liked and respected Peter and I thought I had looked after him pretty well. He had won six, fought twice for Area titles and lost to only two fighters.

Peter carried on boxing until February 1991. He ended his career with nineteen wins against eight losses, including a third challenge for the Area title. It is a creditable record.

Chapter eight
SEAN DALEY

SEAN DALY was a twenty year old heavyweight from Leigh near Wigan when his amateur trainer Richard Jones also from the Wigan area brought him to the gym. I had known Richard for some time through the amateurs where he was also a referee. He asked me to manage Sean whilst he would take out a professional licence and train him. I agreed.

Sean was nice guy and mature for his age. After a few weeks Richard and I felt that he was ready to make his debut so I put him on my own promotion at the Sands Centre, Carlisle on the 22nd of April 1986. I matched him with Gary Fairclough from Chorley who had won two and lost one of his fights to date. I knew Gary well enough since I had rejected him from my gym because I didn't consider him ready for the pros. The match was over four rounds. Sean won every round to secure his first pro start.

Three weeks later I got him a fight with Tony Hallett at the Mayfair Suite, Newcastle-on-Tyne, and Hallett's home town, on the 8th of May. The ref was Fred Potter and the home town decision was a draw.

On the 22nd of May it was a closer to home six rounder against the giant Steve Garber who had beaten Joe Threlfall by default. The fight was at Horwich Leisure centre near Chorley. The big fellow proved too awkward for the inexperienced Sean to deal with and he lost on points. What I was learning about Sean was, at 6' 1" and around fourteen stones, he didn't punch particularly hard. He was a neat, aggressive box/fighter and he had the heart of a Lion. He had been well schooled and if he had possessed a natural hard punch he would have been a very good prospect.

On my Blackpool promotion on the 17th of June 86 I secured a return with Tony Hallett. Sean made no mistake about the decision this time and won every round for his second win

I matched him on my 25th of September show at the Guild Hall, Preston, with Mick Cordon. He was too quick for Mick and won a wide points decision.

Dennie Mancini rang to offer a four rounder in Eindhoven, against Dutchman Ramon Voorn who was making his debut. Dennie insisted that Voorn's manager, Henk Rhuling would only accept a fourteen stone opponent and could I confirm Sean's weight was just over this which I did. The date was for the 20th of October. I told Dennie that I wanted Richard to take Sean but when the tickets arrived they were in my name and it was too complicated to change them.

We arrived at Schipool airport and were met and driven to Eindhoven the day before. We were well treated. At the weigh in Sean weighed 14st 4lbs but I was flabbergasted when Voorn weighed 15st 8lbs. I protested but was told by Rhuling "this is a heavyweight contest" we had been conned by Mancini.

Sean was unconcerned and stormed in as usual with his aggressive boxing style but he lacked the sheer power to hurt Voorn to much and we couldn't really complain when Voorn got the points decision.

I had to argue the toss with the paymaster when it came to getting my expenses paid. I got mad and got paid. They had conned us over the weight so they were not getting away with the cash as well.

On the 18th of November we took Sean to fight Dave Madden in Doncaster. He sailed into him and the referee had to rescue Madden before the end of the first round.

On the 1st of December 86 it was off to Nottingham for a return with Mick Cordon and the result was the same, a wide point's win for Sean.

On the 27th of January 87 Sean fought John Williams at the Ritz Ballroom, Manchester for Nat Basso. Sean made his usual fast start and this time the ref called it off in the second round. It was Sean's third win since the Dutch trip.

Nat called for Sean's services for the 10th of March again at the Ritz. This time it was short notice, only a couple of days. The opponent was Johnny Nelson from the Brendan Ingle stable. Johnny had lost his first three fights but won his last three all on points. He was a couple of inches taller than Sean but half a stone lighter. He had a whipcord physique and the same lightening fast reactions as his stable mate Herol Graham.

The thing about Johnny was that he was motivated by fear. He was so scared of being hit that his adrenaline fuelled reactions made him near impossible to hit. I accepted the match hoping that Sean's fast and aggressive style would be able to close Nelson down, and this is how we instructed him during the warm up.

At the first bell that is exactly what happened. Sean was right on him and chasing Johnny round the ring. Nelson wasn't interested at this at this stage in throwing punches. After about a minute of this action Sean trapped Johnny on the ropes and punched to the body. Johnny grabbed Sean around the back of his head and pulled it down and the same time he raised his right knee in response to Sean's body shots. The next second there was blood pouring from a horrendous cut over Sean's right eye. The ref took one look and waved the fight over.

From the position that Sean's head was in at the moment he got cut, it could not have been caused by a punch or a head clash and I was certain that it was Johnny Nelson's knee that had caused it. The cut was so bad that there could be no other explanation.

I don't know the doctor who came to stitch Sean's eye in the dressing room that night. What I do know is that he was the worst I have ever seen. He seemed to have no idea of what he was doing. The following day Richard Jones rang me to say he had to take Sean to the hospital where they were horrified at the mess that the boxing doctor had made and they had to perform minor surgery to repair it

Johnny Nelson went on to have a long and successful career practicing that style of boxing but it was horrible to watch. Some of his contests were the most boring I have ever had the misfortune to see

Sean had to allow this cut to heal properly before he could even spar again so he took six months off and went on tour around the world returning from Australia in September. I got him a fight on the 6th of October 87 against the five fight undefeated Ian Bulloch at the Ritz again. Bulloch was really a cruiserweight so size was not a problem. Sean was ring rusty and not timing his punches as well as he could, but the fight was fairly even until the fourth when the eye was cut again and the ref stopped it.

Another long lay off meant that Sean was not ready to fight again until well into the New Year. On the 24th of March 88 Terry Toole offered a six rounder against Lennie Howard at the York Hall. Howard had won ten and lost seven. Sean had won seven and lost four and since Howard was lighter than Sean I thought it was a decent match. Once again Sean made a good start and I had it close when the eye went again in the sixth round.

It was time to re-assess Sean's career. He went on another of his walk-abouts and I didn't see him again. The record book shows that he made a comeback in 1995 and had five more contests with a win a draw and three losses

Richard became a manager in his own right and established his own stable. He was one of the few gentlemen I met in the professional boxing business. He was well educated with a responsible job. He is now the Central Area General Secretary.

Chapter nine
IAN BAYLISS

At the beginning of August 1986, IAN BAYLISS came to ask if he could turn professional with me. Ian was twenty years old and his parents were from the West Indies. He had boxed amateur since he was a boy with Preston's other amateur club, Bamber Bridge ABC. He had not aspired to amateur titles but I had seen him box against Preston and Fulwood boys at interclub shows.

He was 5' 7" tall with a solid muscular build and a bone structure that made him a natural middleweight. After the routine discussion about conditions and after watching him spar, I decided I could get on with him and signed him up. He passed the medical tests and his licence was approved.

I quite enjoyed working with him although his technique required some hard work. The techniques, or should I say lack of them, that he had learned in his amateur career explained why he had not achieved more in the ABA's. He settled in well and got on with my other fighters and his style added to the sparring sessions. The one thing I liked about Ian was that was a natural hard puncher. He had good rotation due to his low centre of gravity and although short for a middleweight he had fast hands with plenty of follow through to his punches.

He was quite fit when he came to the gym so by the time my Guild Hall show came around on the 25th of September 86; I felt he was ready for his debut. I booked a twenty two year old Glasgow kid called Kevin Hughes who had fought twice, with one win and a loss. At the weigh in, they both weighed eleven stone nine pounds but Hughes was a good four inches taller. Ian warmed up well and was right in the zone.

At the bell Ian was across the ring fast and he trapped Hughes in his own corner and within ten seconds he had Kevin down and taking a count. He got up but was helpless against the ropes when Ian slammed in a terrific left hook and Kevin Hughes was out like a light. It had lasted seventeen seconds.

After that quick win it was a bit more difficult to get fights for Ian. A couple of months past with many negative telephone calls producing nothing until I got a call from one of the London managers, Harry Holland, who needed a short notice opponent for a show at the Thistle Hotel at Heathrow airport the next day. The opponent was called Freddie James, a West Indian kid based locally.

Ian was fit having been in the gym constantly waiting for a job and when I told him about the short notice he was quite happy with it.

At the weigh in Ian, at 11st 13lbs was two pounds heavier than Freddie and I was pleased to note he was only a couple of inches shorter. We warmed up well and Ian was right in the zone.

At the first bell it was exact re-run of Ian's debut against Hughes. He was across the ring fast and slamming in left and right hooks. Freddie put up a little more resistance and lasted a minute and a half before Ian landed that devastating left hook that had Freddie out for the count.

A couple of weeks later I got a call from Alex Morrison offering Ian a fight at the Plaza Ballroom in Glasgow against ex ABA champion Alex Mullen on the 22nd of December 86. It was over eight rounds but Ian was keen for it after having so far only managed to get less than two minutes pro experience under his belt after training for five months or so.

There was nothing in their weights on the night but Mullen was a six footer so Ian would have to get inside the reach. We warmed up as normal and Ian was in the zone. From the first bell, again Ian was straight into action but this time Mullen was a good mover and when Ian did get close, Alex smothered and held.

Between rounds I was encouraging Ian to keep up with the inside tactics and for the first four rounds he was able to dominate. Half way through the fourth Ian landed a terrific body shot and as Mullen grabbed and held him I saw desperation in Alex's face over Ian's shoulder as he came in to clinch and i knew he was hurt.

When Ian came back to the corner I was alarmed to see that his head was down. He suddenly seemed to have lost heart even though he was well in the fight up to that point. I had to push his head back to get eye contact but I was getting no feedback. It was as if he had become disheartened because he knew he had hit Mullen with some good shots but this time the fighter had taken them without folding.

He went out for the fifth but now Mullen was realising that Ian was not pressurising and he was able to use his reach advantage to score points without getting hit. Ian's heart was no longer in it for the rest of the fight and although there was never any danger of him being stopped, he seemed to be content to just see it out. Mullen rightly got referee Billy Rafferty's decision.

I was seeing the other side of Ian's character and it made me realise that I had known him for such a short time compared to my other fighters, I had a lot to learn about him and a lot of work to do.

In the middle of January I got another call from Harry Holland. This time he had a show in Fulham and he was looking for an opponent for Andy Till on the 18th of February. He wanted to know if Ian could make the middleweight limit of eleven six because Till was only a light middle having won the ABA title at that weight. Ian was back in the gym after the Mullen fight and we felt that he could make the weight without a problem so the match was made.

Ian was in good form on the drive down. We had talked about the Mullen fight and Ian said he become disheartened when Mullen hadn't gone down by the fourth and since, up until that fight, he had never been beyond three rounds. It was understandable.

Ian made the weight comfortably and I was surprised when Till was a couple of pounds heavier. This was London. Why should I be surprised?

From the first bell Ian was his usual aggressive self. Till was a good boxer and Ian once again couldn't get that big hook onto his chin. It was a close fight and this time Ian's head didn't go down between rounds. Referee Nick White gave Andy the deserved decision but Ian had again given a good account of himself.

Andy Till was a genuine hard man who went on to win British Titles and afterwards became a feared and respected knuckle fighter.

I had a bust up with the paymaster after that fight when tried to short change me on the expenses for the trip. Harry Holland was called over and was full of apologies for their error. You would be surprised at the number of times this happens with some of the promoters but I never let them get away with it.

I got a job for Ian Bayliss at a dinner show at the Marton Country Club in Yorkshire on the 2nd of March 87 against Doug Calderwood. They were both middleweights and Doug had only had three fights more than Ian.

Everything went well and once again from the bell Ian was all over Doug. He soon had him on the deck but to give him credit he got back up and tried to make a fight of it. During the rest of the fight Ian Bayliss was the boss and he had Calderwood down again. Even with Referee Arnold Bryson in charge and Calderwood down twice which meant he had lost those rounds by a full point, he couldn't lose. I was amazed and disgusted when Bryson called it a draw. Can anyone explain how a fighter who had been down twice in different rounds and never really in the fight get a draw?

A couple of weeks later and Tommy Miller offered me a fight for Ian on the 6th of April 87 against a fighter making his debut. I was told his name was Slugger O'Toole and he was one of Brendan Ingle's fighters. This made me suspicious straight away. With Ian's record I couldn't see Brendan accepting him for a fighter making his debut. I couldn't find anything in any record books, amateur or pro, for anyone with that name. By this time Harry Warner the referee was now the Central Area Secretary after the death of Ted Tulley. I knew that any new licence applicant would have passed through the office and that the application would have the real name as well as the obvious boxing pseudonym that Brendan had dreamed up. I rang Warner but he said he knew nothing other than the Slugger name. He was telling a blatant lie but I didn't know it then.

Anyway I took the fight at eleven stone ten pounds over six rounds.

Slugger O'Toole proved to be a coloured fighter, just an inch or two taller than Ian and they both weighed in the same. We went through our usual warm up routine. This time the ref was Gerald Watson.

From the bell Ian started the way he always did. O'Toole was obviously a very experienced boxer and he was able to counter punch Ian's attacks. Even so for three rounds Ian was well in there. Brendan Ingle in O'Toole's corner could be heard calling out between rounds for Slugger to stay off the ropes and not exchange punches with Ian. He knew Ian's reputation.

From the middle of the fourth O'Toole began to get on top. Once again Ian's belief seemed to ebb away if he couldn't land those bombs that ended things quickly. Halfway through the fifth referee Watson decided Ian was not fighting back and he called it off. I had no complaints.

At this point I will tell you that Slugger O'Toole was really a fighter by the equally unlikely name of Fidel Castro Smith. He was from the midlands and had been an amateur Champion and International. Brendan Ingle had given him the pseudonym to make it easier to get opponents initially. Warner had known this but had colluded with Ingle to keep it quiet. If I had known the real identity I would not have taken the fight for Ian. O'Toole reverted to his real name and eventually went on to win the British middleweight title.

A couple of months later we were given the opportunity for revenge against an Ingle fighter when Nat Basso offered Ian a fight at the Ritz in Manchester. It was against another Brendan Ingle fighter called Michael Justin. Justin had won one and lost three and I had seen him fight so I accepted it right away. It was on the 9th of June 87.

Ian had got over the O'Toole fight and was well up for the fight. The weights were level and Ian had warmed up well. When the bell rang for the first round it was obvious that Justin was one of the oh so familiar Ingle stylist's. Ever since Brendan's most famous fighter up to that time, Herol "bomber" Graham, hit the scene with his superb lightening fast reactions, hands down and hit-me-if-you-can style, many of Brendan's fighters tried to adopt it.

Justin was one of them but without the speed, reflexes or power of Herol. For the full six rounds Ian hunted him down but couldn't quite hit him clean enough to drop him. He did hit him often enough to win every round AND get the decision. Ian had a few weeks off for the summer break after this fight but he was back in the gym by the end of August.

On the morning of the 14th of September 87, I received a desperate call from matchmaker Charlie Shorey similar to the one I got from him in 85 when he needed Sammy Sampson for Graeme Ahmed. This time he wanted to know if Ian Bayliss was available to fight that evening against Steve McCarthy at the Crest Hotel Bloomsbury. McCarthy had won three out of three. I knew that Ian was fit to fight a six rounder providing the money was right for such a short notice fight, and if I could locate him.

Charlie was in a weak position for negotiating so I got a good purse offer. I then went round to Ian's house but he was not at home. His brother said he would probably be hanging out in the St Georges shopping precinct so I shot into town and sure enough found him. When I told him of the offer he just grinned and said "this is just like the Freddie James fight, lets get it on"

I rang a very relieved Charlie Shorey and at 3pm we left Preston to drive to London. When we arrived at the Crest, all the other boxers had already weighed in. There was no sign of Shorey but found one of the inspectors and he put Ian on the scales where he weighed 11st 10lbs, the weight I had told Charlie he would be. He then saw the doc and passed his medical.

There was still no sign of Charlie Shorey which surprised me because I was sure he would have been looking out for us with gratitude for our short notice appearance. Instead I saw Tommy Miller who had his light heavyweight Crawford Ashley on the bill. I was shattered when he told me that McCarthy had weighed in but his manager Jack Bishop had found out at the last minute that Ian was the short notice sub and when he asked Tommy if he knew him, Tommy told him about Ian's demolition of Hughes and James. On hearing that he told McCarthy to get changed again and they went back to Southampton.

Now I knew why Charlie was avoiding me. I found him in another dressing room getting one of his own fighters ready for the ring. He apologised and offered me £100 expenses, hardly enough to pay for the petrol and a meal on the way home.

I waited until after his boxer had fought then collared Charlie again. Knowing that, having weighed in and passed the doctor, Ian was entitled to claim his full purse. If Shorey needed to be compensated it would have come from Jack Bishop and Steve McCarthy who had pulled out. There followed a stupendous row between us. I called in John Morris who was the BBBofC General Secretary and was at ringside. He informed Shorey that I was correct but he still refused to pay. I took the £100 on the night but told Charlie Shorey that I would be taking it to the next full Board meeting. I paid Ian his purse out of my own pocket and a few weeks later Shorey and I were called before the Board at a tribunal held at HQ. I won the case hands down and Shorey also had to pay my expenses for my second trip to London.

Brendan Ingle had a great record of producing Champions at every level. A couple of months after Ian's win over Michael Justin, he asked me if I was interested in Ian Bayliss challenging his fighter Paul Smith for the Central Area middleweight Title. I always believed in getting my fighters a shot at an Area Title so I jumped at the chance. Brendan wanted the fight for a show he was promoting at the City Hall in Sheffield on the 28th of November87, Smiths home town. The money was decent but more importantly I had seen Smith box on several occasions and had even once tried to get him for a fight with Sammy Sampson at lightmiddle. I fancied the fight for Ian. Paul Smith had fought twenty four times, winning ten losing twelve and drawing two.

We prepared in our usual way for the ten round championship distance. Ian was easy to work with although I still wasn't as sure about his temperament as I was with the boxers I had known for much longer. He did everything I asked of him and the sparring went well. He came to the championship weight of 11st 6lbs with a day or two to spare.

The weigh in for the title fight was at Brendan's Wincobank gym in Sheffield. Ian and Paul Smith both weighed in spot on the limit. Paul was two or three inches taller than Ian. There were quite a few of Brendan's large stable of fighters around including the cocky little thirteen year old Naseem Hamed. Nas was always at the shows featuring Ingle fighters and he could be irritating when he came into the dressing rooms bragging about what they were going to do to the opposition. Johnny Nelson was delegated to drive us to the City Hall, which he did like some sort of rally driver.

As we prepared and Ian got into the zone, he was well up for the fight. From the first bell he took charge and had Smith desperately defending. He clearly won the round and was just as positive in the second. Paul Smith was not one of Brendan's usual hit and run stylists so Ian's power punches were doing damage. By the third Paul was bleeding from the nose and mouth and half way through the round a crunching left hook had him on the floor. He bravely got up at eight but the ref had seen enough and Ian Bayliss was the new Area Champ. He was my third Area title winner after Sammy Sampson and Joe Threlfall.

In mid September a call from Terry Toole offered Ian a fight with ex ABA champion Rod Douglas who was being managed by Mickey Duff. The show was at the Grand Hall, Wembley on the 2nd of December 87. It was on the undercard of a British and Commonwealth heavyweight title fight between Horace Notice and Australian Dean Waters. It was on live BBC TV and I was pretty sure that with all the hype going on about the future of Rod Douglas, the fight would be broadcast. Because of this the purse offer was good.

I discussed it with Ian and he was happy to go for it. No matter how good Douglas was, Ian had the power to equalise if he could land the punch early. It was Douglas's fourth fight after winning his first three.

Ian was his usual phlegmatic self on the journey down to London. He weighed in at 11st 8lbs as did Douglas. Ian warmed up well and showed no sign of nerves going out in front of a big audience and with the TV cameras on him. We were on second so I knew his fight was going in the can.

At the bell Ian was quick out of his corner and the first to lead off. He didn't storm in the way he had in some other fights so maybe he was giving Rod Douglas little too much respect. The action was open with Ian trying to land a right over Rod's left jab but he was slightly out of range. For a couple of minutes it looked even then suddenly Rod Douglas opened up with a powerful combination ending with a powerful right of his own. It hit Ian cleanly on the jaw and as he went down I knew he was knocked out. Our gamble had failed and Ian had been beaten but not beaten up.

We got changed and since it was still early we decided to stay and watch the main event. The fight before it was a light heavyweight scrap between "gypsy" Bobby Frankham and Billy Simms. The ref was Ritchie Davies. Frankham had a big crowd of gypsy supporters on one side of the hall, to our left, and Simms had an equal number on the opposite side, our right.

Frankham was the favourite and at the first bell he rushed across the ring at Simms who immediately fought back. Within seconds, Davies had to warn Frankham for head butting and a few seconds later he stopped the fight and warned him again. The fans were working themselves into a fury. As soon as Ritchie told them to box on, Simms clipped Frankham with punch which dropped him, but he jumped up without a count. They locked horns and were wrestling more than boxing. By this time Ritchie had lost patience and he stopped the fight and sent Frankham to his corner disqualified. At this point Frankham completely lost the plot and threw a punch at the referee, bringing the seconds from both corners rushing in to grab him. Whilst this mayhem was going on in the ring, both sets of supporters who had been screaming across the hall at each other rushed across and began a full blooded riot. Punches and objects were flying and some poor neutral fans were caught in the middle.

All the time this was going on, the BBC cameras were recording it. The MC got in the ring and pleaded for calm and eventually the security guards got it under control. It had been some experience to watch it and it took our minds off Ian's loss. A few days later it was announced that the BBBofC had banned Frankham for life from boxing so ending what seemed like a bright future for him.

After the Douglas fight Ian had a break from training over Christmas 87. He came back to the gym in mid January 88. I was informed that Fidel Castro Smith had been nominated as the leading contender for Ian's Area Title and that he had to make a compulsory defence.

Once again Brendan Ingle wanted the fight for a City Hall, Sheffield promotion on the 24th of February. The money on offer was the going rate at that time and we had to accept or relinquish the Title which was not an option. By that time Smith had won five fights and lost one.

We had five weeks to prepare which, was enough time considering Ian was still in good shape after his short bout at Wembley. At least we knew what to expect with Smith this time. The training went well with plenty of good sparring and Ian was in good shape.

We warmed up well and seemed to be in the zone in spite of the needling from the obnoxious little Naseem Ahmed whom I had to chase out of the dressing room.

From the first bell Ian was not his usual aggressive self. He seemed to give Smith too much respect which robbed him of the advantage of his natural power. Between rounds I tried to motivate Ian to close the distance and get inside Smith's reach advantage. At the same time, Brendan knew of Ian's punch power and he was advising Smith to keep the fight at distance.

In the interval between rounds five and six, Ian's head was down. I was getting no feedback from him and when Fidel Castro Smith opened up with some power punching of his own in the sixth, Ian seemed to crumble and the referee called it off. Ian's title had gone back to the Ingle camp again.

Fidel Castro Smith went on to win the British super middleweight title.

After that fight Ian disappeared from the boxing scene. He never came back to the gym and I heard on the grapevine that he had gone to live in London.

I always got on well with Ian and if he had a problem with the way his career was going or anything else, he never spoke about it. We had some good nights and some not so good. He had been a professional Champion and his name would be in the record books for ever.

He never took a beating and had suffered no serious injuries in his nine professional fights. He was undoubtedly a natural knock out puncher.

I have only seen him once since 1988 and he seemed in good humour.

Chapter ten
PAUL BURKE

PAUL BURKE was another ex Bamber Bridge amateur who came to the gym late in 1986. Like his club mate Ian Bayliss, I quickly established that he was a very talented boxer and again I could not understand why he had not achieved more in the ABA ranks.

He was an entirely different personality from Ian, much more intense and I was to find out, much more complicated. He was keen to learn and adapted to my training regime well. He was 5' 10" tall and the ideal build of a lightweight. He fitted perfectly into the box-fighter category.

At first we got on well and he even came to help me in my Aquarium business where he got on well with Jean and her with him.

By Christmas 86 I began looking for an opponent for Paul's pro debut. I put the word out to all the contacts on my list. Early in January 87 I got a call from Birmingham promoter Ron Gray offering Paul a fight on the 21st of January against one of his own fighters, Steve Brown. Like Paul, Brown had no amateur credentials to talk off but he had won four and lost one in the pros. I accepted the match which was at the Kings Hall, Stoke-on-Trent.

The match was made at 9st 10lbs and on the night Paul was one pound lighter than Brown when he weighed in at the lightweight limit of 9st 9lbs. We warmed up well and Paul was in the zone without seeming to nervous for his debut. From the first bell Paul was in charge and it was Brown who looked as if it was his first fight. The second and third went the same way and I had little to do in the corner except reassure Paul that he was boxing well and in control. Half way through the fourth, Paul whipped over a great left hook and Brown was down and out.

Paul seemed very calm after the fight, almost nonchalant. When I went to Ron Gray to collect the purse he said to me "you have got a good prospect there Jim" I agreed with him.

We were up and running and when the day after Tommy Miller rang me to see if Paul was available for the 30th of January, one week after, to box one of Brendan Ingle's fighters called Paul Marriott who had only had the one pro fight, I accepted. The fight was in Kirby, Liverpool, so I thought that with the venue being neutral for both boxers, we shouldn't need to worry about the ref. I was wrong.

Ron Hackett was the referee. The boys were perfectly matched physically and from the first bell Paul Burke was the better boxer. It was a good fight but I was confident that Paul had won clearly so I was dismayed when Hackett gave the decision to Marriott. It was unbelievable and even Brendan looked over to me and shrugged his shoulders as if to say "some you win, some you lose"

Paul took the loss badly. He knew he had won and was baffled by the decision. I had to explain to him what this business was all about and the fact that he had to be professional about these things and learn the lesson.

The next date for Paul came from Tommy Miller again. It was a six rounder at the Marton Country Cub, Yorkshire on the 2nd of March. The opponent was one of Tommy Gilmour Jnr's fighters from Glasgow called Brian Murphy, who had one win and three losses in his pro career. Paul had worked hard in the gym after his farcical loss and he weighed in four pounds lighter than Murphy at 9st 6lbs.

This time he was taking no chances with referee Freddie Potter. From the first bell, Paul dominated the action and by the end of the round even Potter would have to give it to him. It didn't matter because one minute into the second, that wicked left hook whipped into Murphy and he was down for the count. Paul's mood was much brighter. They took Murphy to hospital for a scan. He was badly concussed

On the 6th of April Paul got his chance for revenge when we were offered a return against Paul Marriott this time in Newcastle-on-Tyne. It was an all night show with the live transmission of the Marvin Hagler v Sugar Ray Leonard being shown on a big screen lowered into the ring after the live boxing. Tickets for that show started at £50!

This time Paul made no mistake with Marriott even though he had beaten him the first time. He was just too good for him and this time he got the points decision. It was daylight before we got home that morning.

Next up for Paul was a trip to the iconic York Hall Bethnal Green on the 30th of April. Frank Maloney rang me looking for an opponent for his fighter Paul Gadney. Gadney had a six win two losses and one draw record against Paul's three wins and a loss that never was. Frank Maloney thought they were on to a good thing. We had an easy drive down and Paul was relaxed and on good form. He warmed up well and was in the zone. Compared with my other fighters, Paul was always more intense pre fight but he kept his nerves under control.

From the first bell he boxed beautifully. He was fast and accurate and Gadney, who himself was not a bad boxer, had no answer to Paul's variety of punches. Even with a London referee, Paul got the well deserved decision.

On the 1st of June 87, Tommy Miller tried to pull a fast one on us. He was matchmaking for the YESC and two weeks before the show he offered a six rounder for Paul against Barry Bacon. Barry had only won one out of twelve fights so I jumped at the chance. At 10am on the morning of the fight, Tommy rang with the bad news that Barry Bacon had pulled out with an injury. However he said not to worry he had found a substitute, a kid called Pat Barrett from Manchester who had only had two professional fights, both wins.

The alarm bells were ringing in my head when I rang Area secretary to check out this Pat "black flash" Barrett. He was in fact signed up to Tommy. He was an ex ABA area champion and had won his two pro starts by stoppage. He was being spoken of as a good prospect (which proved to be true when you now look at his career record). Anyway I had to make a decision on whether to accept or reject the fight. I knew it was a case of Tommy looking for an opponent for his hot prospect and that the Barry Bacon fight was never on and was just a lure. I decided to call his bluff.

I picked Paul up at the usual time for the drive over to Bradford and on the drive I casually told Paul about the change of opponent but disguised my knowledge of the reasons behind it. Paul's confidence was high after his recent performances and didn't want to sow even the slightest seed of doubt.

We went through our usual warm up routine and Paul was well up for the fight. From the first bell Paul boxed the way he had against Gadney. He was beating Barrett to the punch and easily defending against his attacks. By the fifth Paul was well in control and as far as I was concerned, he sealed a win when he dropped Pat for an eight count with a cracking left hook. Tommy Miller's face was a picture when the ref raised Paul's hand without hesitation.

I was delighted with Paul's performances to date. He was learning all the time and I thought that he was happy as well. It was time to ease of for a summer break and it was August when we were all back in the gym and preparing for the new season. I had secured an Area title fight for Sammy Sampson against Dean Wormald on the 15th of September 87 and I got Paul a six round fight on the undercard. The opponent was Marvin P Gray from Newcastle. Marvin was the most experienced fighter that Paul had faced so far with a ten win twelve loss and a draw record and I thought it was the right sort of learning contest for Paul.

With Sammy preparing for a ten rounder and plenty of sparring in the gym, Paul seemed to be training well although after the summer break I began to detect a change in attitude. I couldn't quite put my finger on what it was although I was slightly alarmed when he told me that in the summer he had gone to London and visited the Terry Lawless gym and even sparred there. It did not occur to him that a boxer under contract should not go to another professional gym without the approval of his manager. He denied that he was unhappy with his training and his record so far should have re-enforced that.

On the show, Paul's contest was on the second half of the bill after the Sampson v Wormald fight. Although Sammy lost the decision to Wormald he had fought so well that we were not despondent in the dressing room and Paul seemed to warm up and get in the zone.

I have just reviewed Paul's fight with Marvin on tape because I still can't understand what happened to him and needed to remind myself before I begin to describe it. For two rounds Paul dominated the action. His punches were accurate and hard and Marvin had to show all his toughness and experience to survive them. In round three, for the first minute Paul looked as if he would stop Marvin with the next clean shot that landed, but as the round went on suddenly Gray started to fight back although by the bell I was happy that Paul was three rounds up.

When Paul sat down in interval before the fourth I realised that I was losing touch with him. He avoided eye contact and he was not responding to instructions. At the bell to start the round he boxed neatly for half a minute or so before Marvin began to take charge by his shear aggression. At one point he backed Paul into our corner where his foot slipped on a wet patch and he went down. I wiped the canvass with a towel and there was no count. Paul had virtually stopped fighting back effectively and right on the bell he was taking punishment and was bending forward with his hands just brushing the floor.

When he got back to the corner I tried to refresh him and break through a sort of trance he had fallen into but to no effect. I knew that Marvin P Gray was hurting him, especially to the body, but he had not taken a single big shot that had dazed him, he seemed to have lost the will to fight.

At the start of the fifth again Paul got his jab going but there was no snap to his punches and Marvin was walking through them and relentlessly clubbing him to head and body. Paul's legs were now wobbling and he went down for a count. He wasn't stunned and he turned to me and waited for my signal to get up which he did at eight. It was no good though and just before the end of the round he was down again and without turning to the corner he took Ron Hackett's count and got up just as the bell rang.

I could hardly take in what was happening. From being three rounds up and seeming completely in charge, suddenly from the fourth he was falling apart. Technically, he could still have won the contest if he got his act together and box the way I knew he was capable of, there was still a chance. He was tired but so was Marvin and I have seen fighters rally from the brink before.

But there was no getting through to him between rounds. The lights were on but there was nobody at home. He wasn't listening, he had given up. I was close to calling it off myself but there wasn't a mark on him and although he had been down twice in the round, he hadn't been *knocked* down. I thought there might still be hope but it was in vain. At the start of the round Marvin marched straight in and Paul made no attempt to fight back. His legs had turned to jelly and soon he fell down again and this time the ref quite rightly called it off.

I could hardly believe that the fighter who had just beaten Paul Gadney and then Pat Barrett in consecutive fights would fall apart so quickly. It was early days yet and I came to the conclusion that the sheer dogged determination of the more mature Mervin P Gray, who had taken some good shots early in the fight and had come back from them, had demoralised Paul.

Paul took the defeat hard and my immediate response I am ashamed to say was one of anger with him. I thought that he "bottled" out when I should have realised that, he was still a young man and not as mature as his previous performances indicated.

A couple of months later and Paul (and I) seemed to have got over the trauma. I got another call from Frank Maloney seeking revenge for Paul's win over Paul Gadney. This time it was another of his fighters, Rudi Valentino, again at the York Hall on the 18th of November. Rudi had won four and lost one so it was a good match for Paul.

We had a good trip and we seemed to be getting on fine again. Paul weighed in two pounds heavier than Rudi. We prepared well and Paul was in the zone. Form the first bell Paul was back to the fighter he had been before the Gray debacle. He boxed beautifully just as he had against Gadney and won every round. He was calm and I was getting feedback between rounds. I was relieved and Paul was back on course after a good win. Maloney was as sick as a parrot.

Less than a month later I got a call from Keith Tait offering a four three minute round fight for Paul against one of his fighters called James Jiora. Just like Paul's previous opponent, Jiora had won four and lost one and that was to Marvin P Gray so they had that in common. What's more the show, on the 15th of December 87 was a televised Fight Night and Paul could get on the box for the first time if the producers needed a fill in hence the four rounds distance.

Paul, after a redeeming good performance against Valentino, trained hard and was looking forward to the fight. The show was at the Manningham Sports Centre Bradford. We were there in good time and both boxers weighed in the same at 9st 12lbs. We were the first fight on the bill so I knew it would be in the can if needed for the broadcast.

Paul warmed up in the usual way but seemed a little remote and detached and definitely not in the zone. The hall was a bit sparse and lacking in atmosphere but that doesn't explain Paul's performance. He was at least tree inches taller than Jiora with the resulting reach advantage but he failed to use it. Although he was not as bad as in the

Gray fight, from the first bell it was a different Paul from the one who had outboxed Rudi Valentino less than a month before.

It ended up being a scrappy four rounds with neither of the boxers being better than the other and for the TV crews it was just a chance to get their cameras tuned in. Jiora won a points decision.

Once again there didn't seem to be a logical explanation for Paul's lack lustre performance that night. There were obviously things going on in Paul's head that I didn't understand I couldn't break through. It was coming up to Christmas and a break might help.

After New Year 88 my little chunky friend Frank Maloney was on the phone asking for a return between Paul Burke and Paul Gadney. He was determined to get a win over Paul and maybe the loss to Jiora had encouraged him. He gave us the date of 11th of February 88 and an eight rounder at the Woodville Hall, Gravesend. I hated those South or east of London venues because it meant driving through the Capital late after the show and a long drive home but it was a good fight for Paul against someone he had already beaten and the purse was decent.

Again in training I felt that we were not quite on the same wavelength as we had been pre the Gray fight. Anyway he worked hard for the longer fight, his first eight rounder and he was in a positive mood for the long drag down to Gravesend. Paul weighed in on the lightweight limit of 9st 9lbs, two pounds lighter than Gadney.

The referee was Roy Francis so knew we would get no favours there. Paul warmed up and was in the zone. Unlike the Jiora fight I was getting feedback from him. From the first bell, again it was the Paul Burke I once knew. He boxed well and was comfortable between rounds. Gadney, who had not fought since their last fight, was again putting up some resistance but Paul was winning the rounds. At the end of the fight again I was lost for words when Francis called it a draw. Even Frank Maloney seemed embarrassed by the home town result.

That fight was the last that Paul fought for me. So far he had won six lost three and drawn one. In real terms he had won eight and lost two because one loss and the draw were blatant home town decisions. Somewhere along the way Paul and I had drifted apart. I couldn't see where it had gone wrong. Paul started to arrive at the gym early and was working out on his own. At that point most of my boxers had day jobs so, for sparring purposes, I was conducting evening sessions. When I told Paul that I wanted him in the gym for these sessions for sparring he refused point blank and then said that the others should be coming in for his sessions. From there he then accused me of showing favour to some other boxers that I had known since long before his time.

That annoyed me because as far as I was concerned I had never favoured anyone over another. I gave each boxer what I thought was as much individual time as they needed. This varied from fighter to fighter and if one was training for a title fight for example, he obviously would get more of my time, but all the other fighters accepted this. If I had three or four boxers all in the gym at the same time and at different levels, obviously I couldn't spend as much time with each one as I would have liked but Paul seemed to think I should have been giving him more time.

Perhaps he was right but it didn't prevent my other fighters from achieving titles and he was the only one who complained. I was open to talk to anyone and always encouraged feedback. If Paul had come to me and explained how he felt instead of going in to himself maybe we could have worked it out.

When he first came to the gym I spent a lot of time with Paul, talking to him about boxing and explaining the pros and cons of the business and I thought I was doing a pretty good job of turning him from a lowly amateur, who had achieved nothing so far, into a good young professional. He still had a long way to go but I was sure he would go to the top given his obvious talent, but with this breakdown in our relationship there was no way forward and I told him that.

A few months later I got a call from Jack Tricket the Manchester promoter/manager asking if Paul was free to sign with his stable and I of course agreed. Paul was still under contract but I was not going to hold him to it. He had his first fight away from me on the 21st January 1989 which he won. He was now being trained by Phil Martin in the "Champs Camp" in Manchester. He went on to fulfil my prediction that he would become a very good fighter. When he retired from boxing in 1999 he had fought forty three times winning twenty eight losing thirteen and drawing twice. He became British and Commonwealth lightweight Champion and fought for European and WBO titles. A creditable record in any ones book and I like to think that I set him off in the right way.

I have only seen a few times since and we were on friendly terms. Jean was always fond of him.

Chapter eleven
KEITH HALLIWELL

KEITH HALLIWELL was a nice guy. He had been around the gyms as an amateur for quite a few years when he first turned up in my gym. He was from Wigan and was twenty seven so physically mature and weighing around twelve stones.

At first he didn't ask about turning professional he just wanted to train with the pros and spar with them. I was happy with this for a while and he was a useful spar against Sammy Sampson and Simon McDougal etc; By New Year 1988 he had come on so well that when he finally decided he would like to fight for real I was happy to get him licensed.

He was ready for his pro debut by the time I was taking Kevin Pritchard to fight in London at the Café Royal on the 7th of March 88 and Dennie Mancini found an opponent in the shape of Den Lake who had a two win and one loss record. It was six twos and although Keith was boxing well, he got a nick over his left eye in the third round but I was able to keep it under control. He won the points decision.

On the 30th of March I was offered a six rounder for Keith against Joe McKenzie who had won one and lost two. It seemed right but on the night it didn't work out. Keith boxed well in the first round but got caught early in the second with a big left hook which put him down and the ref stopped it.

After a compulsory break he was back in training and I got him a job for the 13th of June on a Nat Basso AASC show in the Piccadilly Hotel Manchester. He fought a six rounder against the experienced Dave Mowbray and won clearly.

On the 12th of December he knocked out Sean Stringfellow with a peach of a right cross again at the Piccadilly.

With Christmas and New Year 89 out of the way Keith was in action against Morris Thomas at the YESC in Bradford thanks to Graham Lockwood. He started fast that night and Morris didn't know what hit him when Keith let that right hand go again in the first round and it was goodnight Morris.

Nat Basso booked Keith again for the Anglo American Sporting Club at the Piccadilly on the 4th of April. This time the opponent was Carl Thompson who had been a champion kick boxer before turning professional. He was big at six foot one against Keith's five foot ten but also he was a full blown light heavy.

I asked Keith how he felt about it. At this point Thompson had won his four pro starts and Keith had won four and lost one of his so the question was mainly about the weight difference. Keith's confidence was high after his last two KO wins so he was up for it. Nat said that Carl Thompson would "probably" weigh around twelve four.

Keith weighed in on the night at exactly twelve stone and I was dismayed when Thompson weighed twelve eight. I should have known Nat better after all he spoke with forked tongue many times. Not only that, Thompson was a mountain of muscle. He of course went on to win world titles at cruiserweight.

On the night Keith attacked the big guy from the first bell trying to land that power right that he had been successful with twice before. Thompson was content to back off and throw long overhand crosses. A minute into the round before any clean punches had been landed by either; Keith was cut badly over the right eye. I didn't see a punch land on it and it might have been Thompson's head but whatever, the fight was over.

A call from Alex Morrison offered us a fight at the Bellahuston Sports Centre, Glasgow, on the 27th of June 89 against ex Scottish ABA champion, James Wray.

The top of the bill was an International ten rounder between Pat "Black Flash" Barrett and American Robert Trevino. Pat had come a long way since his loss to Paul Burke.

James Wray had had four wins out of four in the pros. The match weight of 12st 2lbs suited us and it was only a four by three minute round fight. We accepted. We also knew we would be up against the Scottish referees as well as James Wray.

Richard Jones travelled with us as a second, he knew Keith well from his amateur days in the Wigan area. We called at the Alex Morrison gym in Duke St, in Glasgow for the weigh in. Both boxers scaled 12st 2lbs and I was pleased to see that Wray was the same size and build as Keith after the physical disadvantages of the Thompson fight. We went for some lunch in Glasgow with Pat Barrett and his trainer Brian Hughes.

I was peed off when I saw that the ref for our fight was Harry Mullen and knew we were a couple of rounds down before the bell rang. The show was televised and we were second on. From the first bell Keith was straight into the attack and dominated the round. The fighters were well matched barring the age advantage of James who was seven years younger. Keith's experience was telling though and by the fourth and final round I was sure he was well in front. This was confirmed at the final bell when Harry Mullen called it a draw. When I look at a photograph I took of the two fighters afterwards, it is Wray whose face tells the story of the fight.

It was time to take a summer break and I didn't see or hear from Keith again until March 1990. He explained he had been busy in his full time job and also he had to consider whether he wanted to carry on with his boxing. His wife wanted him to retire. He had now re-charged his batteries and was ready to give it another go. I told him it had to be his decision at that point. He had fought so well and displayed heart and courage and if he was ready to walk away I would not discourage him, but at the same time I wasn't ready to tell him it was time to call it a day.

It was May when I got a call from Ernie Fossey who was looking for an opponent for Paul McCarthy, brother of Steve McCarthy who was onetime British lightheavy champion. Paul had won fifteen and lost six but in his losses he had been stopped five times. The match was on another big Frank Warren televised bill at Rivermead Leisure Centre in Reading on the 26th of May 90. It was a six threes and the money was decent.

We travelled on our own and at the weigh in both boxers scaled 12st 3lbs. Again they were of similar height and build. At the weigh in Keith was pleased to see one of his old St Helens mates Gary Stretch who was topping the bill. Gary had changed stables since he beat Sammy Sampson for the Area Title when managed by Mike Barrett. He was now with the Frank Warren outfit.

Keith was always easy to prepare. He kept his nerves under control, warmed up well and got into the zone. He started the fight as always, on the front foot and throwing plenty of leather. McCarthy was willing to back pedal and try and keep out of trouble. Keith won the first and second clearly and I was feeling confident when he went out for the third with the instructions to carry on doing what was obviously working for him.

Suddenly there was blood running down his face just like the Thompson fight. The ref brought him to the corner for me to dry the cut so that he could see it properly. I asked him to let it go on so that I could work on it at the bell and he did let them box on. Half a minute later and with Paul McCarthy encouraged by the sight of blood, now attacking for the first time, the referee waved it over. It was a big disappointment because up until the cut I was confident that Keith would land that devastating right hand that had KO'd fighters before.

On the long drive back to Wigan we were able to have a good talk about the future and we agreed that, at thirty years old, Keith had left it a bit late for starting what is always a young mans game. I left the final decision with him.

I thought about what a good professional Keith would have made had he turned pro when he was in his early twenties. I had enjoyed working with him and he had never argued or complained about anything. He worked hard in the gym and was as brave as any man who ever climbed through the ropes.

I didn't hear from him again. I hope he is well and happy.

Chapter twelve
SIMON MCDOUGALL

SIMON McDOUGALL was from Blackpool. He was nineteen and boxing for Lytham St Annes YMCA amateur boxing club when he first came to my gym in 1987. He was considering a professional career but wanted to spar with my boxers for a few months before making the move. He was entered for the ABA championships in early 1988 and I went over to Wythenshawe to watch him in the preliminaries. At 5' 11" he weighed around twelve and a half stones but he was "fleshy" and I estimated at least half a stone overweight. He was obviously talented and courageous but his punching technique was awful and although he won his first fight he lost in the second and was eliminated for that year.

A few weeks later he came back to see me having made up his mind to turn professional. He was a nice young guy who seemed laid back and happy go lucky which belied his passion for fighting. He just loved the sparring but, unfortunately, he also liked to fight in the street as well and his hobby was standing on doors at some of the Blackpool pubs and clubs where he got the chance to throw some punches most weekends. I had a serious talk with him about this and warned him that if he became licensed then the fist fighting would have to stop and he assured me that it would. I had to delay an initial application because he was due in court over a punch up he had with a holiday maker. It turned out that the magistrate threw the case out because it was a six of one half a dozen of the other scenario but it served as a warning to Simon.

He was the most frustrating of all the fighters I had ever worked with simply because he hated all forms of exercise and fitness work. I spent hours in the ring with him correcting his punch angles and his range of punches and whilst I was holding the pads he would be punch perfect but as soon as he was left to punch the heavy bags and speed balls, he was lackadaisical and back to his old ways. I never had a problem getting a 100% effort out of any of the other boxers during circuit training and floor exercises but Simon did the minimum he could get away with. For all that he was a great guy to have in the gym and the other fighters liked working alongside him, maybe it was because he made them look really industrious

He had that natural instinct of distance and timing and the ability to lie on the ropes and avoid punches by swaying back. It is an age old tactic that was made popular by Muhammad Ali's so called "rope-a-dope" against George Foreman but it has been part of the game since roped rings were first used.

By October 1988 Simon was licensed and fit enough for a six round pro debut. Nat Basso offered a six two minute round contest on his AASC show at the Piccadilly Hotel on the 14th of November. His opponent was Andrew Bravado from Manchester who had lost his only other fight. Simon weighed in at 12st 6lbs, a couple of pounds lighter than Andrew. Warming Simon up and getting him in the zone was easy because he never showed any sign of nerves at all and just wanted to get in the ring and fight.

He dominated the action for three rounds before landing a big right hand in the fourth on a by now demoralised Bravado who looked nothing like his name. The ref stopped the contest and Simon had his first win.

After more work in the gym, it was Christmas and New Year 1989 and in spite of my pleading with him to stay fit over the few days off from training he came back to the gym showing signs of the festivities. Tommy Miller wanted Simon for the YESC show in Bradford on the 16th of January and the opponent was Steve Osborne who had lost five out of five fights. The match was made at 12st 10lbs which reflected both boxers Christmas breaks.

Again Simon was nonchalant at the pre fight preparations and this was reflected in the scrappy, lack lustre six rounds which culminated in a point's win for Osborne. I was not happy with Simon but he just shrugged it off.

Pat Brogan was at that show with another fighter and he asked if we wanted a return with Steve nine days later at his show in Stoke on the 25th of January. After Simon's performance I was sure he could do much better a second time against Steve Osborne. Simon was also keen for the fight. It was in Steve Osborne's home town but I didn't think that would matter. It did because after a much better performance, I was sure that Simon was a clear winner but Midlands Area referee Terry O'Conner saw it the other way and gave it to Osborne by half a point.

The 20th of February saw us back at the YESC Bradford against Newcastle hard man Willie Connell. Simon was responding a little better to my urgings and was down to 12st 6lbs for this one. After three rounds I had Simon comfortably ahead and boxing well when in the fourth round he threw a blinding left hook which split Willie Connell's eye wide open and the ref stopped it.

On the 4th of April it was back to The Piccadilly for Nat Basso and six rounds against Lee Woolis who sported a 7-16-1 record. Simon boxed well but lost a fair decision to the cagy experienced Woolis

The next trip was up to Glasgow to the Edmiston Club for Alex Morrison. This was a quite amusing situation. Alex told me he had a fighter called George Ferrie who was making his pro debut. He said that George had been around the gyms for years but was now ready for the pro game. He was a well known hard man around Glasgow, which is saying something, who also worked on the doors.

I should explain at this point that if you lined Simon McDougall up with fifty other young guys of his age, he is probably the last one you would pick as a pro boxer. He was a good looking boy, yet to show any of the facial signs of a boxer. Blonde haired and a light complexion, straight nose and looks more of a choir boy than a fighter. At the weigh in at Morrisons gym in Duke St he weighed in at 12st 2lbs and gave the glowering George Ferrie a cheeky grin. I smiled to myself when Alex pulled me to one side and asked me if Simon would be all right. He was genuinely concerned about this wee boy going in with the hard case. I told him not to worry and assured him that the boy just loved to fight.

The referee was Harry Mullen and I was more concerned about him than Ferrie. From the first bell it was obvious why it had taken Ferrie so long to make up his mind to turn pro. He might have been tough on the corner but Simon was tearing him to pieces. Half way through the first round, Ferrie was down for the first of several counts. The second third and fourth were the same with Ferrie on the deck in each round and Simon cruising. The only thing you could say for George was that he was no quitter even though by now his friends outside the ring were jeering him. By the fifth Simon was beginning to feel sorry for him and actually began to toy with him. He told me afterwards that he didn't see the point in trying to knock him out. I was to see this side of Simon's nature several times in the future. At the final bell even Harry Mullen couldn't get away with a home town decision but I was shocked when he only gave it to Simon by one round. What fight had he been watching? I admit that I am obviously biased when it comes to close decisions but this was ridiculous but at least we got the win.

Simon's next fight was much closer to home when he was offered a six rounder against Burnley's Jimmy Cropper who had a 3-3 record at the Oldham Sports Centre on the 30th of November. There was a bit of local needle to this one, a sort of East Lancs v West Lancs. Simon won a one sided contest on points.

Nat Basso wanted Simon for a show at the Four Hundred Club Manchester on the 7th of December. It was against his own fighter Sean O'Phoenix whom I knew from Sammy Sampson's sparring days in Manchester. Sean had won eleven and lost eight and drawn three. He was a decent fighter and coming so soon after Simon's win over

Cropper, I was dubious. However Simon was keen to fight for another pay day before Christmas.

He was his usual self on the run up to the fight and got as close to the zone as he ever got. Sean O'Phoenix was too good for him that night. Simon was really just going through the motions for four rounds until the fifth when O'Phoenix caught him with a big right that broke his nose and put him down for an eight count for the first time in his career. As he sat down at the end of the round I straightened his nose which had been bent to one side. It is always the best time, if not the only time, to do it. Funnily enough it wasn't bleeding very much and Simon was keen enough to go out for the last round. Sean didn't get close enough to follow up and it was probably Simon's best round of the fight although O'Phoenix deserved a wide point's decision.

After Christmas and New Year 1990 Simon's nose had healed up well. There was no kink in it and, apart from a slight thickening at the bridge you couldn't tell it had been broken. I turned down several fights for him until March just to be sure. We kept up with the training although I had to nag him sometimes to get him in the gym. At the beginning of March 90, Dennie Mancini offered Simon a fight in Eindhoven, Holland, against Eddy Smoulders who had a seven out of seven record at the time. Eddy was an ex-kick boxing champion and at 6' 1" weighing 12st 7lbs, he was a full blown light heavyweight. It was over six three minute rounds on the 7th of April which gave us five weeks to prepare. The purse was the best so far and Simon was keen to go.

We were met at Schipol airport by one of promoter Henk Rhuling's men and driven to Eindhoven on the day before the show. We soon discovered that Eddy Smoulders was a bit of a celebrity in the town and at the weigh in there were TV and newspaper reporters asking questions. Eddy looked much bigger than the 12st 6lbs he weighed in at and at twenty seven years of age was a well matured, muscular specimen compared to the 12st 4lbs, pale and slightly fleshy Simon McDougall. I could see that they were all expecting an early night.

We were well treat though and shown a great deal of respect. Our accommodation was good and we were happy with our preparation. The show was at the local ice rink and we were given our own dressing room which was a first for me. We usually had to share with several others.

Smoulders was roared into the ring by the big home town crowd and we got a respectable cheer. At least I had a helpful house second in the corner. Simon was as unruffled as usual and at the first bell he surprised Smoulders by taking the fight to him. After a flurry of fairly ineffectual left jabs and cuffing right hands, Simon reverted to his normal style and invited Eddy to try and hit him, which he couldn't.

For the full six rounds I could see Eddy Smoulders desperately trying to please his baying fans by landing a significant punch on the slippery Englishman, but Simon was to clever for him and although his punches were not bothering Smoulders, he was landing plenty. At the final bell there was no doubting the winner but Simon had confounded those who thought it was an easy fight for Eddy. Simon got a good cheer from the crowd as we left the ring.

Eddy Smoulders went on to win the European Light heavyweight title and fight for the WBA title. When he retired in 2005 he had fought 39 times and lost only twice.

We were driven back to Amsterdam the following morning but our flight was not until about 6pm that evening so we did a tour of the City. Simon was well amused by it but I was less so. I thought it was a sordid place with its porn shops, cannabis cafes and street beggars. I had the purse money on me and had to stay alert at all times. Simon wanted to buy some porn videos which he said he could copy and make a fortune in Blackpool but I wouldn't give him the cash because I told him we would probably get turned over by the customs in Manchester and they would confiscate them anyway. We of course were stopped and searched and although they were interested in my medical bag, especially the adrenaline solution, there was nothing for them. It was the first of several trips I would make with Simon.

Just over a month later we were off to South Shields to fight Terry French for his manager, Tommy Conroy. It was only a four three minute rounder on the 15th of May. Simon had suffered no bruises against Eddy Smoulders and his nose had caused no problems. French had a 9-8-1 record. Simon was too good for him though and had Terry down for eight in the first before running out a clear winner even on referee Freddie Potter's card.

Dennie Mancini offered Simon a fight in Cayenne French Guyana South America on the 12th of October. It was against local boxer Ray Albert over six threes. It was good money but a long trip to a hot, run down third world country. Simon fought well in atrocious conditions but lost a close points decision. It was a new experience.

We were again closer to home on the 22nd of October where Simon fought Bury's Glen Campbell at the Piccadilly Hotel Manchester. Simon was down to 12st 4lbs and was two lbs lighter than Glen. Up to that fight, Campbell had won five out of five fights and was being hailed as a bright prospect and champion of the future. He was a muscular black kid with a reputation as a puncher. I mention this because it illustrates how referees can be influenced into making bad decisions.

From the first bell Campbell was on the front foot attacking Simon who was content to counterpunch him and then turn him into corners and slip away. Glen was getting more and more frustrated round after round but could not land a solid punch on Simon. After the six rounds that Simon had fought against Eddy Smoulders, who would have blown Glen Away in a round or two, it was child's play. In the interval before the fourth round I told Simon to give it one more round before switching to a more positive action when Glen would be tired.

At the start of the fourth Simon again allowed Glen Campbell to chase him around the ring. Half way through the round Simon retreated to the ropes to tire Glen out by doing his rope -a-dope trick whilst Glen whaled away with futile shots. This was typical Simon McDougall stuff and I was dismayed when referee Roy Snipe suddenly stopped the contest and declared Campbell the winner to save McDougall from further punishment. It was an absolutely ludicrous decision made by a ref who just didn't understand what was happening but thought that the favourite had done enough. Simon was furious to think that someone of Glen Campbell's calibre could say that he had stopped him.

On the 10th of December Graham Lockwood booked Simon for a six rounder at the YESC against Morris Thomas who had a 6-3-1 record. Simon weighed 12st 6lbs for this one and he was in a hurry when he stormed Morris for one and a half rounds before the ref rescued him.

After that quick win Lockwood booked Simon again for the YESC show on the 28th of January 1991. The opposition was Ian Henry from Gateshead who was trained and managed by Tommy Conroy. Ian had won five out of six so far and he was a year older than Simon, a couple if inches taller and around the same weight. In other words they were well matched and this was the first of eventually three meetings between them. It was Simon's first eight rounder and I had stepped up his training, at least I had made him work longer if not any harder. At any rate, he boxed really well that night and deserved his points win.

In the meantime, Glen Campbell had won the Central Area super middleweight title in his only fight since his win over Simon. Glen was managed by Jack Doughty who was a boxing historian and author who wrote the life story of one of Britain's finest ever middleweights, Jock McAvoy the "Rochdale Thunderbolt" (recommended reading for any boxing fan). Jack had a thriving young stable at Shaw near Oldham and promoted shows in the area as I had around Preston in the mid eighties. I spoke to Jack and agreed for Simon to challenge

Glen for the Area Title which was accepted by the board if I could guarantee that he could make the weight comfortably. The lightest that Simon had weighed for a contest was 12st 2lbs but I knew that, with his fleshy physique and the fact that he had never ever tried to get down to a lower weight, 12st wouldn't be a problem.

Coming off two wins, Simon's confidence was high and I sat down with him and emphasised the need to knuckle down to a serious training programme which included a proper diet and abstinence from beer. I had gone through this several times in the past with him only to have broken promises, but this time he did stick to it. He was keen to prove a point against Glen Campbell after his farcical stoppage.

Jack promoted the show in Glen's home town Bury on the 28th of February 91. Simon's training went well and at the 1pm weigh in on the day of the fight he scaled 11st 12 1/4lbs, a few pounds heavier than Campbell. He warmed up well and his concentration before the fight was the best I had known from him. He was in the zone.

The referee was Ron Hackett. From the first bell Simon went out to stamp his authority in contrast to their first meeting. It took the wind out of Glen's sails and Simon won the round. The next five rounds were pretty even affairs with the super fit Campbell being the aggressor but with Simon having no trouble in avoiding his bombs and turning him on the ropes with ease. I told Simon to be more forceful in the seventh which he did and it was obvious that Glen didn't like it when he was pushed onto his back foot. The round was even but in the eighth Simon was even better and I looked across to Glen's corner and saw panic on the faces of his seconds. Glen was almost in tears in his corner before the ninth and I thought there was a chance he was not going to make it out for the start of the round but he did. Simon dominated the action for the round and although Glen tried to rally in the tenth and final round, Simon won that round too. So if you called the fight even at the end of the seventh, Simon won the last three clearly and should have been crowned the Area Champ. Instead, with the crowd booing and to my amazement, Hackett gave the decision to Glen Campbell by half a point. It was another blatant home town decision.

Simon took the decision with a shrug and although he was annoyed he didn't get too upset that is how he was. He took a month off which he deserved and was his old laid back self when he returned to the gym at the end of March.

I got a fight for him on the 23rd of April in Evesham, Worcestershire against Paul Burton whose record was 9-9. It should have been an easy job for Simon but he was so negative that he deservedly lost a points decision.

Simon was going through a spell when he just wouldn't knuckle down to train unless he had a fight coming up and even then his lifestyle was deteriorating and I knew that he was back with his doorman mates and drinking beer. He denied it but I had other people who knew him. His weight was climbing after his 12st championship fight but he just didn't care.

I got him a return fight with Ian Henry, whom he had out pointed in January, at Gateshead on the 10th of May. Tommy Conroy asked for the fight to be at 12st 7lbs plus or minus a pound. Simon weighed in surprisingly heavy at 12st 11lbs against Henry's 12st 3lbs. I wasn't happy and neither was Tommy.

Simon was his usual self at the preparation but not in the zone. For three rounds he was able to control the action. He was stronger than Ian but not as sharp. He began to labour in the fourth and when he sat down at the end of the round and I removed his gumshield I realised his jaw was damaged and his cheek was beginning to swell. I asked him if he was OK to go on or should I call the ref over but he insisted on going on. For the last two rounds he used his experience to fiddle his way through to lose a point's decision. The doctor diagnosed a broken jaw and I took Simon to the hospital where an X-ray confirmed a hairline fracture. Simon was out for two months.

I had another long talk with Simon about his future. He now had won only seven of if his seventeen contests and even allowing for a few dodgy decisions, he wasn't doing himself justice. His refusal to work really hard in training and on his technique was limiting his potential and I was having second thoughts on whether I wanted to be part of it. He was such a great guy that it was hard to walk away from him but he was so frustrating. He promised me that he would get back in harness and train properly and cut down on the night life if I would just get him some fights.

I got him a six rounder in Liverpool on the 30th of September. His jaw had healed well and he was working hard in the gym. The opponent was Doug Calderwood who now had a 6-5-1 record and was a step down from the class of his last few fights. Sure enough Simon weighed in at 12st 6lbs the same as Doug. From the first bell he was back to his best and by the middle of the fourth round the referee had to rescue Doug Calderwood.

The 10th of October came a return with Terry French in Gateshead. By now Terry's record was up to 12-10-1 but I was confident that Simon would repeat his previous win over him. It was another good close fight but this time French got the nod. I didn't feel bad about Simon losing when he fought as well as that.

Dennie Mancini was back with a an offer of another foreign trip, this time to Terni in Italy, about fifty miles north of Rome. It was an eight rounder against the Italian Light heavyweight champion Andrea Magi who was undefeated in eleven fights. The match was at 12st 7lbs and the money was good and Simon jumped at the chance. We flew to Rome and were taken by road to the Town which was up in the mountains. The hotel we were staying at was good and Magi's people were decent, respectful guys for Italians.

At the weigh in we were surprised at how big Magi looked. He was at least 6' 3" tall and although he was only a pound heavier than Simon, he looked a lot bigger.

Simon was as unconcerned as usual and the preparation went well and Simon got in the zone. We had already discussed the tactics and knowing we couldn't expect any favours from the ref I told Simon that I didn't want any heroics. This time, after the experience with Kevin Pritchard in Rome, I made sure we had a house second who I tipped with a few thousand liras (pre euros) before the fight.

From the first bell the big fellow came out looking for a quick win but against Simon he had little chance of that. Simon was much faster and had no trouble turning Magi and landing some of his own pitter patter left jabs. By the third Simon was enjoying himself and this got me a bit worried. It was obvious that Magi had power in his shots but he was getting frustrated at not being able to land anything clean on Simon who was looking a bit to cocky.

In the fourth, inevitably, Simon began to tire against the strong Italian and although he wasn't being hurt there were signs of danger. Sure enough in the fifth, Magi did land a heavy bludgeoning right on Simon which made him hang on for a few seconds. As the referee broke them, Simon went down on one knee. It was only the second time I had seen Simon down the only other time was when Sean O'Phoenix broke his nose. This time Simon looked at me and I gave him the signal to stay down. He rose slowly at nine but the referee knew the body language and called the fight off. Magi was relieved to get the fight over, Simon was unhurt and had only been hit by one hard punch in the five rounds and the crowd cheered their hero. Everyone went home happy.

We were well looked after that night and after breakfast the following morning we were taken to the railway station and given tickets to Rome. I was paid the correct amount plus expenses without a quibble which made a change. On quite a few trips I had to argue the toss before getting paid in full. We arrived in Rome by about 11am and since our flight was late evening I took Simon on a whistle stop tour of the sights in the centre of Rome that I had done with Kevin Pritchard a couple of years before. We were late checking in at Rome airport and literally had to run to the gate!

Simon took time off until after Christmas and New Year 92. He reappeared in mid January weighing around 12st 12lbs. He was in good form and was training quite hard and asking for a fight as soon as possible, he was broke after Christmas. I told him I wouldn't accept anything until he was below twelve seven. A phone call in mid February from Tommy Conroy offered Simon an eight rounder on the 3rd of March against Paul Hitch who had won six out of six all against fighters that Simon had fought and mostly beat. He was offering good money but he wanted Simon to weigh in at close to 12st which of course was out of the question at that short notice. It did give me a lever to use on Simon to encourage him to make the effort to get his weight down to what was his best. We agreed on 12st 4lbs.

The show was on Paul Hitch's home patch of Houghton-le-Springs, Tyne and Wear. At the weigh in, sure enough Hitch was under 12st and Simon made the stipulated 12st 4lbs. The fight was a boring affair. Hitch was by the far the quicker puncher and his footwork round the ring was neat but Simon just couldn't be bothered chasing him around the ring and Paul was not going to exchange punches with him so in the end a points win for Hitch is how it ended.

At that show Tommy Conroy offered Simon another shot at Ian Henry. They were one apiece after their last two meetings so a rubber match on the 11th of March, just eight days after the hitch fight and another eight rounder with decent money, suited Simon. This time the fight was on neutral territory being at the MSC show in Solihull, Birmingham.

Simon had put a couple of pounds on and weighed in at 12st 6lbs pounds with Henry a pound lighter. This time it was a good entertaining eight rounds and we didn't dispute a half point win for Ian Henry although I thought a draw would have been fairer.

Again at that show, Ron Gray, the promoter, offered Simon a third eight rounder in the month against fifty/fifty fighter Nigel Rafferty at the Leofric Hotel, Coventry. Again it was good money and at twelve and a half stones it was right for Simon. The date was 30th of March.

This was one of Simon's now typical performances where he was just laid back and disinterested in the contest. With a 13-12-4 record, Nigel Rafferty too was an experienced survivor and between them the waltzed through eight rounds without hurting one another. Rafferty got the points win.

With three decent purses in the month, Simon again took time away from the gym. He was back looking for work in mid May and surprisingly he was still around the twelve and a half stone mark. He said he was keeping up with his running along with Louis Vietch who was in the gym preparing for a fight and keeping me informed of Simon's goings on.

On Monday the 8th of June 92 I was just starting the gym session at around 7.30pm when I got a call from Matchmaker Graeme Lockwood. He had a YESC show on that night in Bradford. One of their fighters called Mark McBaine was due to fight and had sold quite a few tickets. McBaine weighed around thirteen stone but had only had three contests and had lost them all. His opponent had failed his medical and in desperation Graeme asked if Simon was in the gym and would he fight at such short notice. Naturally they would have to pay over the odds but it would save embarrassment if McBaine could fight. I told him I would call him back if Simon showed up and wanted the fight.

When Simon walked into the gym at around 8pm I told him about the job and, against a losing novice, it would be no harder than the sparring he would be doing that night and he would be getting well paid as well. He jumped at the chance and I rang a relieved Lockwood back and asked him to confirm the purse money before we left Preston, which he did.

I knew the journey to Bradford like the back of my hand and we were there in just over an hour. Simon weighed in at 12st 8lbs, five pounds lighter than McBaine. Things had happened so fast that Simon soon warmed up and for once was in the zone. It was probably the excitement of the short notice that got his adrenaline going but what ever it was, he was ready for the fight.

When the referee called the boxers to the centre of the ring we got our first real look at Mark. He was big, a couple of inches taller than Simon and with big powerful arms and shoulders and a nice set of abs. I had told Simon that I wanted him to impose himself on the novice from the start so that he didn't get to confident and from the first bell Simon battered the poor guy all round the ring. At the end of the round I told Simon he could make it an early night if he wanted to and he nodded agreement.

He started the second in the same way and then he suddenly started to lay back. I at first wondered whether he had hurt a hand or was feeling tired but at the end of the round I realised that it was nothing to do with that. He simply knew he had the fight completely under control and he just didn't want to humiliate Mark in front of his home fans. For the rest of the fight that is how he played it. He allowed Mark to come on to him where he did his rolling on the ropes and slipping tricks just as if he was in the gym, before throwing a flurry of jabs and hooks but without malice. He won every round on the referee's card but at least Mark McBaine got to the final bell and they both got a big cheer from the crowd. On the way home Simon said he didn't see the point in knocking the guy out which would have meant a twenty eight day suspension for him. I always said Simon had a big heart.

Now it was summer again and a busy time in Blackpool. Simon disappeared from the gym for a few weeks. He was back by the end of August hungry for another pay day. Frank Turner, who was matchmaker for Barry Hearns Matchroom outfit offered us an eight rounder in Antwerp Belgium on a big promotion for sky TV on the 6th of October 92. They wanted Simon to fight Gary Delaney over eight rounds on the undercard. Delaney had won seven and drawn one and was an up and coming star. They were looking for a quick KO opponent for Gary and were willing to pay well for one. Unfortunately for them, Simon was not a quick KO victim for anyone. We took the fight at 12st 9lbs.

It was a good well organised show in Belgium where Hearns had established a Matchroom snooker Empire. We shared a dressing room with Bobby Neil, ex-British featherweight champion who had become a successful trainer/manager, who had a couple of fighters on the bill. Simon really got into the atmosphere again and our prep went well. He was in the zone. Gary Delaney was a big light heavy but Simon once again was not fazed by looks and from the first bell he was happy to exchange jabs with Gary.

After an even couple of rounds, Delaney's extra power began to tell and Simon went into defensive mode which he could do very well. Gary was getting more and more frustrated with Simon but even when he did land a half decent shot, Simon shrugged it off. Delaney won by a mile but Simon made him work to the last bell and he earned his money.

Matchroom put on a dinner and show for everyone after the boxing ended. It was a good night and overall, a good trip.

On the 12th of December Hearns was putting on another World Title Show at the Alexandria Pavilion featuring Nigel Benn v Nicky Piper and again Gary Delaney was on the undercard so they asked if Simon would give Gary a return and a second chance to KO him in front of his London fans. I was able to negotiate a good purse

Simon had stayed in the gym and was raring to go and earn some Christmas money. I took Kevin Pritchard to work the corner with me and I took a few of Simons mates as well for the trip.

Again Simon concentrated and focused on the job during preparations, had he at last got the message? He was in the zone as we went out to a huge crowd who had turned out to see Benn and a few other home town fighters. Delaney got a big cheer from the West Hammers. Both fighters had weighed in at 12st 9lbs, which was a bit heavy for Simon but better when he was up against such a big guy.

From the bell it was a near carbon copy of their Antwerp fight. Once again Gary tried to pin Simon down long enough to land his bombs but once again Simon was peppering him with jabs and turning him on the ropes as well as taking the few shots that did get past his guard. As they were raising Gary's hand after the final bell, I got in the ring to put Simons gown on. Gary came over to me and said "that's the last time I want to fight this guy. He is impossible to hit or hurt"

Christmas 92 came and went and it was towards the end of January before Simon was back. It was mid February 93 when I got a call from Tommy Gilmour Jnr asking for Simon for 4th of March in Glasgow. The opponent was Alan Smiles who was an ex ABA Champ but had only had one pro fight which he had won on points. I had vowed to stop dragging fighters up to Scotland only to get raw decisions but a six rounder for Simon against a novice was too much of a temptation so we took it.

It was another pay day and another half point farcical decision from referee Al Hutcheon. Simon hadn't boxed at his best but he had done enough against a poor opponent. I know that anyone who has read about me bleating about bad decisions may think I am a bad loser, but you can ask just about every trainer/manager who ever brought fighters up from England about the bias. Sure I am biased when it comes to my own fighters, but I am as close to the action as it is possible to get and I know whether a fighter is winning or not.

A couple of weeks after the Smile's debacle, Paddy Byrne acting for Mogens Palle offered really good money for Simon to fight Swedish favourite Roland Erickson in Copenhagen, Denmark where I had taken Kevin Pritchard a few years before. The date was 26th of March and it was six rounds at 12st 7lbs. Simon was still in reasonable condition after his March 4th fight and he jumped at the chance. Ericsson had been well fancied until he tripped over a left hook or two and his record stood at 17-4 but he had been stopped in three of his four losses.

Simon was once again switched on. Everything went perfectly in the warm up and he was full of fight for this one. Ericsson didn't have a clue on how to deal with Simon. For four rounds it was scrappy but Simon was dominant and in the fifth he dropped Ericsson and when he got up the referee stopped it. Why did Simon blow so hot and cold? Who would have predicted that result? Not even me!

On the 17th of April it was time for another rubber match. Like Ian Henry before him, Terry French had lost and won against Simon. Again the fight was in the North East at Washington, Tyne-and-wear. Simon was down to 12st 5lbs for this one and just a pound heavier than Terry. Which Simon would turn up for this one?

As always with these two it was a hard even fight, good for the crowd and Terry French got the decision. No complaints.

On the 12th of May we went over to Sheffield to fight Martin Langtry. Simon was up to his old tricks again dodging the training sessions. His weight was going up again and only a month after his fight with Terry French he was up to 12st 12lbs, the heaviest yet and the only reason I accepted the fight was because Langtry had only had one winning fight, but he was a cruiserweight.

Simon was in his laid back "I'm only here for the beer" moods. There was no atmosphere to our warm up; he was just going through the motions. The fight consisted of the novice Langtry bulling Simon around the ring with no idea of how to get to grips. Simon was in pure survival mode. Langtry won on points

Again it was approaching summer and Simon had no time for training. I honestly wondered whether he would bother coming back. For a couple of fights he had really knuckled down then just as quickly he lost interest again. But sure enough after a few weeks away he was back to see if I could get him some money fights. He made all the old promises and he worked hard, by his standards, in the gym. He was still heavy.

To give you some idea of what he was like to deal with, I was at that time talking to a nutritionist about diets for fighters. Nutritionists are all the rage these days but they were few and far between in the eighties and nineties. He had a talk with Simon who agreed to follow a plan for two weeks which involved amongst other things, a controlled intake of calories plus protein drinks etc. As part of the plan Simon could take some special snacks if he felt hungry between meals. We, foolishly, gave Simon a week's supply of the protein drinks and the snacks. This was on the Monday. On the Thursday he asked me if he could have some more. Thinking he had given them away or lost them I asked him why he needed more and he told me he had had got hungry and by Wednesday evening he had finished them all!.... What can you do with someone who thinks like that?...I advised him to forget the plan.

I got an offer for a six round fight with Londoner Mark Prince from Tottenham. It was at the Hammersmith Palais on the 14th of August 93. The show was being headed by a ten rounder between the great Jamaican Mike McCallum and American Glen Thomas. The atmosphere was the most hostile I have ever experienced in boxing. When the national anthems of the two main contestants were being played, the crowd cheered the Americans and booed ours which was being played for Mike McCallum. Reg Gutteridge, the commentator who was at ringside but not working, got up and walked out.

The fight was made at 12st 10lbs and Simon and Mark weighed the same. Mark Prince had only fought three times but had won them all by KO. I got good money for Simon because they thought he was the sacrificial lamb in front of a big home crowd. They were wrong because Simon was too tough and clever for the powerful but crude Londoner, and although Prince deserved the points win he came no where near stopping Simon. Mark Prince went on to win inter continental titles and fight for the WBO title. He had twenty fights and only lost one and Simon was one of only three opponents to take him the distance.

Simon's next fight was on the 4th of October. Again it was a good money fight against another strong, black fighter called Bruce Scott whose record was 8-1 and again he expected an early night. The show was in Mayfair, London. Simon actually weighed in a pound under Scott's 12st 12lbs. Once again Simon frustrated the strong man and it was a closer fight than the Prince affair but the result was the same. The newly crowned WBC heavyweight champion, Lennox Lewis watched this fight and came and shook hands with Simon and congratulated him for his performance against Bruce.

Bruce Scott too went on to win the British and Commonwealth cruiserweight title and fight for the WBO title.

Whilst I was down in London I got Simon a sparring job in Paris with French star Cristophe Tiozzoe who was preparing for a World Title fight. Part of the deal, as well as a hundred pounds a day for the sparring, was an eight rounder against Frenchman Chris Girard on the same bill. The fight was in Romorantin, Loir-et-Cher, France on the 15th of October. Girard had a 22-1 record but he had his hands full before beating Simon on points.

After two contests close together Simon had earned a rest and I turned down work for him until I was offered an eight rounder against comparative novice Stevie Davies at Cottingham, Hull on the 8th of December 93. Steve had a five wins against eight losses record. Simon weighed in at 12st 10lbs. He was far too good for Stevie and had him down a few times before the referee rescued Davies in the fifth.

On the drive back from Hull Simon told me that, on the strength of his earnings from his last few fights, he was taking a Christmas break and had booked a flight to Sydney, Australia in a few days time. He was due back in mid January.

When he re-appeared in the gym around the 16th of January 94 he looked tanned and fit but he was heavy. He insisted that he had trained over in Aussie and had been running but I think he meant from bar to bar. He was broke though and asked me to find a fight for him. There was a big Frank Warren promotion coming up on the 29th of January at the National Ice Rink, Cardiff involving a Naseem Hamed title defence. I had been offered an eight rounder for Simon against the up and coming Swedish star Ole Klemetson who had won ten out of eleven fights but I turned it down although it was for good money. I told Simon about it and he insisted that I call Ernie Fossey and see if the offer was still on and if it was to get some more money for the short notice. I did, it was and yes we could have extra cash.

The deal was only if Simon worked hard in the gym and on the road, which he did. At 1pm on the day, Simon weighed in at 12st 13lbs, two pounds heavier than Ole. With his new Australian sun tan he looked the business and for four rounds he did his usual thing, Jabbing and moving, rolling on the ropes and tying Klemetson up but it was taking its toll on him. Ole was a class act and there was no chance of Simon pulling off a surprise like he had against Eriksson. He went out for a last hurrah in the fifth and did actually land a good right hand to the head of Klemetson but it had little lasting effect. When Simon sat down at the end of the round I knew he was knackered so I called the ref over and told him Simon had hurt his right hand with that last big shot and I was pulling him out. He had earned his money

On the drive back to Blackpool I had another heart to heart with Simon. It was painful to see 'a big strong Boy' as Henry Cooper would call him, with talent, courage, fighting spirit and a big heart, throwing it all away by his lack of dedication to training. He was such a nice guy but he was being influenced by some of the dodgy people he was associating with on the doors in Blackpool. I knew this from some of the scams and shady get rich quick deals he told me about. I advised him to steer clear of them but it was Simon McDougall I was talking to.

The talk seemed to have made an impression. For the next few weeks Simon, for the first time since his preparation for his title fight against Glen Campbell, really knuckled down and worked hard. Ron Gray offered us a six rounder against Birmingham's John Foreman who had a 12-8-1 record. It was at the Tower Ballroom, Edgbaston on the 8th of March 94. John was the Midlands Area light heavy Champion and had been in the top ten of the Boxing News ratings before suffering a few setbacks. The fight against Simon was for his rehabilitation, although it didn't work out that way.

Simon had a three pound weight advantage at the weigh in but was in the best condition he had been for some time, both in head and body. He surprised John Foreman and his backers by taking the fight to him and winning by a mile. It was a much happier drive back home.

This new lease of life helped me make a quick decision when Terry Toole, acting for the unpleasant Mickey Duff, rang me to see if Simon would fight one of Mickey's ex-ABA champions and bright prospect, Monty Wright. Monty had won all five of his pro fights to date which gave me the chance to screw as much money out of them before accepting it. It was for a show in Wright's hometown of Stevenage, Hertfordshire on the 11th of May 94.

Simon was well up for it. The weigh in was in Duff's office in Soho at 1pm on the day before the fight. This was a new regulation that had been introduced to save fighters from losing weight by de-hydration on the day of a fight. Simon and Monty both weighed the same 12st 9lbs. After the weigh in, I took Simon for a good lunch on our way to Stevenage where I had booked a Hotel for the overnight stay. We breakfasted then took it easy before making our way to the venue.

Simon warmed up well before the fight and got in the zone. He was concentrating on the job. It was a pleasure to be with him in the corner that night. He did everything right and made Monty look the novice that he was. Mickey Duff was shouting his usual verbals from the corner trying to influence the referee but it was to no avail and Simons hand was raised at the end of fight.

It was back to the old Simon for the next couple of months. He didn't come back to the gym after the Monty Wright fight and my phone calls to him were ignored. I asked Louis Vietch about him and he told me he was doing his usual thing on the doors and downing the pints after hours. During this period I turned down several fights for him. Both his last opponents wanted returns and on his best form we would have been happy to oblige but with Simon out of circulation I had to refuse them.

He turned up in mid August full of excuses and determined to return to fitness. After a month of hard work and no beer, the weight came off and he was keen to fight as soon as I could find him a job which I did in the form of Scottish light heavy Stephen Wilson. He was one of Tommy Gilmour Jnr's fighters and had won eight out of nine. I had seen him a few times on the circuit and thought Simon would have no trouble handling him even though it was once again in Glasgow. The date was 19th of September and the match was made at 12st 9lbs which Simon just about weighed. Wilson was 12st 5lbs for this fight.

From the beginning Simon was just not interested. He was full of beans on the drive up but during the warm up and pre fight prep he only went through the motions. He was not in the zone. Why was I bothering with him? From the first bell he simply spoiled and held when ever he could. Wilson was sharp and determined and after another round of mauling he was two rounds up, no argument. In the third he cracked a good right cross over Simon's tippy-tap left jab and for the first time in his career Simon was cut over the left eye. The referee stopped a one sided fight.

Stephen Wilson went on, two fights later, to beat Glen Campbell in an eliminator for the British Super middleweight title after which he was KO'd by Joe Calzagie for the British title.

Simon was out to allow the eye to heal and to again decide whether he wanted this business anymore. I was pretty peed off with him, but in December he was back in the gym. Promises, promises, promises… he made them all again but I knew he just wanted some Christmas money. I refused out of hand any offers for him until after New Year 1995.

Alex Morrison was on the phone offering Louis Vietch a Scottish title fight. That is covered in the story of his record but Morrison also offered six threes for Simon against Sean Heron whom he had recently signed. The show was one of Frank Warren's super promotions at the Scottish Exhibition Centre in Glasgow on the 21st January 95, headed by Naseem Hamed's world title defence against Armando Castro plus umpteen other title fights for Sky TV.

Heron had a 13-3 record and was rated by some and overrated by me. Simon had a three pound weight advantage at 12st 13lbs and was up for the fight and intended to make amends for his pathetic performance against Stephen Wilson. As usual with these long shows, the TV producers were calling the shots as to who was on when. We were told that Simon would be on early and we warmed and gloved up in good time. A few minutes before we were due to enter the hall we were told that to fit in with the TV schedule they were cutting our bout from six three minute rounds to four threes. It was out of order but there was nothing we could do about it. The referee was Len Mullen. Simon started fast and was well in control of the first round. In the second Heron resorted to dirty tactics and was butting and holding and hitting. This didn't put Simon off because he enjoyed a good ruck but it didn't make for a nice spectacle. In the third and fourth the ref had to warn Heron on several occasions and Simon was well on top. At the final bell of course Mullen gave it to Heron by half a point. It was ridiculous but by now not surprising. If the fight had gone the six rounds I think Simon would have stopped Sean Heron.

On the 16th of February, Jack Doughty booked Simon for a third and final meeting with Glen Campbell at Bury. Glen's record was now 13-1-1. We had got Simon's weight down to 12st 8lbs by then but the fight was a damp squib. From their two previous encounters they had got to know each others strengths and weaknesses but neither of them seemed interested. It ended in another half point win for Glen Campbell and it was fair enough.

A couple of week's later Simons weight went up dramatically. He was still coming to the gym but he was also drinking beer. He denied it but my Blackpool spies were telling me otherwise. Simon said he was fed up trying to make the light heavyweight limit of twelve and a half stones and he wanted to move up to cruiserweight. I warned him that it was a bad move. Genuine cruisers were a size bigger and stronger than an overblown light heavy with the consequent increase in power. After all a lot of good heavyweights in the past, from Henry Cooper to Rocky Marciano would these days be classed as cruisers.

I was offered a contest for Simon at the Marriott Hotel, Mayfair London where he had previously fought Bruce Scott. It was on the 6th of March and the money was good for eight rounds against John Keeton who had won eight and lost six so far. The match weight was 13st 6lbs and Simon weighed in at 13st 2lbs against Keeton's 13st 5lbs. As predicted, Keeton was just too strong for Simon and he just couldn't hold him off. For three rounds he was able to out speed the big guy but his punches were ineffectual and in the fourth he began to tire. By the middle of the fifth Keeton was well on top when the referee called it off.

On the drive back I told Simon that I was no longer willing to train and match him. I had tried every way I knew to get through to him the fact that if he continued to abuse himself by the lifestyle he was leading and his lack of willingness to train then he was going to get hurt in this business. He had so much talent and so little self discipline and it was hard watching him throw it all away.

I had at that point gone into partnership with him in a new venture in Blackpool which had nothing to do with boxing and I was hoping I could make him see sense and break away from the undesirable characters he was associating with.

He insisted in coming back to the gym and proving to me that he could put his wayward habits behind him and together with my guidance in our new business, he would prove himself. Sure enough he never missed a session for the next four weeks and with his weight below thirteen stone again and no talk of cruiserweights, I relented.

Dennie Mancini offered us a very good purse for Simon to Fight Stefan Angehrn in Berne Switzerland. When I checked Angehrn out he had won ten and had lost one and drawn one. Swiss fighters are as rare as hen's teeth and Stefan's ten wins had been against novices or no hopers. He had been KO'd in his only loss and had drawn his last fight. Simon was keen and after a long talk I was persuaded. The fight was on the 17th of April. Dave Paterson took Simon and according to Dave's report, he was as good as gold. In the fight he was far to clever for Stefan and in the fifth round He knocked him out cold just as he had done to Roland Ericsson in 93

On his return to the gym he was quite rightly full of himself. He said he was beginning to realise that he could have achieved much more if he had listened to me from the start of his career but now, with the summer ahead and working with me in our Blackpool business, he would knuckle down to it. I had heard it so many times before from Simon.

We were back in the gym by August and sure enough Simon was working hard. Because I was seeing him virtually every day I was able to keep a bit of pressure on him and his weight was down to around twelve nine.

I began searching for a decent job for him and rang Trevor Callighan who managed the Central Area Light Heavyweight Champion Michael Gale and he was quite receptive to the idea of a challenge for the title from Simon. We needed a promoter and one came in the form of Barry Hearns whose Matchroom outfit was promoting a show for Sky TV in Sheffield on the 22nd of November 95. He was willing to put the Gale/McDougall title fight on the undercard and he offered a good purse.

The timing was perfect for us to set out a championship training schedule. Michael Gale had a twenty win and one loss one draw record and I had seen him a few times. He was a nice boxer but I thought he was beatable and a win for Simon against a top ten rated fighter could open other doors for him.

The training programme went well and Simon was looking in the best shape he had been in since his title fight with Glen Campbell. Added to that was his experience and improved ringcraft, so I was feeling confident. With two days to go I put Simon on the scales and he was a pound over the championship limit which was perfect. With all the hard work behind him, I wanted him in the gym one more time to shake out and for a final weight check. The next evening, the one before the day of the official weigh in, I waited for Simon to turn up at 7pm as arranged but after an hour he hadn't shown. I managed to get him on his mobile and he made some excuse about not getting to Preston but he was in Steve's weight training gym in Blackpool and that he had got on the scales there and was spot on 12st 7lbs. I wasn't happy and insisted on speaking to Steve who assured me that his scales were accurate and that Simon was the weight he said.

When we left Preston the next morning, Simon was on good form. I took Kevin Pritchard and Steve Hardman with me so I had a perfect corner team. We arrived at Hillsborough Leisure Centre where the weigh in was taking place at 1pm. There was a world title fight topping the bill so the weigh in was the usual carnival for these events. Michael Gale was first on the scales and weighed twelve stone six and a half pounds. Simon stepped on the scales and to my horror was announced as twelve stone NINE and a half pounds. I couldn't believe it and knew then that I should have insisted on Simon coming over to Preston the night before. All that hard work that we had put in seemed to be going out of the window. Simon seemed quite nonchalant about the whole thing but by professionalism was, for the first time ever, on the line.

Fortunately I was able to get the leisure centre manager to open a steam room for us and Steve, Kevin and I got Simon in there with a skipping rope and every sweater and track suit we could muster on him. The boxing rules allow one hour for a boxer to make the weight and after fifty minutes of badgering a reluctant Simon McDougall to sweat it off, we got back on the scales and just made it. Thank goodness for the twenty four hour previous weigh in regulation. Simon would have been in no fit state to fight if the contest had been that night. It was another example of Simon's lackadaisical attitude in spite of everything I had said to him and the golden opportunity he had in front of him.

On the night of the fight we were in the dressing room early. We had been told we would be on before the main event since the fight was going out live. I was still seething inside over what had happened. I was blaming myself as well as Simon. We warmed up well and Steve Hardman and Kevin helped in getting Simon in the zone. For seven rounds Simon fought as well as he had ever done in his career and was well in there for the title. From the eighth round on he began to fade and he was paying the price for his misdemeanour the day before. Michael Gale deserved his one and a half point victory.

We had come to the end of the road. I told Simon that as far as I was concerned his career was over. It had been a roller coaster ride with him with some great highs and deep lows. He was one of the bravest fighters you could ever meet with a heart like a lion but he was also one of the laziest. He never fulfilled his potential which was a shame. Over his career he had been subject to more than his share of dubious decisions. He had earned some decent money but hadn't saved much of it.

Some time after Simons fight with Gale, Louis Vietch told me that he was with Simon that night in Steve's gym. They went on to a club and Simon was drinking beer in spite of Louis pleading with him not to so close to his title fight. That explained why he was overweight and summed up Simons weakness throughout his professional career.

I continued working with him at our Blackpool venture (adventure) for another year before we finally parted in 1996.

Simon made a comeback under his own management in 1997 and had one losing fight. He tried again in 1998 and once more he lost

Tragically Simon failed to break away from the bad influence some people had him under. He slid into bad habits and tragically, in 2002 he died alone at his flat in Blackpool.

Chapter thirteen
BRIAN CULLEN

BRIAN CULLEN was a Dubliner who had come to live in Preston. He was an ex kick boxer and was being managed by Pat Brogan from Stoke. Brian had fought six times as a pro when Pat called me and asked me to train Brian for him.

When Brian came to the gym I got on fine with him. At 5' 6" and just over 10st he was a light welter. He had won three and lost three.

Pat matched him on one of his own shows at Stoke on the 25th of October 88 against a boxer called Erwin Edwards. Under my training regime Brian's weight had dropped to just under 10st. He was an aggressive young Irishman and he started fast only to get clipped by a fast counter punch and went down for a short count. On getting up he rushed straight in and got caught again and was down for an eight count this time.

When he got back to the corner I was relieved to see that he was not dazed and I was getting feedback from him. I was able to calm him down and instructed him go out for the second round and box his way back into the contest. I was learning a lot about Brian fast! He pulled himself together and boxed really well and by the fifth he was back to his aggressive style with the points in the bag and a good win under his belt.

On the 28th of November Pat matched him with the undefeated Hugh Forde who had won all fourteen of his fights to date. The match was made at 9st 10lbs at the Tower Ballroom, Birmingham and was being promoted by Forde's backers. I thought it was a tough match but I was only the trainer.

Brian made the weight easily enough so he was strong, confident and in the zone when he climbed into the ring that night. Hugh was also a boxer with a kick boxing back ground and at 5' 9" he had a big reach advantage. From the bell he needed it because Brian was straight into him.

Forde won the first and second by virtue of a long southpaw right jab and, in true kick boxing style, switching to orthodox every twenty seconds. I instructed Brian to use his footwork to try and trap Hugh on the ropes and in corners so that he could get close enough to land his short powerful hooks. In the third it was beginning to work. Hugh Forde, under pressure, was looking flustered and Brian was getting to him. I felt as though the underdog was turning things around.

In the fourth Brian carried on with his assault until Forde uncorked a peach of a right hook onto Brian's Jaw which checked his attack for a moment. The bell rang and when Brian came to the corner and I was removing his gumshield, I realised that Brian's Jaw was broken. His Lower jaw was slack and he was bleeding from the mouth. I called the ref over and retired him.

Brian was out until the New Year 89 and when he was back in condition I rang Pat Brogan who matched him for the 1st of March against Gary Barron from Leicester, on his Kings Hall, Stoke show. Gary had a three-one-one record.

Brian was his old aggressive self and won a good point's decision.

Pat then matched Brian with the vastly experienced Dean Bramald of Doncaster. At that point Dean had won eighteen lost fifty. The match was at 9st 12lbs on the 3rd of April 89 Brian started in his usual way and for a couple of rounds it was a scrappy affair with Dean using his experience to tie Brian up until in the middle of the third round when Brian once again walked onto a right hand and was down. He got up but the ref decided he was in no fit state to continue and it was over.

Brian was soon back in the gym. He was pretty peed off by the stoppage because he thought that the ref had acted too quickly he hadn't even been dazed. He was out for twenty eight days by the regulations then on the 8th of May Pat matched him with Manchester's Michael Oliver at Nat Basso's Anglo American Sporting club show at the Piccadilly. Oliver had a 6-4-1 record.

This time the fight went the same as now becoming Brian's trade mark style. He steamed straight in, taking shots to land his own. For four rounds it was all action with the clever counterpunching style of Oliver matching Brian's aggression until the fifth when once again a counterpunch right had Brian down and again the ref stepped in. This was becoming a bad habit.

I advised Brian to take a complete break from boxing for a few weeks and assess whether he wanted to continue. He needed some easier fights if did.

He took three months off and when he came back to the gym refreshed in August he told me his contract with Pat had expired and asked me to manage as well as train him. I rang Pat to confirm the contract situation which he did but he was mad with me and accused me of poaching him. I told him what I thought of that and got Brian to ring him and tell him that it was his idea, not mine. It cleared the air and we continued to train

I got Brian a six rounder in Hull against Dave Croft on the 4th of September which he won on points

He then out pointed Steve Booth on the 11th of Sept, Barry North on the 20th Sept, Mick Mulcahy on the 4th of Dec and Brian Ryan on the 24th of Jan 90. Five straight wins.

On the 19th of Feb we went to Doncaster and fought a return with Brian Ryan which Brian Cullen lost on points, before a return with Mick Mulcahy whom he again beat.

On the 15th of May 90 we went into Paul Charter's home patch in South Shields where Brian made one of his storming starts only to get put down in the 5th and again the ref stopped it.

One of Brendan Ingles fighters came next at the Colosseum in Stafford, on the 12th of September. He was Wayne Windle who had a five-seven-two record and I must admit that I was expecting him to be the typical Ingle hit-and-run type. I sent Brian out to trap him on the ropes. Instead Windle held his ground and whacked Brian with a big right hand as he steamed in. Brian got up at eight but he was unsteady and ref Pat Thomas stopped it. It was a big shock to us.

On the 12th of November we got a fight with another experienced fighter in Ray Newby. By now Brian had won eleven and lost nine. He was experienced enough to mix with fighters like Newby who had a twenty win sixteen losses and two draw record. Brian fought well in Stratford-on-Avon but lost on points.

On the 18th of February 1991, Brian out pointed Michael Howell over six rounds.

I got him a fight on the undercard of the Kevin Pritchard v Robert Dickie in Cardiff on the 5th of March. The opponent was Dave Andrews who had won four and lost five of his nine fights. I thought it was a good match for Brian but again he committed boxing suicide when he stormed out and got caught cold again with a right counter. Again he got up but the ref stopped it.

I once again suggested to Brian that he should take time off and reconsider his future. He seemed to run hot and cold and, with a wife and young family, to consider maybe he should hang up his gloves. He was off until September when he returned to the gym after deciding he wanted to give it another go.

I got him a six rounder at the Castle Leisure Centre on the 21st of October, where I had another fighter on the bill. He fought Mike

Calderwood who was much less experienced and easily beat him on points. Once again the lay off seemed to have worked.

Ernie Fossey offered us a fight at the Festival Hall in Basildon, Essex, on the 11th of December 91. It was against Jason Rowland who had won all of his seven fights to date but Brian had the experience. This time it was the fourth before Rowland tagged him with a right hand. He was up and willing but the ref called it off, quite rightly.

This time I told Brian that it really was the end of the road. He took it hard as a typical Irishman. He was a brave man but had gone as far as he was capable in this tough game. Although he had been stopped a few times, he had never taken a long beating, the sort that causes real damage. He had won thirteen against twelve losses and should have been proud of that.

Brian was always a respectful and hard working professional and a pleasure to work with.

Unfortunately I have lost touch with Brian. He did call into the shop some years after he retired from the game to say he had moved away from Preston. We were still on good terms.

Chapter fourteen
STEVE HARDMAN

STEVE HARDMAN was a member of the squad of senior ABA boxers who missed out on the ABA championships in 1982 which saw my departure from the amateur scene. I had known Steve and his younger brother Keith since they were about twelve or thirteen years of age. They joined the Preston and Fulwood club after first spending some time at the rival Bamber Bridge ABC.

They came from a good family and their father, Bob, brought them to the club and encouraged them in the sport. I ran a well disciplined club and stood for no nonsense from the club members. I would not allow the fathers of the boys to interfere during the sessions and I was always wary of the kind of fathers who coerced their sons into boxing against their wishes. Bob was not that sort. He was interested but never interfered.

The boys enjoyed their boxing and thrived on the discipline and consequently became good junior competitors and went on to make that difficult transition from junior to senior boxers.

Steve grew to mature as a light welterweight/welterweight as a senior amateur. He developed a terrific punch and he enjoyed some great KO fights in that last year with me and the P&F club and he was a good prospect for the championships and one of reasons for my anger and disgust at the rotten system that ruled him out.

Like Sammy Sampson, Steve left P&F and joined St Helens ABC where he continued with his amateur career. I lost contact with the Hardman's over the next few years although I heard that Steve had turned professional in 1989 with Mike Atkinson, one of the

Merseyside manager/trainers. He had one contest on the 16th October and drew with Trevor Meikle.

I was therefore surprised when Steve, after eight years away from my coaching, came to see if I would take over managing and training him in the pros. He had been out of the game for a year due to an injury so I telephoned Mike to see what the position was regarding Steve's contract and got confirmation that he had only signed a one year deal and was free to sign up with me.

I told Steve that I would first have to be satisfied that he still had some fights left in him. Eight years was a long time to be away from my style of coaching and he was now twenty nine and had been boxing since he was eleven years old.

He accepted my terms and we set a programme. Sure enough, Steve had gone a long way back in technique but he had retained that grit and determination that I remembered from his amateur days. No one could have trained harder than he did and it was great to see him begin to improve in the sparring sessions. I talked a lot to him and he was good listener.

It was now November 1990 and I was satisfied that he was ready for his first fight under my guidance. I put the word out that he was available for a 6x3 contest at ten and a half stones. I soon got a call from Graham Lockwood offering a fight with Brian Keating at the YESC, by now very familiar to me, on the 10th of December. I accepted.

Steve was thrilled at the opportunity to get back to action. He said he had not felt so ready for a contest since he left my squad at P&F in 82 and said how much he now regretted not turning pro with me at the same time as Sammy Sampson.

At the weigh in Steve was a pound lighter than Keating, who had boxed pro twice before, losing both contests.

From the first bell, Steve took charge and boxed well. Sure there were some signs of the bad habits that he had developed over the last few years, but the great thing about him was that after all the experience he had, when he came back to his corner after each round, he was listening to instruction. His head was screwed on and he did everything he was asked. He won the fight clearly and boy was he pleased with himself. I loved it.

Steve stayed in condition right through the Christmas period and I got another offer for a six rounder on a televised show in Alfreton, Derbyshire, on the 17th of January 91, against home town boy Richard O'Brien, at ten stone nine.

O'Brien was a tougher proposition with a three win two loss and a draw record. Steve's attitude for this fight was the same as for every fight he had for me. He always said "Mr Mac, you make the matches and I will fight them". If all my fighters had that attitude life would have been so much easier.

O'Brien had a weight and height advantage but from the start Steve was the boss. For round after round he dominated the action even having O'Brien down and at one point close to a stoppage but we were on his home ground so the ref gave him every chance to recover. At the end we were satisfied with a clear points win.

Steve came away from that fight without a mark so when Graham Lockwood was on the phone again asking for Steve for another trip to Bradford on the 28th of January, this time against Neil Porter, I was only too pleased to accept.

Porter had won one lost one and drawn two of his previous four contests and was the same weight as Steve. The contest was good and competitive but Steve was clearly the better man and won a wide decision. In this contest I thought that Steve had just about thrown off the bad habits he had developed and he looked good.

Next up, Nat Basso wanted Steve for a return with Trevor Meikle whom he had drawn with in his first contest when he was with Mike Atkinson. It was at the Anglo American Sporting club show at the Piccadilly Hotel, Manchester, on the 11th of February. This would be the ideal measure of Steve's progress because, by this time, Meikle had fought twenty three times since their first meeting and his record now stood at eight wins fourteen losses and five draws.

The match was made at 10st 9lbs and Steve weighed in a pound under. Meikle was the same weight and they were physically well matched.

I don't know what Trevor remembered about their first fight but whatever it was he was in for a shock because Steve had come on so well that he was a different fighter. From the first bell he dominated the action and for six rounds put on a great display of boxing to win clearly on points. It was never easy because Trevor Meikle was a good pro by this time and as tough as they come, but it was all down to Steve's confidence and boxing ability.

That was four wins out of four for Steve since his return to the fold and both he and I were regretting those lost years and what a good fighter he could have been by this time.

Again I got a call from Lockwood and another date at the YESC in Bradford. This time it was for the 25th of March 91 and the opponent was Glasgow's Tommy Milligan. I knew of the Milligan fighting family going way back and although Tommy had only had one pro fight, which he won on points, he was an ex ABA champion and Scottish amateur representative so he would be no pushover. The match was made at around the welterweight limit of 10st 7lbs and on the night Steve weighed ten seven and a half against Milligan's ten four and a half, giving us a three pound weight advantage.

Steve was confident during the preparations and warm up. The ref was Phil Cowsell.

From the first bell I got a shock. Milligan came out fast and was firing in left jabs which Steve didn't seem to have an answer to. Suddenly Steve, under pressure, was reverting to the style he had been practising over those last eight years. He was clumsy and his footwork had deserted him. He lost the first round by a wide margin.

He came back to the corner confused and, for him, disorganised. For the first time in all the contests, amateur and professional, that I had seconded Steve I was not getting feedback from him. He was no better in the second although he did fire off more left jabs but again he was clumsy and un co-ordinated and it was another clear round Tommy Milligan.

The same thing happened between the second and third and Steve went out to take another boxing lesson from Milligan who, by this time must have thought that this professional game was no harder than the amateurs. To give the referee credit, he didn't seem too concerned although I have seen refs stop such one sided fights.

At last, in the interval at the end of the third, I suddenly began to get feedback from Steve. The lights had come back on and It was as if he had just woken up to what was happening and he was responding to my urges to get his hands up and to counter punch Milligan. At the start of the fourth, that is exactly what he did. He met the advancing Scot with his own jab and for the first time in this fight, he forced Milligan to retreat under some solid combinations. Milligan was not deterred and kept his clever boxing going but it was a much closer round although I knew that it would probably go to Milligan again.

During the next interval Steve seemed back to his old self. He was responding to me and his eyes were clear and focused. I urged him to get out in the fifth and take the play away from Milligan with both hands and that is what he did. The fight had turned and Tommy must have realised that this was a lot tougher than he thought. Hardman was living up to his name and it was the Scotsman who was desperately trying to defend in the face of Steve's concerted attack.

At the bell he had pulled one round back but he would need a KO to win the fight.

The sixth and last round followed the same pattern. Milligan was now in trouble and Steve was unloading and trying to land that finishing punch. It wasn't to be and even with Steve on top at the final bell it was Milligan's whose hand was raised. I couldn't argue with it.

In my analysis of the fight, I concluded that early in the first round Milligan must have landed a shot, which I never saw (nor Steve), that had taken away Steve's conscious thought without affecting his motor. This was exactly the opposite of what had happened to Joe Threlfall when Steve Garber hit him behind the ear leaving him clear headed but taking away his motor. It was the same affect that Peter Crook experienced when fought the second half of his fight with Michael Marsden without remembering a thing. There have been many cases recorded in the past of this happening.

In this condition a boxer reverts to the techniques he has been practicing in the past. In Steve's case he had reverted to those mis-spent years until, at the end of the third round, his conscience returned and he was able to think his way back into the fight

He had displayed true grit, strength and determination to survive those three rounds and had the fight been over eight rounds he would have beaten Milligan.

Incidentally, Tommy Milligan only had two more contests after his fight with Steve. Maybe he decided guys like Steve were too tough.

After the Milligan fight Steve had a couple of weeks off before getting back into the gym. He actually was a hard man (no pun intended) to keep away from training, such was his enthusiasm, but fate dealt him a blow when he suffered a rib injury. He popped the cartilage between the short ribs on his left side during a sparring session with Kevin Pritchard. This is a fairly common injury in boxing and even Mike Tyson once suffered from it. It is so painful that the sufferer can't even do sit ups let alone spar and there is no quick solution only rest until it heals. I had to pull him out of a match I had for him in Manchester.

By the end of July he was back in the gym and starting to work hard again. The injury seemed to have healed although I gave instructions to sparring partners not to punch to the body.

At the end of August I got a call from Mike Atkinson, Steve's first manager, asking if Steve would fight Andreas Panayi on the 30th of September in Liverpool. Panayi was an interesting character. He was a Greek-Cypriot who had been working as a bouncer at a nightclub in Cypress and had a reputation for being handy with his fists when he was approached by one of the Atkinson brothers who offered to train and manage him in the pros over here. He had accepted and was now living in St Helens. He was a genuine welterweight and by this time he had boxed seven times, winning four losing two and one draw.

At 5' 8" he was two inches shorter than Steve and he was eight years younger. I expected it to be hard fight but thought that Steve's extra experience might give him an edge.

Training went OK although Steve didn't seem as sharp as he should have been in the last week running up to the fight. We were working a hard schedule aimed at peaking on the 30th so I wasn't too concerned, except I suspected that the rib injury had taken more out of him than he was letting on.

At the weigh in on the day, Steve weighed a pound under the welterweight limit of ten stone seven. Panayi was one pound lighter than him. The Cypriot had an impressive physique and looked the part. Steve was unconcerned.

Panayi made a lively start with an aggressive two handed attack and Steve had to use all his experience and toughness to contain him. Steve did get his left jab going but to little effect.

When Steve came back to the corner he was alert but calm and listened to my instructions. I told him that he had to work the jab and use good defence and footwork and not get involved in a head to head fight at this stage. Steve boxed well in the second and third, tying up the inexperienced Panayi in close and relying on his longer left hand at distance but he was losing the rounds because Panayi was always the aggressor.

In the fourth Steve came under even more pressure and simply looked the older man. Panayi was right on top and had Steve down from a powerful combination for an eight count. Steve once again showed his guts and determination by seeing out the round. When he came back to the corner I was thinking about whether to call it off but at the same time remembering how he had come from behind against Milligan, although Panayi was a much stronger man. Steve was still fully aware and had not been stunned by the knockdown so I decided on giving him one more round.

Steve rallied at the start of the fifth but it was short lived and Panayi was soon back on the attack and Steve was down again. He was up at eight but both the referee and I had seen enough and the contest was stopped. At least Steve was still on his feet and had not stayed down as many others would and that is a sign of a man who never knows he is beat.

It was a big disappointment to both of us but in his last two fights I had seen signs that told me that Steve had passed his peak and that from here on there were more such fights ahead of him and I didn't want to see that. Steve was such a warrior that he would have carried on as long as I found opponents for him and would never refuse a fight.

By this time I had known Steve and his family for the best part of twenty years. Jean and I had been invited to his twenty first birthday party in 1982 and his wedding reception in 1983. By 1991, Steve and his wife Janice had two children, Victoria and Chad. Outside of boxing he came to visit us at home and even now, nineteen years later, he still does.

A few days after the Panayi contest, Steve was back in the gym. I took him to one side for a chat about his future. I explained that after twenty years in boxing, man and boy, with well over one hundred and thirty amateur contests and seven professional fights behind him, I could tell that he was not responding to the training regime he had to follow. Sure he was working just as hard as ever but he simply just had too many miles on the clock and, as a time served motor mechanic, he accepted my analogy.

As always, he accepted my judgement without question and I was pleased when he agreed to take out a trainers licence and stay in the business as a trainer and corner man with me.

One year later, fate took a hand in Steve's future. In October 1992 I received a shocking telephone call from Janice. She told me that Steve had been involved in a serious accident whilst working a night shift as a tipper lorry driver on a motorway repair site. He was in the Royal Preston Hospital so we arranged to meet her and went straight up to see him. He had suffered severe injuries to his right leg plus many lesser injuries to other parts when his cab was crushed by another lorry that had reversed into him at speed.

His unbelievable toughness of body mind and spirit shone through in the stoical manner in which he accepted these injuries had to be seen to be believed and over the weeks that he was hospitalised he astounded everyone attending him. We did what we could to help him and his family and of course he had the support of his own strong family around him.

To cut a long story short, after many trips to hospital for unsuccessful attempts to get his severely damaged right ankle to heal, in October 1994, Steve made the decision to have his leg amputated below the knee. He described making this decision in such a matter of fact way it was as if he was discussing whether to have his hair cut short or not.

A couple of weeks later he told me the date of the operation. As it happened, it was the day after one of Mike Tyson's heavyweight title defences. The operation was set for 2pm and at around 5pm I got a telephone call from Steve. I was surprised because I wasn't expecting to hear from him until the day after when I had arranged to visit him. His first words were "did you watch the Tyson fight last night, what did you think?" I said to him "I thought you were having your op today, have they postponed it?" He laughed and said "No, it's off". I was astounded. I dropped what ever it was that I was doing at the time and went round to the private hospital that he was in which was only a mile from my shop. Sure enough when I went into his room he was lying back with his now severed leg held up on a frame and a big grin on his face.

There could be no one braver in the face of adversity than this guy and it was no surprise when, only a few weeks later, he turned up in the gym on his newly fitted prosthetic limb and insisted on me photographing him sparring with one of the boys so that he could show the photo it to his surgeon!

He is just the same today as I write this in 2010 and is a regular visitor, usually turning up riding one of his motorcycles.

Chapter fifteen
KEVIN PRITCHARD

At the beginning of February 1988 I got a call from Dennie Mancini asking me if I knew KEVIN PRITCHARD from Kirby, Liverpool. He told me that Kevin was living in Preston and that he had signed a contract for Dennie to manage him. I told him that knew of Kevin but that I had never met him. Dennie asked me if I would train him. My reply was that I would take a look at him in the gym and talk to him. If we got on and he showed that he was not a 'shot' fighter I would train him for the usual ten per cent.

Dennie was one of the old school of manger/agents. He knew and worked with all the big time London outfits and was an established 'cuts' man. He was mainly aligned with the Levene/Astaire/Barret/Duff/Lawless set and less inclined to do business with the new "Impostor" outfits of Frank Warren and Barry Hearns. I had made it clear to him in our earlier meetings that I was strictly freelance and would do business with any of them if it benefited by boxers. He accepted this.

When Kevin came to see me we got on fine. He was a nice guy and treated me with respect. I explained to him my philosophy about the sport and of what I would expect. My style was totally different to what he had become used to in the Liverpool gyms. I was not a 'sergeant major' type who would scream and shout orders but I would apply pressure and expect a 100% effort. After all these were professional fighters and by now should know that there are no short cuts to getting fit and no end to the learning curve.

His record at this point ran to eighteen wins, fifteen losses and four draws. He had fought for the Area titles twice but lost both and he had several fights on the continent again losing them but up against top class opposition. He had been in the top ten ratings in the lightweight and super feathers since 1984 but was now considered a 'journey man' who could give anyone a good fight, which is why Dennie had signed him up. In other words he was a steady 25% for him in decent class therefore decent money fights.

I enjoyed working with him from the start. He was already in decent shape and only a pound or two over the super feather limit. He mixed in immediately with the other fighters in the gym and seemed as fresh and enthusiastic as a novice except that he had the moves. He walked the walk.

I rang Dennie and told him that I would gladly train Kevin and that he would need only a few weeks to be ready for a contest. He called me back a couple of days later to say he had booked him for an eight by three minute round top of the bill fight at the Café Royal in London on the 7th of March 88 against Birmingham's Rocky Lawlor. Lawlor was a tough nut managed by 'Nobby' Nobbs who had a reputation of always being able to find an opponent at short or even very short notice

Kevin was chuffed. He told me that he was enjoying his training for the first time in years. Our pad work and the modification of his style were a revelation to him and something he had never appreciated before. I was just as pleased with my work with him.

Dennie also found a fight for another of my fighters, Keith Halliwell, on the bill. It was to be Keith's pr debut.

We drove down to London and met Dennie at the Lonsdale shop he managed in Beak Street, Soho London. Kevin weighed in a pound under the match weight and was a pound heavier than Lawlor. Keith was also spot-on the weight for his fight with Den Lake who had won two and lost one of his three previous fights.

After the weigh in, Dennie even took us for a meal in the café Royal restaurant which he paid for. It was the kind of hospitality we had not experienced before in the South.

I was pleased when Dennie allowed me to work in the ring with Kevin. As his manager and with his record as a cornerman, I half expected Dennie to want to do it himself but said "you know the boy best"

From the first bell I was able to assess Kevin's True form in the contest situation. Lawlor was a real tough handful but Kevin's experience always shone through. He was alert between rounds and I was getting good feedback from him. He had a great range of punches and he needed them all against the hard little Brummie.

By the seventh Kevin was in complete control but seemed content to out box Rocky. In the interval I told Kevin to go out and sustain his attack to make sure that it wasn't even close on the referee's card. He did and a minute into the round he had Lawlor down for a long count. When Rocky got up at nine, Kevin set another blistering attack and the ref jumped in to save Rocky. We had our first win together and Dennie was very pleased.

Keith Halliwell beat Dean Lake by a good margin so it was a happy car ride back up North.

Just a month later we discovered why Dennie Mancini had signed Kevin. He rang to tell me had agreed for Kevin to fight Jean-Marc Renard in Liege in Belgium on the 10th of April which gave us three weeks to get ready. The fight was made at nine stone three pounds which was not a problem, over eight threes.

Renard was the ex European featherweight champion with a thirty six wins against three losses record with one draw. The fight was in his home town so we were up against it and it was a typical lamb to the wolves set up.

Good pro that Kevin was, he didn't give any sign of apprehension and we trained and prepared for a win.

We were met off the plane in Brussels and driven to Liege. Our hotel was nice and we were well looked after. We weighed in spot on the match weight and Jean-Marc was polite and friendly, none of the old intimidation antics that some find so necessary.

The hall was packed and although Jean-Marc was the favourite, Kevin was given a good reception out of respect as we entered the ring. Typically, Renard had an entourage of corner men. Kevin had me and a house second whom I had to pay to hand up the water bottle and spit bucket.

From the first bell, Renard was a classy boxer, but Kevin took the fight to him. It was a case of two good fighters sharing the ring and by the end of the first I was happy with Kevin's performance although I knew which way the ref would have scored it.

The second was a similar round until halfway when Kevin landed a good left hook that shook Renard and made him step back. The round ended with Kevin forcing the fight and I thought that if that hook had landed flush on the jaw instead of a bit higher on the cheek it would have caused a massive upset.

Renard's corner men obviously got a fright because they sent him out with much more purpose in the third. Kevin was still boxing nicely but Renard was now the aggressor. Suddenly, after a flurry of punches there was blood pouring from Kevin's left eyebrow. The ref stopped the fight and after a good look at the cut he waved it off. We were gutted because I thought that had the fight developed into the later rounds, Kevin may have been too strong for the Belgian.

The doctor stitched Kevin's eye in the dressing room. He was a good doc and inserted four stitches then congratulated Kevin on his bravery.

When we got back to the UK I rang Dennie to report on the fight but he had already heard from Renard's promoter who had told him how pleased he had been in the professional way we had handled the fight and how impressed they were in the way Kevin had boxed until the cut. That was nice of them.

Kevin was out of the gym for a few weeks to allow the cut to heal. It was summer time anyway and he needed a break.

By September Kevin was back in harness and working hard with the other boys. I rang Dennie and told him Kevin was ready for another contest. He came back with a date, the 8th of October. The opponent was Gianni De Napoli who was the Italian featherweight champion with thirteen wins, twelve by KO and one on points and no losses. The venue was the Olympic Stadium in Rome, Gianni's home town.

Now fair enough, Kevin was an experienced professional and considered open class meaning that he was good enough fight most boxers, but come on. This was just a case of fighting for money. The chance of pulling off a win means that a fighter must have some advantage, however slim, but here we had nothing. I expressed my thoughts to Mancini but he was the manager and I had already told him that Kevin was fit so I could do nothing about the match.

I told Kevin who accepted it without question and I was careful not to let him know how one sided I felt the match was. As a fighter he had to believe he could win against all odds. The best I could do was to make sure he was as fit as possible and we were still honing his skills.

We hit our first snag when we arrived at Rome airport. we couldn't find our bags at the baggage re-claim area. It took us over an hour before we discovered they had put our bags on the wrong carousel (or we were at the wrong one). By the time we had located them, the guy who had come to meet us at the arrivals gate had gone back to our hotel to report that we had not arrived on the flight.

I had no telephone number for the promoter but I remembered from Dennie's instructions, the name of the Hotel, so we went out front and I haggled with a taxi driver to take us there and got a receipt so I could claim it back in expenses.

When we did arrive they were so relieved that they treated us with kid gloves for the rest of our stay. We were in a nice hotel and the fight was the day after so we could relax. The weigh in was arranged that evening in the Hotel.

We had some advantages after all. Gianni was only 5' 2" tall, giving Kevin a four inch height and reach advantage. He was also one and a half Kilos heavier than Gianni although they insisted on us shedding half a Kilo in spite of Kevin weighing the nine stone three that Dennie had told me the match had been made at.

It wasn't a problem for Kevin because the temperature was quite high in our hotel room and he had a hotel towelling gown, so he put that on and shadowboxed and did a few exercises and he soon had a good sweat on and an hour later they were satisfied with his weight. I think it was more gamesmanship than anything and in any case, by the time Kevin had a meal followed by a short walk in the balmy Rome evening air, he had put the pound back on.

The following morning we were taken to medical centre for the most extensive pre-fight medical I have ever seen, before or since, which included a blood test! Kevin passed it OK.

We were taken to the venue at around 7pm that evening. It was big circular stadium with tiered seating and already there were people filing in. The show was being televised and our fight was going out live. We had a dressing room to ourselves which was good and I assumed that when we got to ringside there would be the usual house second on duty. The referee, Italian of course, came in to have a word with Kevin and fortunately he spoke good English. His instructions were the standard stuff we already knew.

I popped out from time to time to try and assess when we were due to be on but nobody spoke English and couldn't make sense of anyone, but at around 9.30 I got Kevin warmed up and in the zone and it was a good job because suddenly we were called to the ring. No pre-warning or gloves issued. In every other show I had ever attended, a glove whip would bring the gloves and you knew when you had tied and taped them on the action was about to begin.

The ring had a higher apron than usual which was to prove awkward later. I had all the usual paraphernalia that a cornerman needs but there was no sign of a house second working our corner. In Belgium and in France I had to pay a second to work the corner but it was made clear to me beforehand and hadn't been a problem. This time no one came near for me to engage and none of the officials seemed to give a damn.

By contrast Gianni had about five guys around him. All we had was a TV camera being rammed into Kevin's face. The ref came over and inspected Kevin's bandages then we were given the contest gloves to fit. I had taken Kev's dressing gown off and draped over the ropes in our corner. At that point I was trying to work out how I was going to do all of the vital jobs that a corner team have to do on my own. I was still expecting a house second to appear as is mandatory on a BBB of C promotion, but to no avail.

At the first bell, when I would normally be fully concentrating on watching the opening action, especially since I had not seen De Napoli box before, but instead for the first few seconds I was trying to organise myself for the end of the round. The high ring apron made it worse. I had to get the spit bucket ready, the water bottle and sponge, my adrenaline bottle and swabs in case of a cut, Vaseline ready to apply and then up those steep steps. The ring stool was one of those that were on a swivel from the corner post but because there was a thick buffer with an advertising slogan down the corner, when I swung the stool inwards, it pushed against the buffer and had to be held in position until Kevin Sat down.

Unless you have worked a corner in a boxing contest, it is impossible to understand how difficult it is to do all of this single handed and at the same time refresh the fighter and give him the assistance he needs in that one minute interval. He needs reassurance and positive instructions to reinforce his own actions and tactics.

Gianni started fast as we had expected. He obviously was at a big reach disadvantage and had to bob and weave into distance to land his mostly hooked punches. Kevin had good sound footwork and he used it along with a solid left jab but landing it on the fast Italian was proving difficult. Because of my problems in sorting out the corner, the round seemed to be over so quickly and I was clambering up the steps and wrestling with stool and all this with the damn TV idiots shoving their lenses right over my shoulder.

Kevin was calm enough and hadn't taken too many shots. I managed to get him a mouth swill and then wash his gum shield at the same time as encouraging him to keep on the move and turn Gianni on the ropes and not get trapped in corners. I always got good feedback from Kevin so I knew he was alert.

Having got through the first round and interval, I was getting my priorities sorted and was able to concentrate more on the action. De Napoli was good, no question about it. Kevin was able to keep him at distance at this early stage but wasn't able to set himself for a power attack to make his physical advantages count, but he saw out the round without taking a significant punch.

My instructions at the end of the round were to continue with the same tactics. I thought that Kevin's best chances would come after about the fifth when Gianni either began to tire or he became frustrated and would take chances. At least up to this point there was no sign of damage to Kevin's eye which had been cut so badly in his last fight. I needed four hands as it was so if I had to tend to a cut as well it would have been near impossible.

Again in the third De Napoli was out fast and driving Kevin to the ropes. Once or twice Kevin's jab did knock Gianni's head back but the following right hands were off target although there was a glimmer of hope. Once again at the end of the round the Italian had another one in the bag.

Kevin was gasping a bit when he got back to the corner. He had taken a few heavy body shots and he needed some deep breathing to get his wind back. Again I emphasised the need to keep the fight at range. The little guy was too quick with his hands in close.

The fourth started just a same as the first three. Kevin was desperately trying to keep distance between them but Gianni was relentless. Half way through the round and suddenly, for the first time in the fight, Kevin was hurt by a body shot. He tried to get in close and hold but the Italian was not having it and a combination to the head had Kevin down and taking a count. The home crowd were roaring him on and when Kevin got up at eight Gianni was back on him and another fusillade of head shots had him down again. This time Kevin was facing me as he got to one knee but I signalled for him to stay down which he did.

So the Italians got the home town victory on TV that they wanted and Dennie Mancini got his 25% and the gratitude of the Roman promoter for supplying a victim for their gladiator

The Italians were now very friendly and our dressing room was full of back- slappers thanking Kevin for coming and giving their man a good work out. Where were they when I needed someone to hand me up the water and spit bucket during the fight? They couldn't understand English then, now they were speaking it like Italian waiters.

After the show the promoter was generous. He had laid on a big meal at a restaurant for all the home boxers and we were included. They were a nice bunch of guys. They served up course after course of pasta dishes which I don't eat! The wine was good though and I did have some nice deserts. Kevin must have put on a few extra pounds eating my pasta as well as his own!

The following morning we learned that our return flight was not until 7pm. The weather was pleasantly warm so we parked our bags with a porter at the hotel and spent the day exploring Rome, managing to see all the big tourist sites and even legging it all the way up to the Vatican and wandered round the Sistine Chapel. We made it to the airport after beating off the street urchins who were constantly trying to grab our bags!

It had been a hard but interesting trip. This was the fight game at its best and at its worst at the same time.

Again Dennie seemed happy with Kevin's performance although again he had lost. Just turning up and giving it a go was enough for him but not for me, but my hands were tied.

A month later Dennie was back on the phone this time with a home date on the 16th of December. Dennie said he had a Christmas Box for Kevin, an eight round fight against the British Title contender Mark Reefer. It was on a show promoted by Reefer's manager Barry Hearns. Reefer was from Bethnal Green. The money had to be good because normally Dennie Mancini didn't do business with Hearns.

At the time Reefer had won sixteen of twenty fights and one of his losses was in a Commonwealth lightweight title fight. They were in the process of bringing Mark down to the Super Feather division and the fight was made at 9 stone 4 pounds. It wasn't exactly a gift wrapped Christmas box.

Training was going well and I had got to know Kevin pretty well during our trips abroad. He was an intelligent guy, an artist and pretty good chess player!

He was getting better all the time and defied the old saying about teaching old dogs new tricks.

The show was at the International Centre, Brentwood, Essex, but we were instructed to go to the Barry Hearns Matchroom gym for the weigh in. Kevin was spot on the match weight and Reefer was slightly over but not enough to worry about. I had seen Reefer box a couple of times. He had one of those high definition muscular physiques, but I thought he looked 'drawn' at the weight and I suspected that, although he was only 5' 5" tall…an inch shorter than Kevin, he was really a natural lightweight but his management thought he would be stronger in the lower division, a common mistake.

Dennie didn't arrive at the venue until we were in the dressing room and warming up. This time he wanted to work in the ring with me on the outside. I wasn't happy at that but I was still close enough to be able to get my input through to Kevin.

At the opening bell, Reefer came out aggressively but compared to De Napoli in the Rome fight, he was easier to control and Kevin was soon jabbing him and landing cleanly. I thought Kevin had won the round but, with a London referee in charge, it would probably have been marked as a drawn round.

The next four rounds went the same way and it was turning into a good well fought contest with not much between them although I felt that Kevin was now the stronger man and it was Reefer who was feeling the pace. The last two rounds would be interesting.

But it wasn't to be. A minute into the sixth and suddenly there was blood running down Kevin's left cheek. The cut he had suffered against Renard had opened again. The referee didn't give Dennie a chance to work on it because it was the perfect way for the ref to end a close fight with a safe result for the 'house' fighter. The cut didn't even need stitching and was closed with steri-strip stick on sutures.

That was Kevin finished until after Christmas 1988. He had lost his last three under Dennie's management but all against top men and was proving to be a good investment for Dennie who was receiving his 25% of the purse money.

In spite of this, Kevin had not lost his enthusiasm for the game and by New Year 1989; he was back in the gym. Dennie rang to ask if he would be ready for a contest on the 14th of February which I affirmed. He said that Tommy Conroy, the Sunderland manager/trainer, was looking to move his young fighter Harry Escott up in class and wanted Kevin for the opportunity to get him into the ratings. I knew Escott well having seen him box several times. He was only twenty years old at the time and although he had an eleven wins two losses and one draw record, he was nowhere near ready for the improving Kevin Pritchard.

I was glad to take the match and so was Kevin. My relief at the prospect of a fight I knew we would win was dented when a few days later Dennie rang to say he had accepted the fight but that Tommy Conroy was insisting on it being fought over eight two minute rounds instead of eight three minutes. I couldn't believe it. I told Dennie that it was ridicules to expect an experienced fighter like Kevin to fall back to the novice distance of eight twos against a young kid who could run rings round him over two minute rounds and in any case, if they were expecting to move Harry up he should be doing so over the proper distance. I was even more surprised at someone as experienced as Dennie even considering it.

Dennie said to keep training and he would see what he could do. A week before the fight I rang Dennie for the final decision on it and he said "yes it is OK" which I took to mean it was going to be three minute rounds. The weight had to be at the 9st 4lb super feather limit which was no problem for us.

The show was at the Crowtree Leisure Centre, Sunderland on the 14th of February 89. Kevin was spot on the weight and Harry was two pounds lighter. It was then when I talked to Tommy Conroy that I learned that the fight was over two minute rounds after all. Dennie had sold us down the river. I was as mad as hell but I could do nothing about now.

It definitely looked like a man against a boy when referee Arnold Bryson (home town) called them together at the centre of the ring. Just as I had predicted, Harry Escott was buzzing around Kevin firing fast jabs and Kevin was having difficulty in closing him down. It was of no concern at this early stage as I knew that Kevin would, by the middle rounds, be getting his shots in and it would all change. At least I was back in charge in the corner. Kevin was totally unconcerned when he came back to the corner. After just two minutes of action he hadn't even worked up a sweat.

In the second Kevin did step up a gear and chased the kid around the ring but still couldn't quite hit him clean but it was soon all over and he was back to his stool and getting in the mood.

At the bell for the third Kevin was quickly out and carried on from where he left off when suddenly disaster. There was blood again on Kevin. I had not seen Harry land a single solid punch and it may well have been caused by the head when Kevin bundled him to the ropes, but anyway it was enough for Bryson and Kevin's fourth consecutive loss. I still blamed Mancini for accepting a two minute round contest.

By now I was getting concerned for Kevin's future. I knew how much he was enjoying his boxing at the moment but it was clear that he was being abused by his management. He was good enough to be given at least a level playing field at this stage of his career but Mancini had already written him off and was only interested in putting him in with top fighters for the bigger purses.

A week later in the gym I suggested that Kevin should take at least six months off to give his now scarred eyebrow time to heal properly and also decide if this was really what he wanted in his boxing career or would he decide that it was time to call it a day, after all he was twenty nine and had been boxing since he was eleven. He agreed with me and I didn't see him again for the rest of 1989. I was sad to see him go.

I didn't hear from Dennie again regarding Kevin although I saw him frequently and he offered me jobs for my other fighters.

Jean sent Kevin and his partner Sue and daughter Leah a Christmas card as usual, then, just after Christmas I was surprised when they came to see me at our shop. Kevin asked if he could talk to me away from the gym atmosphere.

He told me that he was really missing the game. He felt that he still had not reached the top of his game and could he come back for one more shot. He said that his contract with Dennie had ended and he wanted me to sign him up and look after him. I examined his eye and sure enough it had healed well without too much scar tissue. I said that I would only agree if he could show me that he really was ready to go for at least British Title if I could secure a shot. He said that was his goal so we shook on it.

The next thing I did was to ring John Morris who was the BBB of C general secretary to check if Kevin's contract with Dennie had expired. He was able to confirm that he was free to sign. I then rang Dennie to make sure the air was clear. At first he said as far as he knew Kevin was still tied to him but when I told him I had spoken to Morris he accepted it and wished me luck with Kevin because he said he had no chance of getting Kevin anywhere near the title. At that point in time Barry Hearn was pulling the strings in the super feather division and Dennie was reluctant to work with him.

After studying the ratings I thought I could see a shortcut to the British title. Harry Escott had won seven more fights since his win over Kevin including a win over Joey Jacobs who, in his next fight, had won the British title. I knew from my association with Tommy Conroy that he was hoping to get Harry a title shot in 1990. With his previous cut eye win over Kevin I reckoned they would be happy to fight him again.

First though I had to get Kevin back in harness and get a few wins under his belt. He came back to the gym and the lay off seemed to have re-vitalised him. He worked hard and by the end of February I began to look for a fight for him.

Pat Brogan ran a sporting club based in Stoke-on-Trent and I knew him well. He had a show coming up on the 14th of March and he offered Kevin a contest over six threes against Nigel Haddock. It was just what I was looking for. Haddock had an eleven win six loss and a draw record and he was a natural super featherweight.

Both boxers weighed in just under the weight limit and were well matched physically. The referee was Paul Thomas from the midlands area. Both boxers started fast and for two rounds there was nothing in it.

By the middle of the third Kevin was getting the upper hand and was obviously the harder puncher. In the fourth and fifth the pattern was the same. Haddock took everything Kevin threw at him and came back for more but Kevin was never in any sort of trouble and his eye had stood up the test.

I sent Kevin out to try and force a stoppage in the last round, although I felt there was little doubt about the verdict. Again Haddock was as game as they come and was still there at the final bell. I was astounded when the referee called it a draw. It was another infuriating case of the ref sitting on the fence. Even Pat Brogan thought we were robbed although he was pleased that it had been a great fight for his promotion.

When I went to get the wages from Pat he told me he had had asked the ref how he had come to call it a draw and he had said to Pat that it had been such a good fight he wanted to send both boys home happy. We were not happy because we had been robbed and the ref was incompetent.

Even so, a draw had not done any harm and it made getting another fight slightly easier than say a quick KO would have done.

After another few weeks in the gym I decided to make a serious effort to get Kevin a return with Escott. Tommy Conroy was quite amenable to the idea of an official eliminator between Kevin and Harry but it was a question of who would promote it?

The answer to that came when there was a World title fight show coming up for John Davidson, another of the Tyneside heroes. It was at the Temple Park Centre, South Shields, promoted by Frank Warren on the fight night series. Tommy submitted the match and with TV we got decent money but just as important, the publicity and the opportunity to cement a decent claim for a title fight for Kevin. All he had to do was beat Harry Escott.

The date was set for the 15th of May 1990. It gave us the perfect time to set a programme to peak.

I had a busy gym and plenty of good sparring for Kevin. The preparation went well with no snags or minor injuries.

We drove over to South Shields the day before and Kevin weighed in spot on the weight with Harry half a pound lighter. Harry had definitely matured since his last fight with Kevin but it still looked like a man against a boy.

We were second on the bill so that the TV producers could get our fight 'In the can' for broadcasting if the main event, which was a international fight between John Davidson and a fighter from Thailand who's name I can't remember, ended inside the distance (which it did) when Davidson cut his Thai opponent.

I was a bit concerned when I heard that the referee for our fight was Arnold Bryson, one of the locals and one whom I had seen give some really dodgy decisions when it was a house fighter against an 'opponent'

Our pre fight warm up was perfect and Kevin was well up for the fight and in the zone. Escott didn't start as fast this time which meant that Kevin had no trouble catching him with his much longer reach and fast combinations, but Harry was game and for the first three rounds it was close which meant that Escott would get the points on the referees card.

From the fourth round onwards I asked Kevin to step up the pace. He had trained for a high work rate and now his superiority all round was evident and he was hurting Harry with his power shots but not yet stunning him.

In the fifth Kevin opened a cut under Harry's left eye which affected his confidence and for the next three rounds he was in survival mode. I was confidant at the start of the last round, that even with the fight on Escott's home patch and with Bryson in charge, the win was in the bag, but I sent Kevin out to make sure and he pounded Harry for three minutes which made it safe. Kevin had won clearly and the ref hoisted his hand instantly at the final bell.

This win established Kevin as a legitimate challenger for the British super featherweight title but the question was how to get him a shot.

Since John Doherty had won the inaugural super feather title on my promotion at the Guild Hall, the title had changed hands five times with no champion defending it successfully. The current champion was Joey Jacobs of Manchester who had taken the title from John Doherty who had held it for the second time. The encouraging thing for me was that Harry Escott had beaten Joey in a fight immediately before he won the title so on that form line, Kevin was in with a chance if we could get the fight.

I rang Nat Basso to sound out the possibility of a fight with Jacobs only to be told that Jacobs was already committed to a defence against the undefeated Hugh Forde.

I then rang Frank Turner who was the matchmaker for the Barry Hearn outfit. I thought a return with Mark Reefer billed as an eliminator for the title was a good match. Frank told me that they had already applied to the Board for Reefer to get a direct shot at the championship and in any case they were promoting Hugh Forde who was fighting Joey Jacobs for the title and if he won they were planning a Forde-Reefer title fight in the near future so there was no way they would risk Reefer against Pritchard again.

This was the problem that all "small time" managers face. If they have a fighter who offered the slightest risk to the establishment he is frozen out. Even so, at the same time, I was not going to risk Kevin's status by fighting a middle of the road fighter or any of the up and comers.

The answer to getting Kevin a meaningful fight that was not a risk to his rating came from our old friend Dennie Mancini. He was looking for an opponent for the French featherweight champion, Jacobin Yoma, and he offered Kevin an eight rounder in Cayenne, the capital of French Guiana in South America. Yoma was based in Paris but was a favourite in his home town of Cayenne. He had only had eight fights…seven wins and a draw… and according to Dennie, this was a winnable fight for Kevin and a win could pave the way to an improbable crack at the European title.

The money was good and Kevin was keen to fight. His confidence was high and he said that he would fight these guys with the intention of beating them instead of just going in as an 'opponent' and expecting to lose as he had in the past. The date was set for the 12th of October 1990. I set a routine that would peak him for that date and Kevin trained with enthusiasm.

On the 18th of September Hugh Forde repeated the extraordinary habit of the super featherweight title changing hands at the first defence when he stopped Joey Jacobs in the eleventh round, as predicted by Frank Turner. I watched the fight and thought that Kevin could hold his own with either of them. Forde was now the darling of the Hearns stable and was being touted as a future world champion…a bit prematurely in my opinion. A defence against Reefer was announced for the 20th of October.

Kevin's training was going well at the end of September when I got a call from Frank Turner. He enquired whether I was still interested in Kevin having a shot at the British title. He said that Reefer had been injured in training and with only three weeks to go they were looking for a replacement to fight Forde. I could hardly believe our luck!

At first I told Frank that Kevin was only ticking over in the gym and it was short notice for a title fight. Well I could hardly tell him that Kevin was in fact in full training for a fight on the 12th and was perfectly placed to step up preparations for a twelve round title fight on the 20th.

Anyway I said we would take it. The money was poor for a title fight at only £4,500 plus expenses but Turner said they were not prepared to negotiate more and he would look elsewhere for an opponent if we quibbled. I accepted it.

My problem was, Kevin was under contract to fight Yoma and I had to somehow get out of that contract. I rang Dennie and explained our dilemma. At first he was adamant that Kevin had to fulfil his commitment, but after some persuasion he could see my point that getting Kevin this title fight was perhaps a once in a lifetime chance so he said if I could find a replacement to fight Yoma on the twelfth he would agree to release Kevin.

The next twenty four hours were spent on the phone in desperate attempts to find a boxer who would be acceptable to Yoma's management and ready to fight in ten days time. I finally breathed a sigh of relief when Paddy Byrne offered the services of Ritchie Foster. Ritchie was a Dublin born Irishman based in America but had fought a few times in the UK and had a twenty one wins ten losses and one draw record. Paddy was his agent. Dennie accepted the match on behalf of Yoma's management and I heaved a sigh of relief.

When the contracts arrived from Matchroom, I noted that they included the options that in the event of Kevin winning he would have to fulfil the engagements Forde was already contracted to, which was a defence against Birmingham's Mark Holt on the tenth of November, plus one further defence. That was fine by us except that the purses for these fights were written in at £7,000 each, not much for the defence of a British title on TV. I had no alternative but to accept these conditions but I also knew that the terms in the BBB of C contract stipulate that the promoter must take up these options within twenty four hours of Kevin winning. The clause that referred to TV percentages was struck out in red.

I signed the contract and sent it back by return post with a copy to the BBB of C HQ in London

Kevin was ecstatic at the news of a British title fight, especially coming out of the blue and in only his third fight after signing with me. I revised his training schedule to prepare him for the extra distance but he was already at an advanced state of fitness so we were able to concentrate on perfecting the tactics he needed to beat Hugh Forde.

In 1988 I was training a young Irishman called Brian Cullen who was living in Preston but was under Pat Brogan's management. Pat matched Brian with Hugh Forde, the fight taking place in Birmingham on the 28th of November. It was Forde's fifteenth fight and he was unbeaten.

Brian was a short, aggressive fighter and for three rounds he gave Hugh Forde plenty to think about. It gave me the opportunity to see Forde at close quarters and to note the way he became unbalanced when he was under pressure. He was tall for a super feather at five foot nine inches. He had come into Professional boxing via the Kick boxing fraternity and as a result he was a switcher, meaning he switched from orthodox to southpaw constantly. This is fine when a boxer is in control of the action but not so fine when he is under pressure and is relying on good well drilled defensive techniques.

In the fourth round he landed a solid right cross which broke Brian's jaw and ended the fight prematurely, but I was not that impressed with Hugh Forde.

Armed with this knowledge, the strategy was to weather the inevitable storm that would come in the first few rounds. I reckoned that Kevin would be behind on points by the middle of the twelve round contest, but by that time Forde would be feeling the pace and Kevin could start to pressure him into making mistakes. My main worry was the possibility of a cut but there is little that can be done to prevent this.

We had plenty of good sparring available and Sammy Sampson helped by providing the switching style that he had perfected in the run up to his Area title fight. Kevin displayed how hard he was punching when he broke the jaw of a welterweight sparring partner even with 16oz sparring gloves.

For the contest I assembled a strong back up to work the corner with me. Sammy had retired from boxing himself and was not interested in becoming a trainer but he had taken out a seconds licence so he could assist and I recruited John Bradshaw who shared our gym training other boxers and he was an experienced cornerman.

Kevin was in superb condition and prepared for twelve rounds if necessary. At the 1oclock weigh in he weighed nine stone two and a half pounds…a pound and a half under the championship weight. Forde surprisingly was a half pound over weight and had to go away and lose it. I was chuffed because, to me, it indicated that they were too confident in there preparation and thought Kevin was easy. I was very surprised that Forde's managers and trainers, the Lynch brothers, could be this unprofessional. They were very experienced having taken Pat Cowdell to British, European and world title fights, but this time they had boo booed!

The fight was in Hugh Forde's home town of Dudley and was on live Sky TV. We went through all the hype of Pre fight interviews by the boxing press and TV commentators and at last we were alone, as a team, in the dressing room. Kevin's experience stood him in good stead as we warmed up and got in the zone. We had rehearsed this scenario time and again. The referee was the 'A' class Larry O'Connell and he came into the dressing room to give instructions. We were nervous but controlled.

There was a full house and the atmosphere was electric as we entered the ring with a respectful cheer for Kevin and a great roar for Hugh Forde.

When O'Connell called the boxers to the centre of the ring for final instructions, Forde seemed even taller than I remembered him against Brian Cullen.

From the first bell, the action started exactly as predicted. Forde was out fast with his loose style and fast hands popping out jabs and sure enough leading with his left and then seconds later with his right. Kevin popped out his own jab but even with his long reach he couldn't find the target against the elusive Forde. One up for the champion

I was happy with the round and all I needed to do with Kevin was refresh him in the usual way and tell him to keep his defences high. The second followed the same pattern but Forde was now landing more shots and was supremely confident and Kevin wasn't hurting him at all with the few punches he did land, it was another clear round to Forde.

In the interval before the third I asked Kevin to throw body shots. We had worked on them in the gym and with a tall evasive target like Forde he had more chance of hitting the body and perhaps slowing him down. There was no panic and Kevin had not been hurt.

At the start of the third Kevin fought with more purpose but this left him open to Forde's fast counters. For the first time in the fight Kevin was taking hard shots and the danger of a cut made me get the adrenaline and swabs prepared. It was a clear round to Forde and I realised that the tactic of holding back for five or six rounds was too dangerous and was playing into the hands of Hugh. During the last flurry of punches in the round, the rubber band that was holding Kevin's dreadlocks in place flew off. It was amusing to see Larry O'Connell retrieving it thinking it was Kevin's gum shield that had come out but the bell had sounded anyway.

There was no sign of blood but Kevin's face was reddening. My instructions were to abandon caution and to attack from the start of the fourth instead of the sixth as we had rehearsed. I explained why and he understood. He was ready for the bell and attacked Forde for the first time. It had the desired effect. Suddenly he was putting Hugh Forde onto his back foot where he was more disorganised and Kevin was landing punches. Forde was firing back but with less effect and at around two minutes into the round, Kevin drove him back with a power left jab and, just as predicted, as soon as Forde's back hit the ropes he didn't know which way to turn. In that split second, Kevin slammed over a terrific right cross.

From the moment it landed, Hugh was unconscious. He stiffened and fell sideways to the canvass. Larry O'Connell took up the count but quickly abandoned it to get the doctor into the ring. Kevin leapt into the air on the realisation that he had just become British Champion. I leapt into the ring and hugging Kevin with a mixture of relief and exhilaration. I glanced at the stunned faces at ringside, mostly Forde's promoters and backers and the boxing journo's and TV commentators. This was one of those major upsets of form that boxing throws up from time to time and Kevin Pritchard had become the unlikeliest winner of a Lonsdale belt for some time.

We celebrated in the dressing room and it was a happy car load that drove back to Preston.

I gave Kevin a few days off to celebrate with his family but told him he had to be back in the gym to prepare for his first defence of the title in less than three weeks time to fulfil our contract obligations. The four rounds against Hugh Forde had not taken a lot out of him and he had no injuries of any sort so we could soon be back to full training.

The day after the fight I waited for the phone call from Barry Hearns Matchroom promotions to take up the options, but the day passed with no call and then the second day and the third. Finally four days after the contest Frank Turner rang. He said that they didn't want Kevin to fight Mark Holt but instead wanted him to defend against Mark Reefer on the 25th of November.

I said that would be fine by us but what was the purse offered. He said "the purse is as written in the contract you signed" I told him that if Kevin had been defending against Mark Holt then we would accept the offer but a defence against Reefer was worth a lot more money. He again quoted the contract and I told him to read the small print himself. It states quite clearly that the option has to be taken up within twenty four hours, it was now four days and as far as I was concerned the contract was now null and void.

Frank nearly blew a fuse. He spluttered and cursed then said "you will be hearing from Barry's lawyers" I said "OK but I hope they can read better than you". As soon as he put the phone down I called John Morris at HQ and explained the situation and he confirmed the fact that Matchroom could not bind us to the now expired contract and that I was free to negotiate a new purse. He also pointed out that since Kevin had won the title in a voluntary challenge, he could only defend it against a Board of Control nominated contender Mark Reefer or the leading contender Robert Dickie.

Later that day I got the expected call from Barry Hearn himself. He wanted to know what was going on and why was I refusing to comply with the contract so I again explained it to him. His first reaction was that he had been out of the country during the period of the fight with Forde so could not take up the option in the time frame. I pointed out that he had people hear in the UK who should have been acting for him and he had to agree. So now we had got over the fact that they had boo booed, what did I want for the Reefer fight. I asked for £12.500 plus expenses and he agreed.

We were now able to get Kevin into the best shape of his career for the 25th November. We were already working from a high level of fitness having only had four days off after the Forde fight so we were able to refine specific tactics for Reefer based on Kevin's previous fight with him and Kevin's confidence was high.

We were in the gym one day when John Bradshaw came in with one of his fighters to spar. When I told him that Kevin was fighting Reefer in a couple of weeks he said "I don't think so. I was in the Matchroom gym only two days ago with Carl Crook and Reefer is not in training. In fact he is in dispute with his trainer because he can't do the super featherweight limit so there is no way he will be ready for Kevin in two weeks" I was shocked. I got on the phone to Frank Turner who claimed he knew nothing about it but he would check it out but as far as he was concerned the fight was still on.

Two days later he rang back to say Reefer had caught a dose of flu and the fight would have to be postponed for two weeks and he would call back with the new date. Our training was scheduled to peak Kevin in ten days time but now I had to re-programme. I had to bring him down by resting him for a few days and then pick him up again. It was not a disaster at this stage but I could now see how they were stringing us along. The Matchroom outfit knew that Reefer was not going to make it and probably knew it for weeks. I wondered how long they would have left it if I had not spoken to John Bradshaw and called Frank Turner.

A week later and Kevin was back in the gym. I had not heard from Turner so I began ringing him every day but just got excuses and I was now really concerned. I rang John Morris to see if the Board had been informed of the new date as they should have been for a British title fight. He said they had not been given a date but he would look into it. I told him that if I didn't get a confirmed date within the week I would seek another opponent for Kevin because I couldn't be expected to keep him in training indefinitely. I was shocked when he said that if Kevin fought before meeting the leading contender they would strip him of the title. We were being screwed by Matchroom and now by the BBBofC.

A week before the fight, the Boxing Board notified me that Mark Reefer was no longer fighting at super featherweight. They had now nominated Robert Dickie as the next challenger and had put the fight out to purse offers.

I was now able to take Kevin out of hard training and put him on a maintenance routine until we got a new date after the purse offers came in by the 10th of December 1990. I didn't expect a date before the end of January.

On the 11th of December I got a surprise call from John Morris. He said that the purse offers had been opened and Frank Warren's Sports Network had put in the highest bid of £24.000. In a 60/40 split for champion/challenger this meant that Kevin would get £14.400. That was a bit more like it. The proposed date was late January.

We were delighted and made our plans to fight Robert Dickie. It meant training right through the Christmas period but that was a small price to pay. I knew all about Dickie. He was born in Wales but of Scottish parents and had boxed for Scotland as an amateur. He had actually fought for the professional Scottish bantamweight title though it was one of his two losses to date against twenty one wins and two draws. He had won and defended the British featherweight title and the WBC international super featherweight title, so he was no slouch. I had seen him when he lost the WBC title by sixth round stoppage against Kamel Bou-Ali and I was confidant that Kevin, with his hitting power and the new found confidence of being Champion, would beat him

By Christmas time I still had not received a contract or date for the fight so I rang Ernie Fossey who, as Warren's matchmaker would know what was going on. He said that they had not yet found a venue for the fight but it would be in late January or early February. I was beginning to worry about it but I didn't tell Kevin that so we kept up with our training schedule and of course I had other fighters training and matched during this time.

By mid January, with still no word from the Warren outfit, I rang Dickie's manager Colin Breen to see if he had any news about the fight date only to be told that they were not even in training seriously until they had a confirmed date from Frank Warren. My next call was to John Morris to ask what the Board of Control could do about it. He said that he would look into the matter but there was nothing much they could do. They were after all, as far as Frank Warren was concerned, the Board of no Control.

Once again I had to ask Kevin to step down from his training schedule. He was getting pretty frustrated by this time after the euphoria of winning the title had worn off, the fact was that he had been deprived of his family Christmas and had been in constant training since September 90, with only a few days off after his title win and here we were now in mid January 91.

Between Barry Hearn and now Frank Warren we were being screwed and the Boxing Board were doing nothing to help. John Morris called to say that Sports Network had withdrawn their interest and that that the Board were going to reprimand Frank Warren. That made us feel a lot better and I bet it really worried Warren.

During our travels together Kevin told me he had been adopted when he was only six weeks old. He loved his adoptive parents, the Pritchard's of Kirby, Liverpool, but he had an urge to find his natural parents. I offered to help him find them and he told me he knew he had been born in Ipswich, Suffolk.

Now that he was a British Professional Boxing Champion and was having his fifteen minutes of fame in life, I was pretty sure I could find them and now was a good time to do it. It would give him a different focus for a little while.

I rang the local Lowestoft newspaper and spoke to their sports editor. He was delighted to be able to help since it gave them a great sports news story. He rang me in only a couple of days to say he had found Kevin's Grandmother and the address of his natural mother who was now living in London. He also said he had been in touch with the Town Council and their Civic Leader invited Kevin and his partner to a reception in honour of his achievements for Ipswich.

Kevin was delighted by this news and it got better when I rang the News of the World, spoke to their reporter Fred Burcombe and negotiated a fee for them to cover, live, the reunion of Kevin and his mother. He also found that he had a full blooded sister and brother, two half sisters and three half brothers. A whole new family to meet and get to know!

All of this, plus invites as a guest to local functions up here in the North West, gave Kevin the opportunity to relax before getting back to the grind of full time training.

Just before the end of the month I got a call from our old friend Barry Hearns he was willing to put on the Pritchard/Dickie title fight in Cardiff on the 5th of March if we could agree terms. There would be no options in the contract and we agreed a purse of £12,500 plus expenses, the same as we had agreed for the Reefer fight that never was. It gave us five weeks to bring Kevin back up to a peak after about ten days out of training, which was just about right for us.

The contracts duly arrived with the details as agreed except that this time the clause which allowed Kevin a percentage of any TV money had not been excluded. This is a standard paragraph written in by the Board of Control and if it is not applicable it has to be struck out by the promoter. Hearns had not mentioned the TV clause in our telephone conversation and since I knew that he never promoted without TV, I was going to ask for a share of the fee he would receive for the show. I signed and returned the contract copies to Matchroom and the Board.

I knew I had them bang to rights again because of their carelessness with contracts just as they had been with the Forde contract. I left it for a day or two to make sure they would have received them then I rang HQ. This time I spoke to Simon Block who was the secretary of the Southern Area but based at the Board of Control head office. Simon had the reputation of being an expert in the interpretation of the rule book so I asked him the check the contract for the Dickie fight that I had sent them. I asked him to check the TV clause and confirm my interpretation that, since it had not been struck out, I could demand the payment. He confirmed that that was the case and that it seemed like Matchroom had slipped up. He also checked the copy they had received from Matchroom and it had been signed and was the same.

With a week to go before the fight I rang Barry Hearns and asked him what the money from the TV as going to be. He was at first mystified by my request claiming that he had a deal with the TV company which covered a series of shows without allocating any specific amount for any one show and in any case I had signed the contract accepting the purse. When I pointed out that the contract had left our entitlement open he was absolutely furious. I also told him that for accounting purposes, they must be able to apportion a fee to that particular promotion. After all the bluster he finally agreed to look into it and we would get our percentage. That was one back for the way they had messed us about in October and November. Maybe they would be a little more careful with their contracts in future.

Kevin was working well in the gym and was coming to a peak for the fight. We drove down to Cardiff the day before the show and found the hotel that had been booked for us. At the weigh in Kevin was 9st 3lbs and Dickie was three quarters of a pound lighter. Kevin looked much bigger than Robert and he exuded confidence. John Bradshaw had come down to assist in the corner.

At the weigh in Barry Hearns came to me and said "before you start, you have got your TV money added to your purse" I thanked him and tried not to smirk.

The National Sports Centre in Cardiff was packed with local supporters for Dickie. We had a decent dressing room and our pre fight routine went perfectly. I noticed that Kevin was wearing new shorts and socks for this fight. He took pride in his ring wear and he was always smartly turned out.

We had trained for a fast start against Dickie as opposed to the cautious tactics when he fought Forde. I felt that with Robert Dickie's experience of going the championship distance, Kevin's best bet was to pile on the pressure from the start and rely on catching Dickie early, and from the first bell Kevin did and had Dickie backed up. He was hurting him with heavy two handed combinations and at the bell Robert Dickie was in trouble. When Kevin came back to the corner we were feeling confident.

The second and third went the same way and our confidence was growing although Kevin was now trying to set Dickie up with single big shots instead of pouring on the combinations which we had worked on. Even so, I was expecting an early drive home as Dickie was showing real signs of distress although Kevin was not quite as dominant in the fourth.

Suddenly in the fifth Kevin was not attacking and Dickie, the good pro that he was, sensed that something was wrong with him and for the first time he was on the offensive. Dickie won the round, the first of this contest. When Kevin sat down his face was twisted in distress. I tried to find out what the problem was and he said it was something to do with his foot! I couldn't understand what he meant and thought the only thing could have happened was that he had twisted his ankle although I had not seen anything like that in the round.

Kevin went out for the sixth and he was definitely limping. Dickie, from being out on his feet in the third and fourth, was now on the attack and Kevin was in survival mode. He saw the round out but it was another one back for Dickie.

Again I just could not get through to Kevin, something I had not experienced with him before. Even in his fight with De-Napoli I had been able to get feedback from him but now there was nothing I could do to raise his spirit.

He fought the seventh as he had the sixth. He tried to rally with some shots but it was mostly a case of surviving Dickie's onslaught. Dickie was now concentrating on Kevin's body and some of his punches were way round the back of his elbows and into the kidney region.

I was now seriously considering whether to pull him out of the fight altogether. The title was slipping away and Kevin seemed to be resigned to it. It was hard to take but for the first time since I had worked with Kevin, he was getting hurt far more than he had been in Rome. I had made up my mind that if he couldn't rally in the eighth I was calling it off and I told him so. He didn't respond.

A minute of one way traffic in the round and Kevin went down to a heavy body shot and I knew it was over. As I got him back to his stool he was badly distressed and apologising for having lost the title. I was more concerned about what had happened to him. I still could hardly come to terms with the bizarre way the fight had changed in the fifth. From being on the point of a stoppage win to this in three rounds seemed impossible.

John Bradshaw and I half carried Kevin back to the dressing room. No one noticed because they were too wrapped up in their new local hero.

As soon as Kevin sat down he asked me to take off his right boxing boot. When I did so and slipped off his sock all was revealed. The entire ball of his foot was red raw. It was an ugly sight with a large patch of skin hanging down and blood dripping off it. It was only then that the realisation of what had happened hit me.

Kevin had bought new socks that he was wearing for the first time. They were made of 100% nylon, not cotton as they should have been.

I had not checked them before he put them on. The friction generated during those first four rounds had obviously raised a huge blister which from round five onwards was being torn off inside his boot. The pain must have been excruciating and it had totally broken his concentration in the fight.

Dickie had sensed it and it gave him the opportunity to claw back from the brink of defeat. I still genuinely believe that had Kevin been wearing cotton socks he would have retained the super featherweight tile by stoppage win.

The nylon socks were binned. The only consolation was that the TV money added a few thousand pounds to Kevin's purse.

With all the shenanigans that had gone on before the two title fights I knew the chances of us getting another shot at the title were slim. I had a good talk with Kevin after letting his damaged foot heal. He said that although he had been stopped by body punches which hurt a bit at the time, his only memories of pain in the fight were from his foot. He had not taken concussive head punches or been cut so he wanted to carry on for a while if I could get him some decent money fights.

No one in the top ranks of the British ratings was willing to fight him so I concentrated on the possibilities of a decent win on the continent which might get us in with a shout at the European title. I was in touch with the agents for Daniel Londas the champion and there seemed a real possibility of a Euro Title fight since Kevin had impressed even in losing to Robert Dickie. Somehow it all fizzled out. Perhaps they also watched the Forde KO.

I knew that Paddy Byrne acted as an agent for the Danish promoter Mogens Palle and he managed the Bredahl brothers from Copenhagen. It so happened that they were looking for an opponent for Jimmy Bredahl for a televised show in Copenhagen on the 17th of May which fitted in pretty well with our training schedule. The match was over eight rounds at nine stone four. Spot on. They were willing to pay good money for the ex British champion.

Bredahl had fought and won just nine contests although he was an experienced amateur. Of his nine wins only four were by stoppage but he was being hailed as a future World Champion. We had heard that before with Hugh Forde and look what happened to him.

Kevin seemed to have totally recovered from his foot injury and was working well in the gym and getting plenty of sparring.

We flew into Copenhagen and were met and taken to a five star hotel. Our room was nice and we were treated well by everyone. The weather was good and after our evening meal we went out for a sightseeing stroll.

The following day we were picked up and taken to the weigh in where we met Bredahl and the other fighters on the bill. Jimmy was taller than Kevin but not imposing or arrogant. Both fighters weighed in a pound under the match weight. We shared a dressing room with an American middleweight and his trainers who were nice guys although I had never heard of them.

Paddy Byrne came to see us in the dressing room before fight time and he assured me that the corner would be well staffed and I wouldn't get a repeat of our Rome experience. We went through the usual warm up routine and I had high hopes of a return to winning ways.

From the first bell Jimmy Bredahl boxed well. Kevin was well in it but was not winning the round and although it was close I knew it would go against us.

I told Kevin to start the second much more aggressively and let us see how Jimmy would cope. For two minutes of the round Kevin kept Jimmy Bredahl backed up until he got hit by a fast left hook which caught him clean on the jaw. It put Kevin on his back foot and

Bredahl followed up with some good combinations and at the bell he had pulled the round back.

Kevin was calm in the interval and clear headed. I urged him to repeat the tactics at the start of the third but be aware of the counters by returning his hands high. For the first minute again Kevin was dominating until the same left hook flashed and this time Kevin was hurt and took a count. The referee had seen enough and stopped the fight. Kevin seemed to be going backwards again.

Kevin was not too downhearted. He had been here before and we were still well looked after until we flew home. We had an amusing incident when we checked out of the hotel. Kevin had made a four minute telephone call home from our room after the fight. The hotel receptionist handed me a bill for £78 for this call. I know it is understood that all expenses at the hotel are paid for by the promoter except bar bills and telephone calls but this was ridiculous and I refused to pay it. They made a fuss but I had by this time got our passports from them so I told them to bill me at home. They did but I still didn't pay.

This time I really was ready to ask Kevin to call it a day. For the first time he seemed ready to listen. He still loved the gym work we were now doing and when I asked him to come and help with the training he was keen. I suggested that since it was the beginning of June he should take a few weeks off from the gym, as he had done before then we would make a final decision.

By the end of June he was back. He said he just got bored away from training so he was back working out and running and sparring with the other fighters and beginning coach and advise them. He also came to shows with me to assist in the corner and inevitably the MC at these shows would spot him and introduce him to the crowd. He enjoyed that recognition and had earned it over the years.

In the first week of August 1991 I got a call out of the blue from Ernie Fossey, Frank Warren's matchmaker. He told me that they were now promoting my namesake, the British featherweight champion Colin McMillan. He wanted to know if Kevin could make the nine stone feather weight limit for a challenge for the title on the 4th of September. The money was good and he said he had thought of Kevin as a consolation for the way the Sports Network had let us down the previous Christmas after they won the purse bid for the Dickie fight. That was bullshit but another unlikely championship challenge was tempting. I told him I would speak to Kevin and let him know the following day.

Kevin was astounded at the offer. I put him on the scales and with about a month to go, he still only weighed nine stone three. He was excited by the prospect of another title fight this late in his career and said he definitely wanted to go for it. I rang Ernie and he was pleased but he said the Board of Control would need to see Kevin on the scales before they would sanction the fight to make sure he could do the weight.

This was no problem and Harry Warner, who was now the Central Area secretary, came over to our gym for a cursory weigh in. There was two weeks to go and Kevin weighed nine stone two. The fight was sanctioned

Kevin trained with all his old enthusiasm and I once again had high hopes of another astounding upset from the old warhorse.

At this time my daughter Deborah was managing the YMCA hostel in Holland Park in Kensington, London. She had plenty of room to put us up in comfort so we drove down the day before the weigh in. Kevin was close to the weight limit but to be sure we walked from the Hostel through Holland Park to Kensington High Street where we found a health club. It was a member's only establishment but I went in and blagged the receptionist who called the duty manager. I explained the position to him laying on the importance of the fight and that it was on the telly and they could brag about knowing one of the fighters.

It worked fine and they allowed Kevin to have a nice leisurely forty minutes in the sauna followed by a shower and weigh in on some accurate scales. I waited in the lounge with a coffee and a view of the pool where some rather nice posh birds were frolicking. It's a hard job this boxing training.

Kevin was bang on nine stone so with an overnight dry out he would be fine at the one o'clock weigh in.

The fight was at the York Hall, Bethnal Green which was well known by us. We weighed in at the Bloomsbury Hotel and Kevin and Colin McMillan were both spot on the weight. Colin was slightly taller than Kevin but only half as broad and we definitely had the edge on size. I had seen Colin box several times and he was a fast box fighter with a decent dig but not a knock out specialist. He had an eighteen win one loss record and his loss was on a cut eye against Alan MacKay at the York Hall and I was there that night. It was to be Colin's first defence of the feather weight title.

I drove to the venue and we were there in plenty of time. Everything went well in the dressing room and Barry McGuigun came in to see Kevin whom he knew from the times when they sparred when Barry was in his prime as a feather weight champion

The hall was packed as usual and anyone who has been to the York Hall will know that it always has a unique feel to it. It is soaked in history and nearly everyone in the fight game has been there at some time or other. The ringside audience is always sprinkled with TV stars politicians and gangsters and its hard to tell them apart.

Manchester trainer/manager Phil Martin was there with one of his fighters and he volunteered to work the corner with me and the house second.

For four rounds it was a good fight. Neither boxer was dominant but Kevin was well in the contest but could never quite catch the slick moving much younger man.

From the fifth Colin McMillan's speed and accuracy were beginning to tell and there wasn't a lot I could do to help Kevin solve the problem between rounds. To the end of the sixth Kevin was not being hurt but at the same time he was not able to land anything significant.

At the start of the seventh McMillan went up a gear and was catching Kevin cleanly with shots and there was nothing coming back. The referee quite rightly called it off. McMillan had retained his title and Kevin had fought his last fight. We both knew it.

We picked up a decent cheque and drove back to Preston but not with the dejection that mostly follows a loss.

It was more the acceptance that Kevin's active boxing career was at last over but with a feeling of relief and great satisfaction that here he was with all his faculties intact. He had travelled far and wide tasting triumphs and defeats. He would for ever more be remembered as a British Champion and worthy challenger.

He had made more money in his last five fights than at any time in his career. He was happy and he said his only regret was that he had not teamed up with me years before when, with youth, he could have achieved more but that was history. Now he was looking forward to helping other young fighters.

Incidentally, Hugh Forde's career was ruined by his loss to Kevin. He only fought three times more, winning one and losing the other two. De-Napoli went on to win European and other titles. Dickie only managed one more win and then lost his British title. Jimmy Bredahl went on to win European and world titles before losing to the great Oscar Del-a Hoya. Colin McMillan went on to win the world title. Harry Escott's bubble was burst when he lost to Kevin and never won a title. Reefer did nothing much after the time he ducked Kevin. He won only one of three more fights. Yoma stopped Ritchie Foster in four rounds and went on to win European and World titles including a win over Bredahl.

Kevin joined me in the gym as a trainer and he was a good assistant to me in the corner. He also worked for me in my Blackpool business right up until 2001 before I sold it when my heart failed. Now in 2011 I count him as a friend.

Kevin's fourteen year old son Ruben is just setting off on an amateur career and is already showing that he has inherited some of his dad's talent

Chapter sixteen
LOUIS VIETCH

In January 1991 at the start of a busy gym session Simon McDougal, from Blackpool, who was in training for a Central Area super middleweight title fight, brought two of his mates with him. He introduced them to me. One was a little tubby guy called LOUIS VIETCH and the other was Ted Mahaffy. I knew Mahaffy because I had used him on one of my Blackpool Winter Gardens shows back in 86 when he had been managed by George Hill. They asked if they could train and I told them they could as long as they didn't block any of my pro boxers from the bags and balls. I wasn't interested in watching them although I couldn't help but notice the little fat guy as he pranced around the gym punching the bags and shadow boxing. He obviously had some experience but he was technically useless and obviously unfit

Mahaffy had fought six times as a pro and had lost five with one draw. At the end of the session I was amazed when the tubby little guy with a Glasgow accent came to me and said

"Whit's the chances Jim?"

I said "whit's the chances of what?"

He said "whit's the chances of me turning pro?"

I was flabbergasted at even the thought of it. I asked him how old he was and he said he was twenty seven. He had been around amateur gyms since he was a boy and had fought for various clubs but achieved nothing. My immediate reaction was to chase him out of the place but then I thought, if he had the cheek to come and talk to me about a professional career, I aught to put him straight.

I put him on the scales and at five feet two inches tall he weighed ten stone ten pounds. I checked his wrist and noted how small his hands were and said "Look Louis, at best you are only a bantamweight which is eight stone six pounds. At twenty seven most of the lighter division boxers are already at retirement age yet you are expecting to start. Your chances of turning pro are nil or even less than that"

He was persistent though and asked me how he could lose weight. He said he hadn't weighed eight six since he was about sixteen. I explained to him the necessity of a good diet and a training programme but more importantly the discipline it takes to follow both and said I didn't think he would have either of those qualities and I had no time to waste on him with my busy schedule.

Finally he said "will you set me programme and advise me on a diet and do some work with me"

I agreed to do the first two of those things but I told him that I wouldn't waste time on the third request until he had lost at least two stones in weight. I asked him about his eating habits at the moment and he confirmed my suspicions. He ate mostly fast food and drank at least two large bottles of 'pop' a day. He hated greens and fish and the only chicken he ate was Kentucky fried. I outlined how he would have to change his eating habits drastically and thought that would be the end of it. I also told Ted Mahaffy that I had no time for street fighters with no discipline which is what he was and, unlike Louis, he did take no for an answer and that was the last I saw of him in the gym.

On the other hand, Louis turned up at every gym session with Simon, and some times when Simon didn't turn up! I still refused to do any work with him thinking he will soon get fed up, but no, there he was week after week.

He was happy to do his own thing at first but then he asked if he could join in the sparring sessions. He kept the other boys amused by his cheeky banter and jokes and when I finally allowed him into the ring, it gave the fighters a bit of light relief from the intensity of serious combat. Louis only asset at this point was his footwork. He had a good pair of legs on him, probably due to carrying that dumpy body around for years, and for about two minutes of a round he could move quite quickly providing good target practice for Kevin, Steve Hardman and Rob Stewart. They didn't take advantage of him which is probably why he kept coming.

This went on until around the end of June 91 when we took a break for summer. I really didn't expect Louis Vietch to turn up again so I was surprised when he reappeared as the fighter's commenced training again in mid August. First of all I was amazed at how much weight he had lost. He asked me to put him on the scales which he tipped at an incredible eight stones six. He said "I knew I had lost a lota weight because I had tae go oot and Buy new clays" (New clothes in English)

After having made the effort and unbelievably achieved the target I had set back in January, I had to honour my word and begin a coaching programme which was a bit of a nightmare.

When you begin to coach a boxer from scratch, at least you can teach correct technique without having to break all the bad habits that have become ingrained by years of practicing bad. Louis had never been coached in his life and as a result he hadn't a clue about what he was doing. Everything was wrong with his punching and defences and he didn't know ringcraft from witchcraft.

But he was a willing pupil. Any coach who uses Tech pads will tell you about the pain you get in the elbows even when the incoming punches are correct and well timed and you are prepared to absorb them. The trouble with novices is that they mistime their punches and frequently strike the pads at bad angles sending excruciating pains into the joints. When you are practicing combinations by presenting the pads in a way that draws a flow of punch angles from both hands from experienced professionals it is hard enough, but with Louis it was murder and took me back to place I thought I had left behind years ago.

He made good progress though and as I began to see some of the techniques from the pad work being carried through to the sparring sessions, for the first time I began to think that he had defied logic and maybe he was going to reach a standard where I could apply for a licence for him. When I told him this he was absolutely thrilled. He said "Jim, if a get a pro licence and even only have wan fight I will have achieved ma life's dream" He was now twenty eight years old.

Louis was married to the sister of Brian McCue, the Blackpool heavyweight. He had a baby son whom they called "wee Louis"

Before taking the next step toward a professional career, there was one more thing I needed to know about Louis. It was obvious he had the courage to get him this far. He had shown determination by sticking to a training programme for nine months and the discipline to change his eating habits and drop two and a half stones in weight. But would he have the bottle when he was under pressure in the ring? Would that prove to be the reason why he had not taken this step towards a professional career when he was in his youth? There was only one way to find out.

I spoke to Kevin Pritchard before the next sparring session and gave him instructions, out of the earshot of Louis. I prepared Louis with a head guard and body protector and called time. Kevin, who was in championship condition, didn't hold back and Louis suddenly felt what it was like to feel shots slamming into him. Kevin was clever enough to know when to ease off and allow Louis to stay in there for round after round. I half expected him to either cower with his hands clamped to his head or just give in but instead he battled away, absorbing some hard shots to body and head.

Between rounds I was in his corner giving him instructions just as I would in a real contest situation. I let it go on for the full six by three minute rounds at the end of which Louis was still on his feet, only just, but he had proved that he had the heart to go on when the going got tough. He was about to realise his dream of becoming a professional boxer.

I arranged for his medical and MMR scan which I paid for up front because Louis was always broke and in the first week of September 1991 his licence was approved

I put the word out to the area matchmakers that I had a novice flyweight available and a week or two later I got a call from Tommy Miller who had an eighteen year old ready to make his debut. His name was Tucker Thomas from Leeds who had boxed amateur but was not an ABA champion or anything like it. We made the match for the 9th of October 1991 at 8st 4lbs over six two minute rounds. It was a dinner show over in West Hartlepool so there were no casual spectators allowed

Louis was excited at the prospect and worked harder than ever for the next two weeks. The day before the match he weighed 8st 2lbs.

I picked up Louis along with Kevin, whom I was going to use in the corner with me, in the afternoon of the fight. Louis was positively hyper during the trip and talked constantly so we were glad when we got to the venue.

We were called to the scales and I got my first look at Tucker. He looked even younger than his eighteen years and even had a young boy's soft physique but he was at least four or five inches taller. Next to him Louis looked more like his Dad! Louis got on the scales and I was surprised when he weighed exactly eight stone.

Tucker on the other hand weighed in at eight stones seven pounds, three pounds over the match weight. I was furious. Seven pounds at flyweight is a lot to give away especially in a pro debut so I immediately called the match off.

Tommy Miller was not at the show and Tuckers trainer claimed he had not been told what weight the match had been made at. I got hold of the shows promoter, ex heavyweight pro John Spencer, and told him that since Louis had made the weight and passed the doctor, as per the Board regulation I was claiming the purse and he agreed that seven pounds was too much to give at flyweight

By this time Louis and Kevin had gone to the dressing room. When I told them that I had called it off, Louis was devastated. After all the build up and with the adrenaline pumping he pleaded with me to let him fight. He said the weight would make no difference and in any case, three of his mates had travelled over from Blackpool and had blagged their way into the hall by paying £20 a piece to stand at the back.

I took Kevin to one side and discussed it with him and we agreed that it would probably do Louis more harm physiologically to miss the fight and with his maturity against the young looking Tucker Thomas, what harm would he come to? I found John Spencer and told him the fight was back on, much to his relief. I questioned Louis as to why he was so light and he told me, against my instructions, he had 'dried out' for twenty four hours before the fight. I was not amused.

As we got Louis ready for ring I told him I was allowing Kevin to act as chief second and that he must listen to him between rounds. He was bursting with confidence and didn't seem nervous at all which is unusual for a debuting fighter. When the bell rang to start the first round I was appalled by Louis action. It was as if I had never even spoken to him since the first night I saw him in the gym, never mind the hours both I and Kevin had worked with him.

He was rushing at Tucker with no semblance of style or technique, hands down and swinging punches. The young kid, who displayed a neat amateurish style, had no trouble in hitting Louis with his left jabs and the occasional right cross as he side stepped Louis rushes with ease. I told Kevin he had to get a grip on him at the end of the round.

Kevin was obviously not getting through because at the bell to start the second round the action was exactly the same. For two rounds Louis had hardly landed a worth while punch and I was glad that Tucker was as soft and light punching as he looked. Again Kevin couldn't get through to Louis in the second interval and the third round was exactly the same as the first two. I told Kevin that I would take over at the end of the round. Louis was clearly three rounds down and going nowhere.

As he sat down I slapped a wet sponge in his face then slammed his head into the corner pad. His eyes popped wide open and I knew I had his attention and he could see I was angry. It was not the way I usually worked the corner but I had to break the trance he seemed to be in. I instructed him to get his boxing under control, to stop rushing in, get his hands up and look at the target and punch straight instead of the swinging punches that Thomas could see coming a mile off. I demanded some feedback so that I was sure he was listening. I only had a minute to get through but it worked.

At the start of the fourth there was no rushing. Tucker was by now feeling confident enough to come forward himself with left jab. Lois immediately banged over a counter punch and within seconds the whole fight changed. Tucker was hurt and unlike his amateur three round contests, he was only half way through this one. He got on his bike again but this time Louis was hunting him down instead of rushing him and a minute and a half into the round he had Tucker pinned on the ropes and helpless to defend against a barrage of now correctly delivered blows which dropped him for the count.

Louis was over the moon at his first win. I didn't put a dampener on his celebrations then but I knew what I was going to do with him the next time he came to the gym!

When I asked him for an explanation over his diabolical start to the Tucker fight, he admitted that he had lost control in the excitement of the moment and his brain was out of gear. He had reverted to his old style as soon as the thought process went into auto mode. He still needed time for the newly learned techniques to imprint on his sub-conscious brain.

On the 11th of November I got him a six rounder at the YESC through matchmaker Graeme Lockwood. It was against Shaun Norman who was making his pro debut. Louis weighed in again at eight stone proving that he was indeed a flyweight.

For four rounds against Norman, Louis boxed well and the bout was even. In the fifth Louis lost his way again half way through the round and became slightly disorganised under an attack. He turned away from Shaun and ran to one side. Referee Mickey Vann interpreted this action as a retirement and stopped the contest. Louis wasn't hurt at all and was as surprised as I was at the sudden ending. It was another lesson learned.

There was nothing for us over the Christmas period and the next date was to be the first of many trips north of the border. I have mentioned many times before futility of trying to get a decision in Glasgow rings, but you have to go where the fights are and when Alex Morrison offered Louis a six rounder against a young up and coming Neil Armstrong, we took it. Armstrong was just twenty one and had a good amateur record but just two pro fights, both wins. It was at the Hospitality Inn on the 12th of March 92.

The match was made at 8st 4lbs. Louis weighed eight three Armstrong was two pounds lighter. The ref was Billy Rafferty. It was a good fast contest and both boys boxed well. The younger Armstrong was the neater boxer but Louis was the aggressor. At the end it was no surprise when the ref hoisted Armstrong's hand and we were not complaining. Louis had given a good account of himself

A month later we were off to Glasgow again for Morrison. This time I had high hopes because the match was against local fighter Mark Robertson. I had seen Mark box a couple of times and he had one win four losses and a draw. The weights were the same at eight two. The ref was Len Mullen. The fight was scrappy due to Robertson holding at every opportunity. I was amazed when Mullen gave the fight to Mark by half a point. Louis was robbed.

We got one of those occasional opportunities to pull off an upset when I got a call from Frank Maloney. He was managing Mickey Cantwell who had been a five times ABA flyweight champion but now had won five out of five pro contests. He was offering good money for Louis to box a six by three minute rounder on the under card of the Alexander Palace, London, show featuring our old friend Colin McMillan fighting Maurizio Stecca for the World Featherweight Title.

I knew Cantwell and in spite of his achievements, I considered it distinctly possible that Louis would be too tough for him. Mickey was a lovely boxer but had no power and certainly not a stopping punch. In boxing terms "he couldn't burst a paper bag". Louis was over the moon at the prospect of featuring on a World Championship bill with all the personalities and journalists who would be keeping an eye on Cantwell as well as the TV coverage. Who would have dreamed of this just a year before?

We trained hard for the fight and I concentrated on Louis getting in close and punching to the body. One of the encouraging things for me was the fact that Cantwell was only a year younger than Louis! I thought that there was a good chance of the biggest upset of the season.

We had a good drive down. I hired a mini bus because Louis wanted to bring a few of his mates plus my corner team. Louis weighed in at eight stone two pounds, a pound lighter than Mickey Cantwell.

I had known Frank Maloney for years when he was just a small time manager and promoter. He had been one of Frank Warren's "gophers" before striking out on his own. Suddenly he was in the news chasing Olympic Super Heavyweight gold medallist Lenox Lewis around America with an open cheque. It turned out that Frank was the boxing front man for Rodger Levitt, a big time financier who seemed like he had money to burn. He wanted to become an instant "big shot" in the boxing world and Lenox was to be his passport in. It elevated Frank Maloney instantly to the big time and he couldn't go wrong with the superb Lenox Lewis who was hammering his way to the very top.

Rodger Levitt's financial empire was made of straw and it burst into flames burning the fingers of a lot of showbiz and sports personalities who had been conned by the crook who went down owing about £10,000,000. He was convicted of fraud and castigated by the boxing fraternity.

I had taken boxers down to London to box on Franks shows and I had used his fighters on mine. This time Frank was a lot less amiable and it was either because he was beginning to believe his own publicity or he was worried about Louis!

I found a place in the dressing room and I began to prepare the tapes and bandages. Louis was in good spirits and as cheeky as ever. As the preliminary fights got under way Louis and Kevin went into the arena to get a feel of the atmosphere. They came back ten minutes later and a total change had come over Louis mood. He looked positively pale and withdrawn and all in the space of a few minutes.

I asked him what was wrong, thinking maybe that just going out to ringside and seeing all the personalities in the ring side seats had overawed him. He and Kevin told me that Louis had spotted Jim Watt and Reg Gutteridge who were doing the TV commentaries. Louis had gone over and spoke to Jim and when he heard that Louis was fighting Mickey Cantwell he began to tell Louis how good Cantwell was and what a great left jab he had. It had intimidated Louis in spite of the fact that I had gone over and over this in the gym and impressed on him that Cantwell couldn't hurt him with his punches and the importance of Louis intimidating Mickey in the ring from the first bell.

I cursed Jim Watt and told Louis to get a grip of him self. This was no time to lose his bottle and by the time I had got him warmed up he seemed to be in the zone.

From the first bell I realised that he was still letting Watt's comments worry him. He was standing off and let Mickey dictate with his neat fast jabbing style instead of closing him down and roughing him up. At the bell Cantwell had won the round by a mile. More worrying was the fact that when Louis sat down I wasn't able to get through to him. There was no feedback and I knew he wasn't listening to instructions.

The second and third rounds were the same pattern. Cantwell was getting things his own way and I wasn't able to break Louis out of his trance. In the fourth suddenly Louis woke up. He began to realise that although Mickey was hitting him cleanly with his powder puff jab they were not hurting him and for the first time he began to fight back.

Between the fourth and fifth Louis began to focus on my urging and for the next two rounds he was driving forward and beginning to hurt the fast tiring Cantwell. At the last bell Mickey had well won the fight but only because Louis had thrown away his chance.

We analysed the fight in the gym a few days later and Louis vowed that he would listen to me in the future and not allow himself to be influenced by other people. He was as good as his word in his next contest. It was a return to Glasgow but this time to Glasgow's other big promoter, Tommy Gilmour Jnr.

Tommy was managing the ex Scottish International amateur Paul Weir. Paul had only had the one winning fight but was being talked of as a future champion. He was even smaller than Louis and, at only seven stone ten pounds; he was three pounds lighter than Louis when they met at the Albany Hotel on the 9th of July 92. This time Louis was not overawed at being the underdog but, although trying his best to overpower Paul, he could never catch the quick slick style of Weir and lost on points. This time there was never any question of a home town decision but Louis had acquitted himself with honour.

On the 11th of September it was back to Glasgow on an Alex Morrison promotion at the Holiday Inn for a return with Neil Armstrong. Since their last fight, Armstrong had only had one more contest which was drawn. Louis had fought three times in between. Louis had come on a lot since their first meeting and it showed, that is to everyone except Len Mullen the referee. After six good fast rounds I was dismayed to see Armstrong's hand being raised. As the saying goes, "We wuz robbed"

On the 26th of October it was a trip over to Cleethorpes in Lincolnshire and a very close point's loss to Nick Tooley. It could easily have been a draw.

The 14th of December saw us back at the YESC where Louis boxed a draw with a Trevor Callighan managed kid called Lyndon Kershaw. Lyndon was only twenty years old and had won his first pro fight after a decent amateur career. After a crowd pleasing six rounds the ref called it a draw. It had been another good performance from Louis.

With Christmas 1992 over, Louis came back to the gym and I was pleased to find that he still weighed just a pound or two over the flyweight limit. I was able to pick up the training schedule where we left off after his last fight.

Alex Morrison was back on the phone. He wanted Louis for another fight with Armstrong on the 29th of January. We agreed that Louis had been robbed in their second fight and that a third match would prove who the better man was.

Neil's record now stood at five wins and a draw. Their third meeting was another close affair and it was no surprise when the ref gave Armstrong the nod by half a point. Were we ever going to get a fair deal in Glasgow? That would be wishful thinking.

A week after the Armstrong fight I got a call from Terry Toole who acted as matchmaker for the Mickey Duff stable. Duff had taken over the management of Mickey Cantwell from Frank Maloney and Cantwell hadn't fought again since his fight with Louis in 92. He was offering decent money for Louis to box an eight by three minutes return with Mickey as the top of the bill fight for a show at the Lewisham Theatre, London.

This was great news for Louis who was desperate for a return with Cantwell now that he knew he had blown his first chance. We had four weeks to prepare and the match was made at the flyweight limit of 8st.

I took Steve Hardman with us to work with me in the corner as Kevin was working away at the time. Everything went well and Louis and Mickey were both exactly on the mark on the scales. Mickey Duff was his usual bolshi self and reinforced my feelings of dislike for the man. The referee was Tony Walker

On the night our preparation went perfectly. Louis was in the zone and brimming with confidence. From the first bell Louis was doing what I had asked the first time they fought and he was all over Mickey from start to finish of the round. I could hear Mickey Duff screaming instructions to Cantwell from the corner but he was too busy defending himself from the punches Louis was unloading on him.

Cantwell was a good experienced boxer and he got his jab working a little better in the second, but Louis was making all the running and he won the round. The third followed the same pattern and at the bell I had Louis three rounds up.

In the fourth Cantwell stepped up a gear and for the first time was out scoring Louis by keeping the fight at distance with some neat footwork and his fast jab. He won the round but I knew he wouldn't be able to hold Louis off for eight rounds.

I told Louis to force the pace again in fifth and rough Mickey Cantwell up in close. Whilst he was doing this Mickey Duff was screaming at the ref to warn Louis but he wasn't doing anything illegal so there was nothing to warn him about. At the bell I saw Mickey Duff run around the ring apron to Tony Walker, who had gone to a neutral corner, and tell him to stop Louis from using rough tactics. It quite amused me and I told Louis that our tactics were working. Louis gave me one of his cheeky grins.

Cantwell was game enough and was starting the rounds well but again Louis was too strong for him and he was finishing them in charge, which is normally good from a round winning point of view.

At the start of the eighth I was confident that Louis had pulled off a surprise win against Cantwell. The round was even because Louis was himself tired by this time. At the final bell I could hardly believe it when Tony Walker held up both their arms and called it a draw. Again Louis had been robbed. He wasn't despondent though because a draw against Mickey Cantwell in his home town and with big shot Mickey Duff trying to influencing the ref, it was as good as a win anywhere else. We drove back to Blackpool with our heads held high.

A month later we were invited to Glasgow again by Tommy Gilmour Jnr this time for a six rounder against Middlesbrough flyweight Neil Parry. The match was made at eight stone three pounds and at the time Parry had a six win fourteen loss and two draw record. It was a straight forward under card bout on a championship show and Tommy said he was offering us an even match for a change. Louis was becoming popular with the Glasgow fans because he always put on a good show. He probably told Parry the same. Anyway Louis took advantage of it and won a clear points decision.

Not to be out outdone by his Glasgow promoter rival, Alex Morrison was on the phone again offering Louis a fourth (and final) fight against Neil Armstrong. This time it was to be fought at the Ice Rink in Paisley, Louis hometown. It was over ten three minute rounds for what Alex called "The Caledonian Flyweight Title"

The money was decent and he offered Louis a percentage of ticket sales. Louis was delighted because all his extended family and friends were still in the Paisley/Glasgow area. There was also a huge amount of prestige for him to be fighting for any sort of title, even if it was an Alex Morrison invention, in his hometown.

We had plenty of time to prepare for Louis first ten rounder and he worked hard. I had two other boxers on the bill so it was good for all of them to be training together and travelling as a team. With the experience of three previous bouts against Neil we knew exactly what to prepare for and having beaten him the last time although not getting the decision, Louis was confident.

Both boxers weighed in spot on the flyweight limit. This time they had appointed Arnold Bryson from the North East as referee who would supposedly be neutral since both fighters were Scots. Louis had sold a lot of tickets so had plenty of support from the crowd.

It was another good hard fought contest. For seven rounds it was dead even and I couldn't be sure whether Louis was just ahead so I urged him to make an all out effort from the eighth onwards. He responded well and was finishing stronger than the much younger Armstrong. The last round was ding dong and again I was dismayed when Bryson gave the decision to Armstrong by half a point.

Louis Vietch had again fought with courage and distinction and handled the result well. He was disappointed but not discouraged and I was beginning to wonder what he had to do convince these referees that he was not just getting into the ring to fill the corner as a journeyman loser. He was working hard and always fought to win not just go through the motions.

I gave him a few weeks off which he deserved but emphasised the importance of not getting too far out of condition because at his age, he was now thirty, any weight he piled on may be even more difficult to shed. He made a promise that he would keep up with his running and would be ready to get back to it whenever I called him.

I had a meeting with Trevor Callighan in September and we decided to apply to the Council for Louis Vietch to Fight Lyndon Kershaw whom Louis had drawn with, for the vacant Central Area Title. It was duly approved and we found a promoter over in Hull who was keen to stage it. The date was for the 7th of October 1993.

Louis could hardly believe his luck when I rang him to get back to the gym. The little fat no-hoper of just two years ago was going to fight another ten round championship contest, it was unbelievable.

Again Louis worked hard. He had been as good as his word and when he came back after his summer break he was only two or three pounds above the weight. We dropped quickly back into the routine that had produced his good performance against Armstrong and again we knew what we were up against.

I took Kevin with me this time and both Louis and Lyndon were spot on the weight. Henry Cooper (he was not yet a Sir) was guest of honour and Louis was impressed when he came to have a word with him.

It was a cracking l contest. Louis was at his best and I was getting good feedback between rounds. Both fighters were performing well and again by the seventh and eighth rounds there wasn't much in it. Louis once again responded to my instructions to impose himself in the final rounds against the tiring younger man and this time it worked because it was Louis hand that was raised at the final bell. Louis Vietch was the new Central Area Champion. It meant as much to Louis as a world title does to some pampered and protected prima donna.

There was no belt issued by the BBBofC for Area champions but I was so pleased with Louis performance that I commissioned a belt for him and I paid for it myself. It became his pride and joy.

A month later we were off to Glasgow again for Tommy Gilmour against James Drummond who was one of his fighters. It was a top of the bill eight rounder at the Albany. Drummond had a seven win seven loss and two draw record but had fought twice for the British Title, losing both times. He had KO'd Keith Parry in his last fight so it was not an easy task for the new Central Area champ.

Drummond was two pounds heavier than Louis and my heart dropped when I saw that Len Mullen refereeing.

It was another good close fight and I thought we were in with a chance of the verdict but it was a forlorn hope and Drummond got a half point decision. Again Louis had shown that he was not far off British Championship calibre.

By way of consolation Tommy gave Louis another six rounder on the under card of the Paul Weir/Josue Camacho World Title fight at the Kelvin Hall Glasgow, on the 2nd of February 94. The opponent was Ian Bailie who had only had four fights, all losses. Louis outclassed him and the referee rescued Bailie in the first round after Louis had had him down twice.

Just over a month later it was Louis first foreign trip. Agent Paddy Byrne offered good money for Louis to fight Denmark's Jasper D Jensen. It was to be Jenson's debut after winning an Olympic medal for Denmark. The fight was in Aakirkeby, Denmark on the 25th of March over six three minute rounds at eight stone two.

I let Kevin Pritchard take Louis this time. They got on well and at the time I had other commitments in the gym and besides it would be a good experience for both of them. They were pleased to be 'cut loose' as it were.

Everything went well on the trip and Louis once again fought with his usual fire and determination but after a close fight Jenson was given the nod. It is worth noting that Jenson went on to win thirty eight out of forty pro contests winning and defending the European and IBO World Titles along the way.

Reading between the lines of Kevin's report of the trip, they got up to more mischief after the fight than they would have done if I had taken them!!

After the Jenson fight I was struggling to find an easier fight for Louis. He deserved to be fighting someone at his own level. By now he had had seventeen fights with four wins eleven losses and two draws. He had only been stopped once and that was a bit of a farce and several of the decisions were of the home town variety. He deserved a break even though he was the Central Area Champ.

My search was proving futile so when I got a call from Johnny Griffin, the Leicester promoter, offering Louis a six rounder against Irishman Vince Feeney nick named The Sligo Kid, and I took it. Feeney was an ex Irish amateur international and was being touted as a future champ. He had won six lost two and had one draw in the professional ranks and I thought that with the extra experience this might be another opportunity for Louis to score an upset.

The match was made at eight stone four on the 24th of May 94 in Leicester. We travelled down on our own this time because I had another boxer fighting at another show and Kevin was taking him. Steve Hardman was incapacitated.

Louis and the Kid weighed in at the same eight stone three pounds. I had a row with the Midland Area officials over the disgraceful state of the gloves they brought to us. They must have been ten years old and had been worn several times that night. They were soggy with sweat and positively dangerous, especially after the experience I had with Brian Wareing in Yarmouth years before. I refused them and they found another pair that was acceptable. It just illustrated again how little the Board inspectors cared about the safety of the fighters.

After that hiccup, we warmed up well and Louis was in the zone. The referee was Jim Pridding, one of the better refs in my opinion. From the first bell I knew that The Kid was going to be a handful for Louis. For once he was not able to get into the fight early on. Feeney was just too clever and he looked all of the ten years younger than Louis that he was. Louis drew two of the six rounds and lost the other four. I couldn't complain about the decision but Louis was there trying up to the last bell.

It was summer again and another lay off for Louis with the same warning. It was September when I got a call from Trevor Callighan. His young flyweight Lyndon Kershaw, whom Louis had beaten for the title, had been nominated as the leading contender for the Area title. Ron Gray, the Birmingham promoter was keen to promote the fight as the top off the bill for a Midlands Sporting Club show in Solihull on the 2nd of November 94.

The money was right and it gave us plenty of time to prepare for a title fight. Louis was well up for it. Lyndon Kershaw had now won eight and had only lost once and drawn once against Louis.

Louis was confident and had prepared well. Both boxers weighed in at 7 stone thirteen pounds. We warmed up well and got in the zone. Louis was proud to get into the ring with his championship belt draped over his shoulder. It was another fast and entertaining fight but by now Louis had the measure of young Lyndon and he was a worthy winner and still Central Area flyweight champion.

Christmas was soon upon us but there would be no pudding for Louis. Alex Morrison offered us a fight that Louis couldn't refuse.

Frank Warren was staging one of his big thirteen fight promotions at the SEC in Glasgow featuring Naseem Hamed defending his featherweight world title against Armando Castro. Morrison was responsible for making up the under card and he wanted Louis for a challenge to James Murray's Scottish Bantamweight title. Morrison was managing Murray and he also offered another of my boxers, Simon McDougal, a six rounder against Sean Heron. Simon was of course a mate of Louis from Blackpool

Louis was over the moon at the prospect of fighting for a Scottish title, especially at the SEC and on such a prestigious show but there was only one snag. Morrison was only offering us £1.200 for the fight which was not enough for a title. He claimed that he had a limited budget for the preliminary fights but he suggested that if Louis could sell tickets he would pay him twelve and a half per cent commission on tickets sold just as he had in Paisley. That suited Louis fine and he said he was not concerned about moving up a division to get the chance at the title. Murray had a twelve wins and one loss record, so he wasn't as experienced as Louis and at 5' 4" he was only two inches taller.

A week after it was all agreed I got a shock when Morrison called to say that although the Scottish Area Council had approved the match for the title, it had been vetoed by the Board HQ in London on the grounds that a reigning Area Champion could not challenge for another Area title even at a different weight. It would mean that Louis would either have to relinquish his flyweight title or fight Murray in a non title bout. Neither of these scenarios was acceptable but, as I have said before, I knew the BBBofC rule book inside out and backwards and I knew that there was no such ruling in it. I told Morrison that I would sort it.

I rang HQ and asked to speak to the general secretary John Morris. He was not in the office but I was told that Simon Block, the Southern Area secretary, was there and that he was the expert on the rule book. When I told him what my call was about he said yes he knew about the bantamweight championship application and it was he who had vetoed it. I questioned him about the rule and he said it was quite plainly set down so I asked him to quote the actual page the rule was on and the clause. The line went quiet for a while then Simon came back on and asked if he could he call me back in an hour.

He was as good as his word and called back but his superiority tone had disappeared. He had to admit that there was no such rule in the current rule book. He said he was sure that it had been there in previous rule books but it had for some reason been left out of the current one and because of that there was no reason to block the fight! He was a bit embarrassed that someone north of Watford Gap knew the rules better than he did.

I rang Morrison to tell him that the title fight was back on.

Kevin and Dave Paterson travelled to Glasgow with me as well as my son in law Bob Coyle so I had a strong corner team. Simon was in good form as well as Louis. The bonus on ticket sales that Louis had sold came to £375 and I told him I was not going to take a percentage of that part of the purse. He was happy.

I hated those big fight bills. The evening drags on and on and there is usually a panic when the TV producers are calling the shots about who is on when and it all has to be timed so that the live broadcast of the main event is spot on time. We were told that Simon was going on in the first half of the bill so I got him ready first. It was just as well because the glove whip came rushing in to say we had to get gloved up quick, we were on next. A few minutes later he was back to say that Simon's fight had been cut from six rounds to four rounds to fit into a time slot. This is not on when you have prepared a fighter for a specific distance but we could do nothing about it although I made a mental note that they would still have to pay for a six rounder.

Simon was very experienced by this time and it didn't faze him at all. This fight is described in Simon's chapter.

There were further delays and switches and the organisation was terrible. Finally it was time for Louis to get to the ring. We had warmed up and then sat down a couple of times with false alarms. The hall was packed and both boxers got a great reception.

From the first bell Murray was just too strong for Louis. The move up from flyweight was too much and although Louis gave it his usual gutsy performance, by the third he was being driven round the ring and after two minutes of the round the ref stopped it. It was the first time Louis had been genuinely stopped. The long wait before we got into the ring hadn't helped! At least he had fought for a Scottish title!

By the time we got changed we were about the last of the boxers to get to the cashier. Catherine Morrison, Alex's daughter was paying out with one of Warrens men. When I checked the money there was only the basic purse and expenses in the envelope. I asked Katherine for the Louis ticket money and she said she knew nothing about it. The Frank Warren accountant said that Frank never gave commission on ticket sales and it was a private deal between me and Alex. When I asked where Alex was Katherine said he had already left the hall and had gone to night club to a reception laid on by the promoters. I was as mad as hell and determined to sort it out before we left Glasgow although it was now 1am and I should really be getting the boxers home. Eventually I found someone who knew where the club was that Morrison had gone to.

We were travelling in Dave Paterson's Land Cruiser so we loaded up and went round to this club. I left them parked up outside the door and I went in to find Morrison. The place was packed and the music was blaring when I spotted Morrison propping up the bar surrounded by his cohorts. Alex Morrison is 6' 2" and a huge ex heavyweight boxer himself and his mates were all massive at least they looked it in that situation. I barged in between them and first thing Alex said was "hello Jim, can I get you a drink". He could see I was mad but when I asked him for Louis money he said "just give Catherine a ring in the morning and she will send you a cheque, I don't carry money around with me" What could I do? I had to leave it that way and we had a miserable drive back to Blackpool and Preston. It even snowed on the A74 to cap a frustrating night. I vowed I would never do business with that crook again and I didn't.

I didn't take my 25% off Louis purse so he didn't lose out. I said I would wait for Morrison's cheque. I rang time after time but it as a waste of a call. We had been screwed but there was nothing in writing so I couldn't ask the Board to help me recover it. I am still waiting for it Alex.

There was a tragic sequel to James Murray's career. He had two more winning fights after Louis before challenging Drew Docherty for the British Title. In that fight he suffered a brain injury and died.

A couple of months went by before I got a call from Tommy Gilmour Jnr. He offered us a six by threes against his young up and coming ex ABA champion Keith Knox. It was a show he was promoting in Knox's home town of Irving on the west coast of Scotland. It was on the 5th of April 95

At least it made a change from Glasgow, but the referee was Len Mullen so we were up against it.

Dave Paterson came as my second. Louis weighed in at eight stone one and three quarter pounds. Knox was eight two. It was a cracking good contest with the younger faster Knox trying to keep out of the way of an aggressive Louis who was back to his old self after his false start with James Murray. I was hopeful of the decision but, guess what, Mullen called it a draw. Why did we keep going back to Scotland?

The best thing about managing and training Louis Vietch was that no matter what the decision was he was never downhearted. He would have fought King Kong if I could make the match for the right money. He was a professional fighter in every sense of the word.

He proved it a couple of months later. He was back in the gym training after the Knox fight but when it got to the end of May with no offers on the table I told him to take a summer break. I had turned down fights for him from matchmakers who were asking for him to give away a lot of weight to bantam and featherweights.

On the 13th of June I got one of those oh so familiar desperate phone calls from John Gaynor. He was matchmaking a show at the Frontier Club in Batley, Yorkshire. His main event was an eight rounder featuring home town fighter Adey Benton and the show was for the next day, the 14th. It was a sell out because Benton was making a come back in front of his home fans after losing a British Bantamweight challenge fight against Drew Docherty in Glasgow.

Benton's opponent had withdrawn at the last minute and John had spent the last twenty four hours desperately trying to find a substitute. The show depended on Benton fighting because he sold most of the tickets. As a last hope Gaynor asked me if Louis was available. He said they were willing to pay above the odds for short notice. The original opponent was getting £600 for the fight. I told John that Louis was out of the gym for the summer and I wouldn't even ring for less than £1,200, double the standard purse for the fight. I didn't really want the fight anyway because I knew that Benton was a tough kid even for a bantam let alone a flyweight. He had to consult with Benton's manager, Keith Tait, first but he called back within a few minutes and said they would pay it.

I rang Louis and explained the situation. I asked him what he weighed and said about eight six, the bantamweight limit. He said he was still very fit…he had only been out of the gym for a couple of weeks… and when I told him the purse he said without hesitation "I'll take it". I emphasised that Benton was a tough little fighter but Louis said "don't worry Jim, ah kin handle him but see if you can get a bit more money out of them"

When I rang Gaynor back he could hardly believe his luck until I asked him for £1.500. He consulted and came back with £1,300 max. I accepted.

There was no one available at short notice to work the corner with me so it was just me and Louis who drove to Batley. At the weigh in Louis was smack on the eight stone six as was Benton. The amusing thing was that Benton was trying to be mean and menacing and he was glaring at Louis who just laughed in his face. Even I was impressed by Louis attitude, but would it be the same when the bell rang?

We were called out of the dressing room and asked to wait at the back of the stage for a big introduction. Benton was on the other side of the stage, oiled up and still trying to intimidate Louis who was still finding it all amusing.

The place was packed and although we got a cheer when Louis was introduced as the Central Area Champ, they nearly brought the house down when they introduced Adey. The referee was Mickey Vann who was by this time a star class ref.

When the bell rang for the start of the first round I was amazed when Benton marched out with his hands right down by his waist. He had absolutely no respect for Louis at all and must have thought that since he was only a flyweight and a short notice one at that, it was going to be an easy night. He was right but not in the way he thought it would. Louis was straight on him and landing left and right hands bang on target. Benson threw a few weak jabs back but it was all Louis. Suddenly towards the end of the round, Louis hit Benton with a terrific right cross smack on the chin, his legs unhinged and although he didn't go down, he was badly hurt. The bell rang before Louis could follow up but when he got back to the corner I told him that Benton was hurt. He said "aye I know Jim I'll get him in the next round" It was an almost surreal feeling!

When the bell rang for the second, Benton didn't seem to have learned anything from what had happened in the first. He still had his hands down and was wide open. After a few opening jabs, Louis again slammed over the big right hand. This time Benton went down as if he had been shot. Mickey Vann took up the count but Adey was out although by instinct he was struggling to get up. Mickey half carried him back to his corner.

I leapt into the ring and picked Louis up and swung him round in a circle, I was so elated and relieved. As I put him down Mickey Vann walked over to raise Louis hand and just at that moment I was aware of someone rushing past me. It was a young guy who had jumped into the ring from the steps in our corner. Louis had his back to him when he swung a right hand that landed on the back of Louis head and knocked him across the ring.

For an instant I was frozen, as was Mickey Vann who was facing me. The realisation of what had just happened hit and I launched my self at this maniac. Mickey was closest to him and grabbed him round the waist, turning him to face me. I grabbed him by both ears and was just about to give him a Glasgow kiss when he lashed out with his right again. The punch landed smack on my left ear and the searing pain told me that it had burst my eardrum.

All of this was happening at breakneck speed. Before I could do anything more, the guy disappeared beneath a team of security guards who were at ringside to prevent anyone getting into the ring. They weren't very good at doing that but they were now all piling on top of the idiot. They bundled him away and the MC tried to calm the crowd who had been stunned by the way their hero had been destroyed by Louis.

We got back to the dressing room and the duty doctor examined me and confirmed that my ear drum was perforated. It was the second time I had suffered this injury but the first time was genuinely done in the ring with a gloved hand years before not by a bare knuckle. It caused me to suffer from tinnitus in my left ear which has continued to this day.

Louis also had a bruise on the back of his head from the first punch the madman threw. We discovered that it was Benton's brother who had been incensed at Louis knocking out his sibling. I was incensed as well and went out to find a policeman to arrest him for assault. There was a whole squad of police outside but they refused to come in for fear of starting a riot. I was pretty mad at them and called them cowards.

The following day a policeman called to see me at home. He had been informed by the Yorkshire Police force of the incident and came to see if I wanted to follow through on the assault charges. I told them too true I did and Benton was eventually arrested tried and found guilty of assault. I was awarded £1,000 criminal compensation. I never did find out what Benton's penalty was except that he was banned sine die from any boxing show by the BBBofC.

The only amusing thing to come out of it was that the whole thing was captured on TV. I have a copy and it appeared on National TV in a programme called "Foul" and was available as a VHS tape. It was once shown on network TV on Boxing Day!

The win over Benton caused quite a stir in the business and the phone never stopped for a day or two. Finally I got an offer we couldn't turn down.

Lennox Lewis was scheduled to defend his Heavyweight title at the Point in Dublin against Australian Justin Fortune on the 2nd of July 95. Did we fancy a return with Vince Feeney on the undercard? You can imagine Louis response to that! It was a hometown fight for Vince but we were getting decent money and after Louis last performance against Feeney he even fancied he could turn the tables. There was also the prestige of fighting on a big bill again with the high profile audience that Lennox Lewis was sure to attract.

It was only a four three minute rounds affair, which was not favourable for Louis who would have preferred at least eight rounds to wear Feeney down, but we had to accept it. At least it was decent money.

We flew over the day before the fight. We were in a nice hotel and there were lots of boxing personalities for Louis to rub shoulders with such as World Super Middleweight Champion Steve Collins who was a really nice guy and spent quite a while chatting to us. At the weigh in, Louis weighed eight stone five, two and a half pounds more than Vince Feeney. It was only two weeks since the Benton fight and he didn't have time to lose much weight from the eight six he weighed for that fight.

The Point is quite a spectacular venue and it was fairly well packed. We were there in plenty of time so we got a chance to go out front and see who was who. It was quite funny when Louis introduced himself to Liam Neeson, who is about six feet six inches tall and I can still hear him saying as he looked up at Liam "aye Liam I thought you were great in Rob Roy". Liam said "aye Louis and I thought you were great fighting Vince Feeney"

For Louis and Vince Feeney's fight the referee was a blast from the past for me. He was Freddie Teidt, the great Irish welterweight of my era both as an amateur and a professional.

From the first bell it was exactly what I had expected. Vince was fast both with his hands and feet. He buzzed round Louis and was careful not to get involved in exchanges where Louis extra power would tell. The four round distance was nowhere near long enough to tire Feeney and as hard as Louis fought, he could not catch Vince with a shot hard enough to slow him down. Feeney won well and we didn't grumble.

It had been a good trip and Louis wasn't hurt which is the main thing.

Louis had the rest of the summer off but was back in the gym by September and again he was as good as his word and was only a couple of pounds over his training weight.

At the beginning of October I got the golden chance I had been hoping for.

Tommy Gilmour offered us another fight with Keith Knox. This time it was a ten round official eliminator for the British Flyweight title and the Scottish flyweight championship. The date was for Monday the 20th of November 95 and it was at the Albany Hotel. Because it was an official eliminator I wasn't worried about it being a local referee. It had to be a neutral star class ref.

Once again it brought out the best in Louis in the gym. He worked his socks off and did everything I asked of him. With his previous drawn fight with Knox we had learned all we needed to know to plan the fight down to the last detail.

What I didn't know was that the referee nominated for Louis fight was Roy Francis, the A star referee. Just by coincidence, Francis had been one of the judges at a Tommy Gilmour show on the Saturday when Gilmour fighter Paul Weir had defended his World Title. Instead of going back to London, Francis had stayed up at the Albany. When we arrived after our drive up from Preston and Blackpool we walked into the Albany and found Francis, Gilmour and a few others having a cosy little coffee break!

Anyway, we were not concerned. Louis had the beating of Knox with or without a partisan referee. Or so we thought. Louis weighed in at exactly eight stone. Knox was one pound lighter.

We warmed up well and Louis was in the zone. I could sense the confidence that Louis was exuding these days. It came from the knowledge he had gained over these last few years, the fact that with experience he knew he could go the distance with any flyweight in the Country and just the sheer pleasure he got from being a professional boxer. He was never overawed by any situation.

From the first bell Louis was the boss. He was catching Keith with the jab and in close he was using his experience to land uppercuts and hooks to the body.

At the bell he had won the round well. He was alert I was getting good feedback from him. I couldn't have wished for more.

For round after round the pattern was the same. Don't get me wrong, Keith Knox was trying his best and it was not entirely one sided but Louis was winning the rounds on my card and I was sure that with Francis's experience he must surely be seeing it the same way.

By the fifth I was so confident that it was not so much whether Louis would win on points but more a question of whether Knox would last the distance. Louis was totally dominating the fight when, after hammering Knox on the ropes Francis called "Break" and I saw blood on Louis forehead. Now Louis had never been cut in a fight before. Knox wasn't landing enough punches to have caused a cut so it could only have been a head clash. Roy Francis called "stop boxing" and brought Louis to our corner. I had sterile gauze ready and I wiped the blood away. It was a tiny cut above the hairline confirming to me that it was a butt not a punch that had caused it. Francis was satisfied and I was relieved because I knew it wasn't a stopping injury. They boxed on and Louis took up where he had left off.

By the time the bell rang to end the round, I had the adrenaline swabs and Vaseline ready and as soon as Louis sat down I got to work on it. I reassured Louis that it wasn't bad and that I wanted him to step up the pace because Knox was about finished. The bell rang and he was eagerly off his stool and backing Knox to the ropes again, totally in charge. Suddenly there was a small trickle of blood running down the side of Louis face. It was only a dribble but it was the chance needed to save the home town boy.

At first I couldn't believe Francis was stopping the fight. I have seen cuts right on the eye lid far worse than this tiny cut on the forehead and I was incensed. As I jumped into the ring to protest, Roy Francis jumped out of the ring on the other side. He quite rightly seemed embarrassed of what he had done. Of all the bad decisions I have seen this one hurt most because if the injustice of it. I am the first to want to protect my fighters from injury, but this was ridiculous.

When we got back to the dressing room the doctor looked at the cut and said it didn't need stitches. Francis did not even use the option of asking the doctors opinion before stopping the fight which is the usual action.

Louis eye didn't need stitching but we had been stitched up good and proper. Afterwards, whilst I was packing up in the dressing room, Louis went out front to speak to one of his friends when he saw Francis at ringside. He went over to complain to him and Francis had the cheek to say that if it was any consolation he had Louis in front on points and he only stopped the fight to save Louis career for the future. The B*****d had just put the boot in on Louis career.

After this eliminator, Keith Knox got a shot at the vacant British title against Louis old foe Mickey Cantwell who was the other leading contender. He lost that one but did go on to win the British title at a later date. If Louis had not been robbed in that fight I am certain that he would have gone on to stop Cantwell and would have been the British Flyweight Champion.

When I got back to Preston I was still fuming and Jean said to me "It is time you were getting out of this crooked business or you're going to have a heart attack"

She was not far from the truth.

After the Christmas 95 and New Year 96 celebrations, we were back in the gym. By this time my stable of fighters was down to the lowest number since I first turned pro with Sammy Sampson. To be honest I was not feeling physically as strong and fit as I used to be and as an active coach I felt I needed to be able to put the boxers under pressure with the pads. My right elbow was now in a chronic state after thousands of rounds of impact from thousands and thousands of punches.

Besides the physical aspect the fact was that I was getting sick and tired of seeing boxers being abused by the system. I knew right from the start what the game was all about and crooks and conmen I would be dealing with. I also made sure that the boxers I signed up knew this as well. I promised each of them that I would do everything I could to protect them from the vultures and stand by them until either they or I felt we had come as far as we could. I was sure I had fulfilled my end of the bargain.

What I didn't know was just how difficult, nay impossible, it was to buck the system. Yes, I met some honest and genuine men in the business and a few I would be proud to call a friend but at the same time it was a battle against a closed shop at the top unless you were willing to cow tow to the main players. Talent and ability alone couldn't get a boxer very far. There was always someone who wanted a piece of the action. If a boxer was too good you couldn't get a fight for him unless it was an overmatch. The trick was to try and beat the system as we did a few times, but you only got the odd chance and then after that the doors closed.

Anyway, back to the Louis Vietch story. At the end of January 96 I was informed that the young Liverpool flyweight Peter Culshaw had been nominated as mandatory challenger for Louis Area Title. Culshaw was an ex ABA champion and had a seven wins and a draw pro record. I had seen him box as a pro and I wasn't too concerned for Louis. He was ten years younger and four inches taller than Louis and as his nick-name "The Choir Boy" suggests he was built not unlike Louis first professional opponent Tucker Thomas.

Culshaw was managed by an unsavoury Liverpool outfit, Munro & Hyland who were employing John Gaynor as their matchmaker and it was he who called me to say that they wanted to promote the fight in, of all places, Barrow-in-Furness, Cumbria on the 5th of March.

We had plenty of time to peak by that date and I had both Kevin Pritchard and Steve Hardman available in the Gym. Steve was once again living up to his name. In 1992 he was involved in a serious motorway accident which, in 94, resulted in him losing his right leg below the knee. He didn't let a little thing like that phase him and he was back sparring on his prosthetic limb and when he was dressed he didn't even walk with a limp.

On the day before the contest we went over to Liverpool for the weigh in which was now mandatory the day before the fight. Louis weighed in smack on eight stone and Culshaw was one pound lighter. John Gaynor asked me if I knew of a boxing oriented doctor in the Barrow district which would save them the expense of bringing an out of area doctor all the way up to Barrow. I had visited Barrow with amateurs many times but that was fifteen years previously so there was no one I could help them with.

We had prepared tactics to deal with the choirboy. Louis was his usual confident self and by the time we drove as a team to Barrow I was confident we had got over the disappointment of the Keith Knox incident.

We soon found a good spot in the dressing room to prepare. I saw John Gaynor and asked him if had managed to find a doctor, by regulation there has to be two doctors in attendance at a show. He told me that he had been put in touch with an amateur football club who used a local Doctor who had agreed to attend. He then said this Asian doctor had never attended a boxing show before but a doctor was a doctor. This was to turn out to be significant. The Board regulations also state that a venue has to be within thirty minutes drive of a Neurological unit in a hospital. Since Preston, which is a least an hour and a half away by the fastest car, was the nearest with this facility, I don't know how the Liverpool promoters got away with that one.

We were a confident team going to the corner. Louis was in the zone and was being encouraged by the presence of Kevin and Steve as well as me. I can't remember the name of the referee except that I know he was a scouser.

The tactic we had evolved was for Louis to get in close and work Culshaw to the body and generally rough him up as he had done with Cantwell and Knox and from the first bell that is what he did. We were happy with him at the end of the round and we set him out to do the same in the second.

By the end of the second round, the neat boxing Culshaw was not enjoying the aggressive attention he was receiving from the tough guy Louis Vietch and his corner men were distinctly disconcerted.

As the bell sounded for the third I said to Kevin and Steve "I can't see Culshaw surviving this for long" and they both agreed with grins on their faces. Suddenly there was a trace of blood on Louis forehead. For a second I was hoping it was from Culshaw's nose which had bled from the first, but then the ref called for them to stop boxing and he led Louis back to our corner for me to wipe the blood away. It was the same spot that Knox had cut with his head but it was not serious. The ref, who was himself not experienced, then said "I want the doc to have a quick look and he called up the Asian football doctor who had never seen a boxing cut up until that moment. He seemed totally flustered, but after a look at the wound which had stopped bleeding any way, he said to the ref "I think it is OK" The ref then said to the doc. "OK but it is your decision". At that the Doctor seemed to panic and said "Oh, I think you should stop it".

It was a total farce once again. Here was a Doctor with no experience talking to a weak referee who had anticipated a Culshaw white wash colluding to stop a contest which was so important to my boxer's career with a cut that, as an experienced second, I should at the very least have been given a round or two to work on. The fight was going away from Culshaw the favourite and promoter's boy and again we were being openly robbed.

I was completely beside myself with anger at the injustice. I tried to get the doctor to come and examine Louis eye in the dressing room and justify the decision but he had mysteriously disappeared and instead they sent in two paramedics who were attending the show. They looked at the so called 'cut' and decided that once again it didn't need stitching. Who ever heard of a contest ending with a cut eye which was so slight that it didn't need at least one stitch? Now it had happened for the second time in two fights.

This was to be the last time I would attend a professional boxing show. I will not expand this statement until I write the epilogue of this book.

Chapter seventeen
ROB STEWART

After the summer break of 1991 we were back in the gym when Trevor Thompson who was an amateur trainer from Blackburn came to see me with a fighter from Darwin near Blackburn. His name was ROB STEWART and he was twenty six years old and at 5' 8" he weighed around ten stone. Trevor told me that Rob had boxed amateur for a few years and was now fancying a pro career and would I take a look at him and see what I thought.

Rob was strong kid and in pretty good condition. I let him spar him with a couple of my experienced fighters and it was obvious that was a decent boxer. We had a talk and I liked his attitude. Trevor didn't want to be involved in the pro business.

Rob quickly fell in with the squad and I did my usual work with him. He was a hard worker and by 14th of October he was ready for his pro debut. I got him a six rounder at 10st 1lb on Nat Basso's show at the Piccadilly against Gary Pagden of Boston in Lincolnshire. It was Gary's pro debut as well. On the night Rob boxed really well and won every round for his first win as a pro.

Nat also liked his style and offered another contest at the Castle Leisure Centre, Bury a couple of weeks later on the 21st of October. This time the opponent was a kid called Ricky Sackfield who had won both his contests to date. Again Rob boxed neatly to win well. Ricky put up a much better fight and I was beginning to see the sort of stuff Rob was made of. He was essentially a box-fighter with a good sharp left jab and a decent range of punches even at this early stage. More importantly he showed that he had the heart and courage to come right back after taking a shot. I was pleased with what I saw in that fight.

On the 4th of December I got him on the Pat Brogan North Staffordshire SC show at Trentham Gardens, Stoke. His opponent was Dean Carr who had a two win three loss record. Rob showed how he was improving by winning all of the first four rounds before dropping Dean in the fifth and the ref stopped the one way contest.

Next up was Rob's first TV show. It was on a Frank Warren Fight Night show at the Town Hall Stockport on the 21st of January 92. His opponent, Chris Aston, had also won three fights and had lost one. Rob was now getting used to my pre fight warm up routine and was in the zone. It was just as well because Chris was also up for a fight and as a result the two of them went at it hammer and tongs for three rounds.

In the first, Aston displayed his kick boxing background by his very square on style as if he wasn't sure whether he was an orthodox or a southpaw but he was a willing, free punching hooker, but Rob was beating him to the punch with his fast and accurate left jabs. By the end of the round there wasn't much in it. The second was fought at the same furious pace but now Rob was showing a much wider range of punches catching Chris with right crosses and uppercuts and for me he won the round. Chris was still very strong at the start of the third and unwilling to take a backward step but in the final minute Rob was catching him with full blooded shots and I detected a slight wobble in Chris's legs.

In the interval before the fourth and last round I warned Rob that Chris would start fast to try and redeem the fight but it wouldn't last long and sure enough for half a minute that is what happened. Rob matched him though punch for punch until suddenly Rob was landing power shots that had Chris in trouble. Half a minute before the final bell referee Phil Cowsell called it off to save Chris Aston from further punishment. It was Rob's fourth victory.

This fight was the first on the bill so I knew it was going in the TV can and if the main event was over early, it would be shown. It was and Rob Stewart was on TV in a more entertaining fight than the main event.

On the 24th of February Graham Lockwood booked Rob for a six rounder against Tony Banks at the YESC Bradford. Banks had a 5-4-2 record and we fancied the job. It was another great little fight but more of a boxing match than the scrap with Aston. I thought Rob was unlucky to only get a draw but there wasn't a lot in it so we didn't complain.

Alex Morrison offered us Rob's first eight rounder against ex Scottish ABA champion Alan Peacock who had an 8-8 pro record. It was at the Hospitality Inn in Glasgow on the 4th of March. I knew the venue so very well and I also knew what to expect from the referee.

It was a match made at 10st 2lbs and both the boxers weighed the same. The referee was Billy Rafferty. The boxer's styles were well suited and by the start of the last round they had put on a cracking fight but I was sure that Rob was at least two rounds up. Rafferty called it a draw, so I was right.

I agreed terms with Jack Tricket for Rob Stewart to challenge Richard Burton (no, not that one) for the Central Area Light welterweight title. Rob had only had six fights so far but he was twenty seven and was so well thought of that there were no objections and I wasn't going to pass on the chance of a title for him. Burton was an interesting character who was born in Jamaica and had his first five pro fights in the USA. He was five years younger than Rob. He had now fought eighteen winning fifteen with two losses and a draw. The show was at Stockport on the 24th of September 92

Our training programme went well and Rob got plenty of sparring. He was well up for the fight and confident. On the night everything was fine. Our pre fight warm up was good and Rob was in the zone. The referee was Ron Hackett, not one of my favourites.

Burton was a few inches taller than Rob but not enough to cause us concern. Both boxers had weighed in half a pound under 10st. From the first bell Rob carried the fight to Burton and had a good opening round. For all the extra experience that Richard had, you couldn't tell for the next seven rounds. Rob used every punch in the book and matched Burton with every move.

I thought that Burton was definitely tiring more than Rob in the ninth and tenth rounds and although it had been a good fight I reckoned that Rob had won it by three rounds. I was once again astounded when Hackett gave it to Burton by half a point. It was a blatant case of the ref favouring the "expected" winner. Rob had been robbed.

Incidentally, it might be no coincidence, but this was the last time that Burton fought. I like to think that it was because of the beating he took from Rob!

I gave Rob a good rest after this disappointing result. He had until the New Year 93 off but was back in the gym none the worse for his experience, in January 93. I got a match for him on the 25th of February at Burnley which was just up the road from his hometown. His opponent was Alan Ingle from Scotland who had won two out of four fights. Alan was one of Tommy Gilmour's fighters.

Rob was right back to his best with a wide points win.

We got a call for a fight in Glasgow again this time from Tommy Gilmour Jnr who was seeking revenge for Robs win over Ingle. The fight offered was at the Albany in Glasgow on the 29th of March and it was an eight rounder against Peter Bradley of Glasgow. Bradley was a class fighter who had won an eliminator for the British lightweight title. He was an ex ABA featherweight champion. His record stood at fought thirty, won twenty four lost six. Two of his losses had been to Paul Burke, one of my ex-fighters and Paul's his old nemesis Marvin P Gray. More importantly he had lost two of his last three. I felt that Rob would be strong enough to beat him.

Rob made his usual fast start and won the opening two rounds by virtue of his superior power. The third was a little more even but I thought Rob was well in it. In the fourth Bradley got his slick boxing abilities going but Rob was the boss and rocked Peter with a cracking left hook. Half way through the fifth there was a clash of heads which caused a bruise beside Rob's right eye. It was nothing serious but it was unbelievably enough for the ref to wave the fight over thus saving the hometown fighter. It confirmed to me that it was a waste of time bringing fighters to Glasgow.

Once again this was Peter Bradley's last fight. He never fought again after his tussle with Rob. It tells its own story.

But I still hadn't learned the lesson. Alex Morrison offered Rob a fight at Paisley Ice rink on the Louis Vietch v Neil Anderson bill on the 29th of May. The opponent was the undefeated in eight Allan McDowell who was a southpaw.

I heard about a good young amateur from Wigan called Lee Blundell so I invited him over to our gym to give Rob some southpaw sparring. Lee was really a light middle but he gave Rob some good sessions.

We travelled up to Paisley the day before. I had Rob, Louis and Steve Scott on the bill. I had agreed with Alex to bring Rob in under 10st because he said McDowell was really a lightweight. At the weigh in he was two pounds lighter than Rob. Rob made a good fast start and his southpaw sparring stood him in good stead. He was so much stronger than McDowell but it was a good even fight with Rob just that bit more positive and the heavier puncher. At the last bell I reckoned Rob was ahead by two rounds and the referee confirmed it by calling it a draw. It was all so obvious.

The next date for Rob was at Middleton for promoter Jack Doughty on the 13th of September 93. The opponent was the very experienced Liverpudlian, John Smith who by this time had an 8-40-5 record and had fought just about every light-welter and welterweight in Britain.

It was an entertaining six rounder and this time we couldn't argue with a draw

On the 27th of October, Mickey Duff's matchmaker Terry Toole offered us a six rounder at West Bromwich against ex ABA champion Mark Elliot. The match was at 10st 2lbs and both boxers were a pound inside the weight. Elliot had won six out of six. The fighters were well matched physically although Rob was the stronger man. It was a hard fight with both fighters throwing plenty of leather. Mickey Duff was as usual screaming at the ref every time the fighters got close complaining about Rob using his head. Rob was never a dirty fighter and it was just Duffs way of trying to influence an otherwise close fight. At the end the ref gave Elliott the decision. We didn't expect anything else but it was fair enough.

The 2nd of December saw Rob fighting Chris Saunders of Sheffield on Brendan Ingles show at Sheffield town Hall. Saunders was a decent experienced pro who was comparatively conventional for an Ingle fighter. It was only a four three minute rounder and Rob stormed it to win on points.

After Christmas and New Year 94 I got a call from Ernie Fossey asking for Rob for an eight rounder at Dagenham against local undefeated prospect Paul Ryan on the 17th of February 94. Paul had already won ten out of ten. I talked this one over with Rob because we knew it was an "into the Lions den" scenario. The money was decent and Rob said he was up for it

The training went well and I had no qualms about Rob's condition. Both boxers scaled ten two at the weigh in. As we warmed up and started to get in the zone I felt that for the first time since we had been together, Rob and I were not quite connecting. He seemed a bit remote and it flashed through my mind that this was the way it felt years before with Paul Burke.

From the first bell the usually positive Rob was now tentative and allowing Ryan to dominate. There were flashes of the Rob I knew but they were not sustained. For two rounds this continued and I was not happy, but in the third suddenly Rob put a good combination together and for a minute I thought we had turned the corner. It didn't last though and at the bell to end the third, Ryan was back on top. I sent Rob out for the fourth with instructions to push Ryan onto his back foot and let some of his power shots going but it was in vain. Instead Ryan came on strong and with Rob not really fighting back the referee stopped the fight. I was frustrated. It was if Rob was carrying an injury because I had never seen him capitulate before. It was just not in his nature.

Anyway, it was over and it was the first time that Rob had been genuinely stopped apart from the farcical stoppage against Peter Bradley. After we got showered and changed we went for a meal before the long drag back to Darwin and it was then I found out the problem.

Rob told me that he had been struggling with the fact that he was facing a life style change. His long term girlfriend was a PA for the managing director of a big company who had asked her to go with him to work in Bermuda. She wanted the job but wanted Rob to go with her which meant leaving everything behind including his work as a landscape gardener and of course his boxing. He had more or less made the decision to go hence his concentration on this fight was lacking.

I was relieved that it wasn't anything more serious and I wished him luck. It was too good an opportunity for a young man in his position to pass up and it at least explained why his mind was not on the job.

With the decision made I was sorry to see him go. It had been a pleasure working with him. He trained hard, never complained and could hold his head high with his performances in the ring

In the time scale of his departure there was time for one last hurrah. Jack Doughty, in association with Barry Hearns new cable TV company was putting on a show at the Castle Leisure Centre, Bury. It was as close to home as Rob was likely to fight and with the date of 25th April we had plenty of time to get Rob ready to fight one of Jack Doughty's stable, Blue Butterworth. Blue was from Burnley and had won seven out of eight fights so far. He was being talked about as a rising star in the area.

With the move to Bermuda settled in his mind, Rob was back to his old self and raring to go. Both boys weighed in a couple of pounds over 10st and both were as fit as butcher's dogs.

I had no problem getting Rob warmed up and in the zone. From the first bell he was back to his best and he needed to be. Blue Butterworth had come to fight and there was plenty of rivalry between them. For me Rob's punches were always the harder and were landing cleanly but it was never going to be easy. When one fighter seemed to be getting on top the other would come roaring back. By the start of the sixth round, Rob's out and out superior strength won through and he was punishing Blue right up to the final bell. He got the decision deservedly.

The fight was shown on TV and I still enjoy watching my recording of it even all these years after.

So that was the end of Rob Stewart's professional career. He ended up with a record of eight wins four losses and four draws and the admiration of all who had the good fortune to watch him box. I certainly remember him as one of the best pro boxers I worked with. I saw him once when he came back from Bermuda for a holiday. He told me he had joined an amateur club on the island as was still enjoying his boxing.

The last I heard of Rob he was back home and studying to become a quantity surveyor. I bet he made it.

Chapter eighteen
STEVE SCOTT

STEVE SCOTT ran a Muay Thai kick boxing school in conjunction with John Ryan and I shared their gym in Church Row Preston. John Ryan was an interesting character. He was an actor and stuntman who had acted as Sean Connery's stunt double as well as playing parts in other films and TV plays. He played a leading role in a Coronation Street story line for a while. John was the trainer and coach and Steve was one of his fighters who won a British Muay Thai kick-boxing title as well as training other fighters in that discipline.

Just after New Year 1992 Steve approached me to ask if I would coach and manage him as a professional boxer. It was more of an exercise to improve his western style boxing skills than the ambition of winning professional titles. We agreed that he would have to give up his kick boxing whilst he was under my management and he would have to convince me that he was serious about his training.

He was twenty six and at 5' 10" and around eleven stone, a light middleweight. He was a good pupil and a dedicated and disciplined trainer as most of the Muay Thai exponents that I ever observed were. I had Rob Stewart fighting on an Alex Morrison show at the Hospitality Inn Glasgow on the 4th of March 92. I got Steve on the undercard to make his pro debut against home town fighter Allan Grainger over six two minute rounds. Grainger had a 3-2 record.

Steve fought quite well on the night although losing on points he didn't disappoint. He became the first and only fighter that I managed who lost on his professional debut.

Three weeks later on the 26th of March I took Steve to Hull where he boxed a six rounder against Rob Stevenson and again he lost a narrow points decision but he had shown improvement.

He didn't fight again until the 14th of September when we went to the YESC Bradford to fight Danny Harper. It was Danny's pro debut and I thought Steve unlucky to only get a draw. The one thing I was learning about Steve was that he was a tough guy. He took punches well and never stopped trying. No matter the decision he accepted it without complaint. You cannot ask for more from a fighter.

On the 27th of October 92 we were off to Cradley heath, Birmingham to fight Steve Levene who was making his debut. Steve Sailed out in his usual confidant style. He caught Levene cold and dropped him for an eight count. He didn't let him off the hook and the ref had to stop it for Steve Scott to taste his first win in the pros. He was as pleased as punch.

Ron Gray, who had promoted that show, invited us back to Birmingham only three days later on the 30th. This time the opponent was James Campbell who had won three and lost two. Again Steve fought well but this time the ref gave the point's win to Campbell.

The 26th of November saw us off to Hull again for a return with Rob Stevenson. This time Steve was a much better fighter than the first time and won a good points decision.

Graham offered us a fight at the YESC against Kevin Spratt on the 14th of December. Kevin had a 19-7-2 record by this time. He had been an Area champion at light welterweight but I reckoned that as he was now up to light middle, a good stone heavier than his best weight, Steve could handle him. It was a hard fight and at one point I thought Steve had Kevin in trouble, but his experience pulled him through and at the final bell Spratt got the decision.

On the 28th of January 93 we went down to London to fight Steve McNess at the Elephant and Castle Leisure Centre. McNess, with a

2-2 record was too sharp for Steve and won well. Steve was certainly getting the experience in Western Style fighting.

The 22nd of February saw us off to Birmingham again for a return with James Campbell but again Steve lost a close decision.

Steve went to Peterborough on the 4th of March to fight the experienced Eddie Collins who had a 7-18-1 record. I had another fighter on that night in Scotland so I sent Kevin Pritchard to look after Steve. It worked because Steve did to Eddie what he had done to Steve Levene and stopped him in the first round to record his third win.

Next was a trip to Scotland to fight an Alex Morrison fighter called Colin Wallace who was making his debut? It was the same old story. After six hard fought rounds, of course Wallace got the verdict. We didn't expect anything else.

Steve's next opponent was another Scot but this time the fight was at the YESC Bradford on the 26th of April. The result was the same though, another six round points loss and another good hard fight. Steve was a tough cookie.

We got the chance of a return against Colin Wallace on the 29th of May at Paisley along with Louis Vietch and Rob Stewart on the bill. This time I was confident that Steve had won after six rounds but we were never going to get a decision in Scotland unless it was by KO. Wallace was declared the winner.

The 11th of June 93 saw us in Gateshead fighting local boy Dave Whittle who had an 8-7-2 record. Steve fought really well and I was pleased with how much better he was boxing these days but it was hopeless to expect a decision from Freddie Potter. Dave whittle got it. Maybe it was fair enough

On the 27th of September Nat Basso invited us to his show in Manchester to fight debuting fighter Alan Cessay. Steve was determined to stop the rot of these decisions always going against him even though he was fighting his heart out. He totally dominated the fancied Cessay and this time got the well deserved decision.

The 3rd of November 93 saw us down in Worcester fighting Andre Wharton who had racked up a 7-1-1 record. This time there could be no argument over the six round decision. Wharton was too good for Steve but there was no way he was going to stop the ex kick boxer

Steve Scott added to his country wide experience when I took him to Northampton to fight the 9-I record fighter Kevin Mabbutt. These were hard fights for Steve but he was happy to take them. He had never been stopped in his seventeen contests to date and never been cut or taken a beating. That night, once again Steve battled all the way through six hard rounds of give and take to see the home town fighter get the decision. It was not a bad decision but it was a close fight

On the 17th of February 1994 I had Rob Stewart fighting on a frank Warren show in Dagenham. I was offered an eight round undercard fight for Steve against one of Warren's stable fighters, Jamie Robinson who had at that time won ten and lost one. It again was a tough fight and I gave Steve the option of turning it down but instead he was keen to go.

It was a bad decision by me because on the night, although Steve steamed straight into Jamie, he was out of his depth and in the second a super left hook had Steve down and out for the first…and last…time in his professional career.

We both decided that he had done enough to improve his Western Style boxing techniques. It was time to revert to his Muay Thai career. I had enjoyed working with Steve. He was a decent young man who always trained hard and never complained. He was strong and brave and never once let me, himself or any of the many promoters he had fought for, down. He ended his career with a 4-14-1 record.

I have lost touch with Steve so don't know how successful the rest of his Muay Thai career went.

John Ryan emigrated to California where they added a "St" to his name so that he became John St Ryan. He was in many films and I saw him in a leading role in a TV series. He now owns a ranch about a three hour drive north of Los Angeles where he trains horses. I met him again just last Year at a local agricultural show that he was visiting whilst over on holiday. We recalled the kick boxing days and he invited Jean and I to visit his ranch anytime we are stateside. We might take him up on it. He has a website and you can Google it

Chapter nineteen
LEE BLUNDELL

LEE BLUNDELL, the young southpaw light middleweight who had come over from Wigan to spar with Rob Stewart in preparation for his fight in Paisley, had talked to me about turning professional after the 1994 ABA championships. I went over to watch him in the preliminaries but he disappointingly got stopped in the second round of his bout when looking good. As they do in the amateurs, the referee stopped his bout when Lee suffered a small nick over an eye even though he was wearing a headguard. Anyway it helped him make his mind up and by the end of February he was in my gym with his pro licence approved.

At six feet two inches and a little over eleven stones in weight, he was very tall for a light middle. That combined with his natural southpaw stance made him a good prospect. Lee had been well schooled in the amateurs and along with his natural talent, fast hands and a good temperament he had everything required for a successful career and I had high hopes for him.

The initial requirement was to increase his strength and stamina and to work on his ringcraft and punch angles and he was a willing pupil. By the end of March I started looking for an opportunity for his debut. It came on the same Barry Hearns promoted show, where Rob Stewart was fighting Blue Butterworth, at Bury on the 25th of April 94

I was offered Robert Harper from Doncaster as an opponent. He had lost all four of his previous fights. At 5' 8" he was giving away a lot of reach to Lee but he was four pounds heavier.

The fight was on cable TV with Barry McGuigun commentating. The ref was Roy Snipe. From the first bell Lee fulfilled all his promise. His right jab was bang on target and the shorter Harper was being out classed. Near the end of the round Harper was bending forward with his arms half round Lee's hips when he blatantly punched Lee right in the crown jewels from below. I had never seen anything like it and even Barry McGuigun was astounded when you hear his commentary. The ref gave Harper a lecture but the bell ended the round before they could box on. In the interval I told Lee to stay cool and pick his punches in the second. Brian Harper was there for the taking and after dropping the hapless Harper for an eight count, Roy Snipe called it off and Lee had got his pro career off to a positive start.

Dean Powell rang to offer me a six rounder at the Town Hall, Acton, London for Lee on the 20th of May against Freddie Yomofio. Freddie had lost both of his previous fights. The fight was made at 11st 4lbs.

We had an easy drive down and at the weigh in Lee scaled 11st 3lbs. Freddie was five pounds over the agreed weight but when I challenged Dean he just shrugged his shoulders. I was used to it by now. Lee did have four inches in height advantage.

From the first bell Lee was the far superior boxer. He won the first four rounds clearly and his speed around the ring left the heavier man flummoxed. I realised in the interval after the fourth that Lee was tiring from his own efforts and I had to slow him down or there was the danger of him blowing up in the fifth. He was much more controlled after the bell and picked his punches rather than waste them. It did encourage Freddie a little and he was making a renewed effort.

For the last round I told Lee to stay under control for the first half of the round and then step it up again, confident of the decision. After a few seconds of the last round Lee opened up with a blistering combination of punches and Freddie was reeling when the ref called it off. It was stoppage number two for Lee.

Dean Powell came over to our corner and said to me "you have got a good lad there Jim" I knew it.

Over the next few weeks I tried to find an opponent for Lee only to come up against a brick wall. His two stoppage wins had been noted and offers were few and far between so I gave him a summer break from the gym. He was back in training in August when Alex Morrison came on the phone looking for an opponent for one of his fighters on the 8th of September 94 at the Hospitality Inn Glasgow, I jumped at the chance. His fighter was Gordon Bair. I knew Blair well having seen him several times and knowing that, at his best, he was a welterweight. He had made a good start in his professional career after being a top amateur, but he had a bad run in 92/93 losing nine out of eleven fights. Now he was up to light middleweight with a 14-14-1 record and at 5' 10" he would also be giving away a lot in height to Lee

Alex was reluctant to accept Lee for the fight, but I didn't have another fighter at the weight so a day or two later he rang to say the fight was on for Lee providing he was no heavier than 11st 4lbs. I wasn't too bothered about the referee as I was confident of Lee's ability not to need one. How wrong can you be?

At the weigh in, Lee scaled 11st 3lbs against Gordon's 11st 2lbs. The referee was Al Hutcheon, who had given some awful decisions against English fighters that I had seen or been victim of over the years. Lee was unconcerned and we warmed up and got well into the zone. From the first bell Lee was all over Gordon Blair who was only about three years older than him but looked at least ten years older. Lee won the first by such a margin that the ref should have given him it by a full point.

Lee was cool between rounds and focused. He started the second fast and by the middle of the round Blair was dropped by a cracking right hook and I thought that it was all over but somehow Gordon dragged himself up and for the rest of the round he just about survived. That was a 10/9 round to Lee.

The third was a carbon copy of the previous round except that it was super combination that dropped Blair. This time when he got up at nine and Lee was raining punches on him I was shouting at Hutcheon to stop this one sided beating. It was another 10/9 round to Lee.

The fourth was the same and again Blair went down, this time just to avoid the onslaught. By virtue of the fact that he to take a count, it meant another 10/9 round. When Lee came to the corner after the fourth he was breathing heavily. It was from the sheer effort and work rate he had maintained for four rounds. What was holding Blair up, apart from the ref, was a mystery to me. I sent Lee out for the fifth with instructions to take it a bit easier and resort to good boxing and footwork.

With the pressure off him, Gordon Blair for the first time in the contest, attempted to lead off with his left but his punches were ineffective and at best I would have called it an even round points wise. Blair would have to knock Lee out to get any sort of result.

As it was, due to fatigue in Lee from all the punches he had thrown and Blair from all the punches he had taken, the sixth was a tame affair and maybe drawn. With at least a half point from the first and a full point from each of the next three from the knock downs how on earth could Al Hutcheon call the fight a draw??? For that is what he did. It was incredulous. I was so angry at the blatant bias of this decision that I went to Hutcheon and asked him how he could possibly justify it. He refused to talk to me and stormed away.

Lee knew he had won and seemed to take it OK. It had been another lesson in this sometimes sordid business. It had also exposed the fact that there was still a lot of work to do with Lee in the gym. He was fast and stylish and with a good range of punches but he needed to toughen up. He was not as physically strong as a top class light middle or middleweight had to be. I began to increase the resistance element in his training.

It was still difficult to find the right sort of opponents and it took many hours of phone calls before Pat Brogan offered a six rounder on his Trentham Gardens, Stoke show on the 7th of December 94. The opponent he offered was Kesem Clayton of Coventry.

I knew Kesem from way back in 1986 when I saw his pro debut at welterweight. He was in the same dressing room as us and I saw him many times after that. He was a genuinely nice guy whose record now stood at 12-17-2 and he was now operating as a middleweight. He had been in with a lot of good fighters such as Robin Reid, Steve Foster, Cornelius Carr and RW Smith whom he had beaten, but he had lost his last nine fights and he was approaching the end of his career. It would be a good learning contest for Lee.

On the night Lee was two pounds heavier than Kesem at 11st 6lbs. It was a one sided affair with Lee dominating the first before zeroing in in the second and dropping Kesem for an eight count. On rising Lee steamed in and the ref stopped it. Later Kesem had the courtesy to come to our dressing room to shake Lee's hand and tell him that he was sure he had a big future ahead of him

The only problem with another quick win was that it would make it even more difficult for me to find his next opponent. Lee had a break for Christmas but I had to decide on the way forward with this talented and potentially very good fighter. I came to the conclusion that in order to secure the build up and exposure that it would take to ensure Lee Blundell's future, we had to tie into one of the big promoters with TV contracts which meant Frank Warren, Barry Hearns or Mickey Duff.

I ruled Duff out since I detested the guy with his supercilious and arrogant attitude. After my experience with Barry Hearns and the Kevin Pritchard episode, I wasn't exactly on his Christmas card list, which left the Warren outfit. I rang Ernie Fossey whom I had always got on with and whose opinion I respected. I explained the situation to him and he said he would speak to one or two people who had seen Lee box and then call me back. Some would have seen Lee's fight on cable TV plus experienced observers such as Alex Morrison and Dean Powell had seen him in action.

At the beginning of January 1995, Ernie called me back. He said they would be willing to take a look at Lee and if he impressed we could talk about a promotional deal. He said that they had a big promotion, one of Warren's super shows featuring Frank Bruno and numerous other stars, on the 18th of February at the West Country Showground, Shepton Mallet. The show was in conjunction with Chris Sanigar. Sanigar was an ex pro who was training and managing a stable in Bristol. He was a devout Christian and always signed off with "god be with you" One of his fighters, a middleweight called Glen Catley, was also vying for a promotional deal. If Lee could do a job on Glen then he would be in a prime position.

This was exactly the sort of deal I had been hoping for. First of all, with a promotion like this everyone who was anyone in boxing would be at ringside including the TV cameras and all of the boxing journalists. Secondly, although Catley was a tough opponent, the fact that he had lost one contest as well as winning ten meant that he was beatable. I did my home work on him including obtaining a video of one of his fights. Glen was a year younger than Lee and at 5' 8", much shorter. The only class fighter he had fought was Carlos Colarusso who had stopped him in five rounds in his one loss.

We had six weeks to prepare which was just right from the fitness level Lee was at and, at 11st 7lbs the contest weight was right. Lee worked hard and was in good shape psychologically. I studied the video and decided that Lee had to use his obvious reach advantage and keep the fight at distance for the first four rounds at least. Good footwork was the key to staying off the ropes and out of the corners for these were the areas where Catley would be trying to trap him with his short hooks and power shots

The weigh in for the fight was at 1pm on the 17th and we drove down the day before that. Chris Sanigar had booked us into the hotel where all the visiting boxers and their entourages were staying and where the weigh in was taking place. I took Steve Hardman and Dave Paterson to work the corner with me and Dave drove us down in his Landcruiser. We were all in good heart at this stage.

The weigh in was interesting. It took place on the stage in the hotel ballroom. There was a rope barrier across the room halfway down to keep all the press and TV cameras back and only the boxers and their seconds, trainers and managers were allowed onto the stage. Lee weighed in at eleven stone six and a half and Catley was eleven six. The fighters shook hands and Lee was very confidant.

Frank Bruno was fighting the Argentinean Rudolfo Marin and when the main event fighters were called to the scales, I was standing next to Rudolfo who took off his dressing gown and stepped onto the scales. He did a big lat spread and at 6' 4" he looked massive as he tipped the scales at 17st 4lbs. He raised his arms above his head and gave a big grin for the cameras. He got off the scales and as he put his dressing gown back on, big Frank pushed his way through the crowd with his trainer, George Francis in front. They stepped up to the scales and Frank stripped off his dressing gown and everyone gasped. He was absolutely enormous with muscles on his muscles he had been oiled up and had a slight sweat on. He stepped on the scales and his weight was announced at 18st 2lbs I looked up at Rudolfo. He seemed to shrink before my eyes and turn even paler than his usual sallow skin colour. You could almost hear him thinking "what am doing here?".

The actual fight lasted one and a half minutes of the first round before Frank landed a huge right cross and the ref could have counted to a hundred. Rudolfo had lost the fight the moment big Frank stepped on the scales.

After that little story back to what turned out to be the worst case of abuse that even this cruel business had dished up so far. We made our way from Bristol to Shepton Mallet to arrive at the venue at around six fifteen. We had been told that because there were thirteen fights scheduled for that night with separate TV transmissions to the UK and Scandinavia, the first bout would go on at 7pm sharp and we could expect to be third on the bill.

There was a six three minute round fight on first followed by a twelve round British welterweight title fight then we would probably be on next. We were directed to what was supposed to be our dressing room which turned out to be a ladies toilet with a cardboard sign stuck on the door with Lee's and a few other boxers names on it. We were the first in and I was appalled to find that there were only a couple wooden chairs between everyone and apart from a row of cubicles and a wash basin that was it. Not only that but it was February and the place was freezing. I told the lads not unpack their bags just to wait until I went to sort it out.

I grabbed hold of the first BBBofC inspector I could find and told him in no uncertain terms that I was not having it. He said he would find someone to see if there was somewhere better. Instead of that I found Ernie Fossey myself and after a few minutes he took us to a dressing room on the other side of the hall. It was spacious and warm and turned out to be the dressing room set aside for the American trainer, Emanuel Steward, who was with the Danish fighter Ollie Klemetson and Norwegian heavyweight Bryan Forbes whose fights were being televised live to Scandinavia. Emanuel had no problem with us sharing and turned out to be friendly guy. We set up our camp and as I was cutting the tapes Lee was getting into his boxing gear. I sent Steve Hardman out front to keep us informed with what was going on in the hall and sure enough, although there were not many people in the place yet, he came back to say that they were getting ready for the first bout in the ring.

I bandaged Lee's hands and looked at my watch. It was 7.17pm. Just as I was finishing, the glove whip came in with Lee's gloves and asked me if I could have Lee warmed up as soon as the British title fight started. It was between the Chris Sanigar managed fighter Ross Hale from Bristol who was the champion and he was defending his title against Birmingham's Malcolm Melville. Hale was a strong favourite and the glove whip said he didn't think the fight would last long.

Lee was calm and confidant as he stretched then went through our usual pre fight routine. Steve came in to say that the title fight was just about to start and I sent him back out to keep us posted. I greased and oiled Lee and we went through a punch sequence to get his heart rate up, raise a sweat and to get the adrenaline flowing. I then put a towel around his shoulders under his dressing gown because I knew it would be cold on the walk to the ring. Steve came running back to say that Melville was down for an eight count in the first round and he didn't think it would last much longer. The timing was perfect; Lee was raring to go and was pacing up and down the dressing room and banging his gloves together. Minutes went past before Steve came back again to say that not only had Malcolm Melville survived the second round, he was fighting back and Hale seemed to be struggling!

I then realised that I had to calm Lee down and get him to sit for while and try to relax. With the adrenaline already flowing that is no easy task but I thought to myself 'well Catley will be in the same position'. As the fight dragged on I was dismayed when I realised that it was going to go the distance. As the last round started the whip came in to see if Lee was ready to go so once again I got Lee to throw some more punches to loosen up again.

Suddenly the whip was back to say that the TV producers had said there was only time for another four rounder before the main Frank Bruno event and now we would not be on until after that. I was so frustrated but helpless to do anything except take Lee's gloves off again and try once more to get him to relax. Angry as I was I could not let Lee see that I was getting wound up.

The big fight didn't last long as I have said. Marin was paralyzed with fear and fell over when Frank banged him with a right hand. Worse than that though, Steve came in to tell me that Glen Catley was out at ringside fully dressed. He had not even begun to get ready for his fight with Lee so the Sanigar camp knew all along that they were not going to be on until the second half of the bill. We had been stitched up.

Not only that, the live Scandinavian broadcast with Klemetson and Forbes was just starting so we would have to wait until that finished. They were both taken the distance and as a result when we finally got the call, the Lee Blundell/Glen Catley fight was the last on the bill. We went out to an almost deserted hall at exactly 12.45am. Lee had been ready to fight five hours ago. Instead of the worlds press and TV cameras there was only a group of Catley supporters from Bristol in the audience and Ernie Fossey alone at ringside besides the officials.

In spite of everything, Lee started exactly as we had planned and he won the first three rounds clearly by virtue of his superior boxing and sharper punching. Catley had no answer to Lee's southpaw style. In the fourth, inevitably, Lee began to slow a fraction but it was enough for Glen Catley to begin to land a few heavy shots but it was still a close round and overall Lee was ahead on points. By the fifth, not only was all that wasted adrenaline from earlier in the evening taking its toll, Lee was mentally wasted. He lost the fifth.

I tried to motivate him to go out and survive the final round in the hope that the ref was scoring it the same as I was but it was futile. Catley knew that Lee was weakened and he stormed in until he landed a crushing right hook that broke Lee's nose and dropped him. He beat the count but it was all over.

It had been a disastrous experience. I knew we had been set up but I couldn't do a thing about it. If the fight had gone on early when it was supposed too, I honestly think that Lee Blundell would have out pointed Glen Catley and looked good doing it. Even if Ross Hale had knocked Malcolm Melville out in the first round, Glen Catley would not have been ready for the ring because they knew all along that the fight was scheduled for the second half of the bill. There was no way they were going to let Catley be exposed whilst the media were watching. Who had told the whip to bring the gloves for Lee and tell us to be ready not once but twice? I tried to find him to ask but by the time we got out of the ring he was nowhere to be seen and even Ernie Fossey had gone by the time we were back in the dressing room.

It was a bad set back for us. I rang Fossey a day or two after and all he would say was "your kid lost to good fighter but if he has what it takes he will come back from it". He reckoned he had no idea of what I was talking about when I asked him why we had been told to warm up when there was no way we were getting in the ring until the second half of the bill. He said that that Chris "holier than thou" Sanigar was running the undercard.

Catley went on to have a very successful career winning British and World titles at Super Middleweight.

It took a while for Lee's nose to heal but in the meantime we worked on his strength. Dave Paterson was a successful businessman and I was talking to him about a sponsorship deal for Lee.

I was offered a six two minute round fight for Lee in London against Howard Eastman who, like Lee had only had five pro contests all which he had won but he had been taken the distance by Andy Peach who had a one win in eleven starts record. I didn't commit Lee to this fight until I had sounded out his state of mind after the Catley disaster. When I realised that he was still ring shy I knew he would need a more gentle return. His confidence had been shaken.

Before I could do this he came to say that he wanted to leave my stable and join Jack Doughty's over in Shaw near Oldham. I was pretty disappointed but his mind was made up and I was not in the habit of trying to persuade a fighter after he has made up his mind or of making him false promises.

Lee went on to have a pretty successful career. He boxed on until 2007 and ended with a twenty three wins, five losses and two draws record and won a central Area Title and a World Boxing Foundation Intercontinental middleweight title. He never made it to a British title but he can be proud of his achievements.

He was one that got away.

Chapter twenty
BRIAN WAREING

I have mentioned before that BRIAN WAREING joined my stable after his second bout with Peter Crook. I put him on my promotion at the Sands Centre in Carlisle, Cumberland on the 22nd of April 86. I had booked the Sands Centre since I knew that Carlisle was a "boxing" town having visited it many times with amateur boxers and I thought if I featured the British Cumberland Wrestling Champion, Joe Threlfall, on the bill it could be a successful show. It wasn't because Joe went down with a dose of flu and was out of the gym and I had other problems with the show which I won't go into.

I matched Brian with a kid called Steve Harwood who had a five wins nine losses and one draw record. Brian boxed beautifully just as he had against Peter and this time he won by a clear margin.

Brian had the summer off. He was the head chef at the Savoy Hotel in Lord Street, Southport and was busy during the summer months. When he returned to training in August he worked hard and was a good sparring partner for my other boxers. I looked for a fight for him.

Frank Maloney rang looking an opponent for one of his fighters called Mark Dinnadge who had fought and won four. Six twos at ten stone four pounds looked a good match for Brian. It was at Lewisham Theatre, London, on the twenty sixth of September.

Brian weighed in at ten three, four pounds heavier than Mark. The first round went OK with Brian fighting his usual orthodox style and it ended even.

In the second round Brian again started well but got hit with a very hard right counter over his left jab and he went down. Roy Francis was the ref and he took up the count. Brian was up at eight and seemed OK but thirty seconds later Dinnadge got him this time with a left hook and Brian was down again and hurt. Again he was up at eight but Francis had seen enough and called it off.

It is a long trip home from London after a loss like that.

On the 30th of January 1987 I got Brian a fight with a Tommy Farrell of Liverpool, who had won two out of two. Brian boxed his ears off and scored a wide point's win.

A month later on the 26th February he knocked out Lancaster's Frank Harrington in the second round at the Borough Hall, Hartlepool.

On the 24th of April I got him a six rounder with another of his old Liverpool mates, John Smith, whom he out pointed handsomely.

Graham Lockwood, the matchmaker who seemed to be calling me every other day for fighters, offered a fight for Brian in Great Yarmouth on the 13th June 87. It was a six rounder against Oliver Henry, a local boy with a six win six loss and a draw record in a match made at 10st 2lbs. The purse and expenses for the long cross country trip were OK so we accepted.

The show was at the Hippodrome Circus in Yarmouth, put on by a new promoter. When we got there it was a bit chaotic. The promoter didn't seem to know what he was doing and the weigh in etc was totally disorganised. When we did get on the scales both Brian and Oliver were one pound under the match weight.

As show time approached I realised why the promoter was agitated. There was hardly anybody in the place. Having been in a similar position as a promoter, I could understand to some extent his feelings, but at least we were always highly organised and everyone new what they were doing.

I was shocked when the glove whip brought the contest gloves for me to put on Brian. I thought they were joking because, although brand new, they were more like children's toy gloves than professional boxing contest gloves. They were made of some sort of imitation suede material and were stuffed with what felt was kapok or even cotton waste which could easily be split and separated.

I immediately complained and asked to see the BBBofC OIC. After a while, Graham Lockwood came and said that the gloves had been approved by Ray Clarke, the ex Board secretary who was acting as chief inspector for the show and that nobody else had complained. At that time there was a lot of fuss being made about the introduction of a compulsory MMR scan for new licence applicants, in place of the existing scull ex-Ray, to make boxing safer and to protect the fighters, yet here we were at the sharp end of the sport being allowed to send boxers into the ring at this level with what was only one step up from bare knuckles. I had made the point but there was nothing I could do at that stage.

I warmed Brian up and everything was fine with him. When we got into the ring there were only about a hundred spectators, cheering for Oliver Henry. They were probably all his extended family.

At the bell both boxers opened with an exchange of left jabs and Brian was boxing in his usual style with hands held high and neat footwork. After a minute or so of the round, Henry made a sudden rush at Brian who stepped back to the ropes and turning him neatly caught him with his jab. I was planning the tactics for the second round when suddenly Henry let fly with a big right swing over Brian's left lead which hit Brian on his left ear. Normally it would have caused nothing more than a shake of the head but instead Brian sank to his knees with his left hand clutching his ear. I was astounded to see blood pouring from under his glove and down his arm onto the canvas and as the ref started to count I jumped into the ring, at which point the ref also saw the blood and immediately called for the doctor. In the meantime I got Brian back to the corner and onto the stool and applied a clean towel to his ear. When the doctor arrived into the corner I took the towel away to disclose that the punch had severed the outer rim of his ear, for more than an inch long, clean through.

It was obvious to me that no gloved hand could have possibly caused a wound like that. The padding in those ridicules gloves must have split in such a way that there was only a thin leather layer over the taped and bandaged knuckles. That is the only way that injury could have been caused. As soon as I realised what the injury was like I went immediately to Henry's corner to inspect his gloves only to find that they had already, within a couple of minutes of the end of the fight, removed the gloves with the boxer still in the ring, something that is completely unheard of either before or since that fight. It stank and yet the officials including the referee; let them get away with it.

The doctor came to the dressing room and on a further examination said that because of the location of the wound in the cartilage of the ear it was not possible to stitch it so he closed it with plastic sutures. When I asked him for his opinion on the nature of the injury and whether it could have been caused by a padded glove, he just shrugged his shoulders.

Brian was in a lot of pain and I was good and mad. I ranted at the officials and at Oliver Henry's manager Gordon Holmes, who I was sure knew what had gone on.

The debacle of that show didn't end there. When I went get paid out I was told that the promoter had been relying on the ticket money on the gate to pay the boxers and because the walk up had been so poor there was only enough cash to pay part of the expenses. He couldn't guarantee a cheque would get cleared for the rest of the purse and I was told that I would have to wait for the Board of Control to pay out from his bank guarantee which took several weeks. I paid Brian myself because I didn't consider it fair to ask him to wait for his purse, especially after the way he had been abused. It was an example of the dirty side of the game.

It was a long and miserable drive from Great Yarmouth to Southport and the sun was rising before I got back to Preston.

I made a written complaint to the Board regarding the gloves and the general low standard of the promotion. I received a reply along the lines of there would be a full investigation at Southern Council level and that I would receive the balance of the purse and expenses in due course. I eventually got the money but the farce of the gloves was quietly swept under the carpet.

Brian was out of the gym until August and when he came back we got him back into shape. He never put on weight between breaks because he kept up with his running and he was not a drinker. His work as a chef meant that he ate well and on the right stuff.

Ernie Fossey wanted Brian for one of Frank Warrens shows at the York Hall, Bethnal Green on 22nd September, to box Roy Rowland. Rowland had won four out of four but was not known as a puncher. We knew we wouldn't get any favours on one Warren's promotions against the hometown boy, but the money was above the going rate and Brian was keen to fight in London and on a televised show.

Their weights were the same on the night and Brian had a height advantage.

From the bell, Rowland was obviously well up for the fight and was the aggressor. Brian was his usual composed self until the last minute of the round when Rowland landed a really good left hook which had Brian hanging on. The ref broke them and Rowland stepped in with the same punch and Brian was down. He took the count on his knee and it was an early shower and return drive to Southport.

On the drive back I had good talk with Brian. I felt that with a steady job and a wife and family to consider, was this the way he wanted to continue with his career? He agreed that it was time to evaluate his position in boxing and I left him that morning after dropping him off at home, to think things over. He decided to call it a day.

I had enjoyed our brief time together. He had always worked hard in training and he was brave and honest and a decent man. I have a lot of respect for him

EPILOGUE

When I decided to walk away from Boxing in March 1996 I was doing what I had promised I would do from the start. I always knew the sort of people who ran the professional boxing business. I went into it with my eyes open and I felt that when the time came when I no longer wanted to be associated with them I would go. After the Louis Vietch v Peter Culshaw debacle, that time had come.

Louis was the last boxer in my stable and I had a talk with him about his future. Typically, he felt that he still wanted to fight on and as a mature fighter with plenty of experience and a good head on his shoulders, I knew he was capable of managing himself. He went on to have another fifteen fights, regaining the Area title in the process and fighting another British title eliminator. He never got the British title shot that he deserved.

After he retired he became a trainer/manager/promoter in his own right. Of all the boxers I was associated with, perhaps Louis started from the lowest point as far as potential is concerned. On remembering how I felt on seeing him on that first visit to my gym, winning an Area championship, fighting for two Scottish titles and being a genuine contender for a British title were so far from reality that I would have laughed at any one who suggested it. He has every right to be proud of his achievements and I hope he still has his belt.

He was a good friend to Simon McDougal and did as much as anyone could ask to try and make him see the errors of his ways but to no avail.

I haven't seen Louis for some time but when he reads this book he will call me

I really started something that day when I let the tubby little Louis Vietch train in my gym!

I look back with pleasure and pride on those years. I was proud to stand in the ring with those young boxers. There were highs and lows but I was never ashamed of any one of them. I made mistakes but not that many and more importantly my intentions were always good.

Professional Boxing was, is and always will be, controlled by the big money men. Quite rightly the emerging stars from the amateur ranks, especially with titles and Olympic medals, gravitate to the promoters with TV contracts and the trainers with reputations who cannot go far wrong with that sort of talent. Good luck to them and I have the greatest respect for some of them who have dedicated their whole lives to the business.

But the sport could not exist without the small time provincial managers and trainers who provide year in year out, the "opponents" for these sometimes pampered and protected Stars.

For myself I am just as proud of taking raw novice fighters, with no hope of the big time according to some so called experts, and seeing them emerge as good, well respected professional fighters. I didn't help all of my fighters to achieve their potential and I am sorry about that, but others reached the bar I had set for them and a few actually jumped over it!

I am on good terms with all of my ex-boxers, some of whom I see regularly others I have only seen occasionally since they retired. I can shake them by the hand and look them in the eye because during our time together I always tried to do my best for them and I never screwed them financially. The rules of the BBBofC allow the manager of a boxer under contract to take 25% in commission from their purse. They also allow for the trainer to get 10%. As a manager/trainer that would have allowed me to legitimately take 35% of their gross purse.

I never did. I agreed when signing a boxer that I would take only 10% from them until they were earning good money for the longer distance fights and then only the 25% of those bigger purses. From the day they signed up I never once charged any of them a gym fee or took 35%.

I kept immaculate records of every penny my boxers earned and held them for seven years after they retired or left my management after which I shredded them. This is necessary to comply with the law and of course I needed them for my annual tax returns. Many a time I expected one or other of my boxers to come to me with an income tax demand but funnily enough no one ever did except Kevin Pritchard just once. If they had I would have had all the details to hand.

I went through a full blown tax investigation myself just after my last boxing promotion. It was a nasty experience and not one I would wish on anyone (on second thoughts there are a few I would wish it on). I came through it with flying colours.

I still loved the sport and many of the people I met in it. It was just some that I could no longer stomach.

When I was young I was lucky. Boxing was so simple then. There were only eight weight divisions and one world champion in each of them. You knew who the best boxers in the world were, without question. I knew every champion at every weight going back to the 1800's. Even before that my imagination was fired by the exploits of the great fighters of the Prize ring the bare knuckle days. My bible written by Viscount Knebworth describes it so vividly

Jumping forward to the post John L Sullivan days, the Queensbury rules and gloved boxing. The early twentieth century produced some marvellous fighters who are legends of the sport. I won't begin with names or this book would go on for another three hundred pages at least

It is hard to believe how tough the sport was in the twenties thirties and forties. Fighters were motivated by the poverty of the times and the chance to break out of it. Believe me when I say that what is known as poverty in the twenty first century is luxury compared to those days. Professional boxers would fight, even as novices, over ten and fifteen rounds twice and three times a *week*. Champions forged out of the cauldron of the depression were the hardest of all time.

If there had been, for instance, a super middleweight division of twelve stones in the days of Rochdale's Jock McAvoy, he would have been the world champion for years instead of being forced to jump from the middleweight limit of eleven stone six pounds to fight light heavyweights a stone heavier because the middle weights wouldn't fight him!. To learn more about this period you should read Jack Doughty's book "the Rochdale Thunderbolt" and the fight scene of the period.

One advantage of old age (probably the only one) is that you can rely on the experience of having seen it all before. There is absolutely nothing new in boxing or in the preparation and training of boxers. It has all been done before although under different guises and conditions. There have always been and will be again, great talented fighters. Men with superb skills, tremendous power, blindingly fast reflexes and knock out punches. They come and they go.

The new kids on the block quite rightly think that the fighters of their era are the best ever. I know I did when I was growing up.

I have sometimes been asked who the best boxer I ever trained or managed was. I have too much respect for all my ex-boxers to answer that question but what I can say is that the boxer with the most potential I ever trained never turned professional. Gary Bully was North West extra junior champion at eleven years of age. One of the abiding memories of my early days of coaching was the sheer pleasure of watching Gary spar with Alan Dickinson, another fine young boxer.

At age fifteen and sixteen Gary won back to back Junior ABA titles in London. At just seventeen and boxing his first season as a senior, he won the East Lancs ABA title and in the next round of the championships he came up against the twenty six year old four times ABA champion and England representative, George Gilbody. He was winning the fight when Gilbody cut Gary's eye with his head. There were no head guards worn in 1981. Gilbody went on to win the title.

Gary Bully had everything needed by a boxer to go all the way to the top except perhaps the dedication. It was his exclusion with the rest of my squad when he was the favourite to win the title in 1982 which caused my greatest disappointment. That decision may have changed history. I would have stayed with the amateurs and maybe I could have guided Gary Bully to who knows where. That's life

You don't have to have been a great boxer yourself to be a trainer and coach…but it helps.

You don't have to have experienced the feeling of standing in a dressing room gloved up with the adrenaline butterflies fluttering in your belly and then walking out to the ring with the lights blazing overhead…but it helps.

You don't have to have climbed through the ropes where suddenly there is only you, the referee and a guy waiting to knock your head off and you his…but it helps.

You don't have to have swapped punches with intent with someone you have never seen before in your life and then at the final bell hugged him like he was your best friend….but it helps.

You don't have to have had the experience of walking over to an opponent who you are certain you are going to KO only to wake up in the dressing after the fight is all over asking your trainer what happened to be told you had been decked with the first punch the wimp threw at you but you got up and lost on points without remembering a thing…..but it helps.

You don't have to know what it feels like to walk over to an opponent and knock him out with three left jabs and a right hook…but it helps.

You don't have to have hit an opponent's head so hard that you felt the bones crunching and breaking in your un-bandaged hands and the searing pain go up your arm only to see him get up at five and proceed to beat the crap out of you for the next three rounds….but it helps.

I was never a champion boxer. I fought for ten years in the amateurs and experienced all the things I have mentioned above. I didn't have lightening fast reflexes but I was strong. I smashed my right hand on Joe Jacobs head in my last fight before leaving 3Para in 1955. Two years later, with my hand seemingly better I was on the point of turning pro having got my self into great condition. Unfortunately instead I lost a contest with a dumper truck I was driving on a building site in Kirby. It pinned me down for a submission with a double fracture of the pelvis, broken bones in my spine crushed kidneys and god knows what else. I recovered after a year off work. Any further thoughts of boxing were shelved for ever, until I put my experience to good use when I began coaching.

I was what is known as an active coach which meant that I got involved with the boxers in the ring and in other parts of the fitness programmes. Towards the end of my coaching career I was finding that the physical part was getting harder and harder. I put it down to age and that, as well as the disappointments with decisions and the rest, is what led to my retirement from the game. I didn't realise it at the time, but I was suffering from heart disease.

Just a few years after retiring, I began to suffer from angina. On examination I was found to have three 99% blockages of three descending arteries on the front of my heart and a 70% blockage on the rear. Fortunately I had not yet suffered a heart attack. We paid money to get a quick quadruple heart by-pass at the Blackpool Victoria Hospital. It was a complete success and within six months of the op, I felt ten years younger. The problem was genetic and not as a result of life style. That was nine years ago and I am still as fit as a butchers dog.

I couldn't have done all this without the help and support of my wife Jean. Throughout the early years in the professional game, she kept the Aquarium business going and even put up with me squandering our savings on the disastrous venture into promoting. She always waited up for me into the wee small hours of the morning for my return from our many long drives back from boxing shows all over the country. She was always supportive of my boxers and treated them like members of the family with words of praise or commiseration. She was (is) a world champion.

The End

Jim McMillan

Jim McMillan (11) George Lovell Jock
McMillan Danny McMillan (13)
Circa 1947

Sammy Sampson with Joe Threlfall

Karl Ince

Joe Threlfall throws a straight left at Roy Smith

Simon McDougal

Kevin Pritchard

Peter Crook lands a perfect right cross on Michael Marsden

Keith Halliwell gets in the zone

Gary Bully throws a right cross at George Gilbody 1981

Rob Stewart